Learn Word 97

FAITHE WEMPEN

PRIMA PUBLISHING

To Margaret

P is a registered trademark of Prima Publishing, a division of Prima Communications, Inc. In a Weekend is a trademark of Prima Publishing, a division of Prima Communications, Inc. Prima Publishing is a registered trademark of Prima Communications, Inc. Prima Publishing, Rocklin, California 95677.

©1997 by Faithe Wempen. All rights reserved. No part of this book may be reproduced or transmitted in any form or by any means, electronic or mechanical, including photocopying, recording, or by any information storage or retrieval system without written permission from Prima Publishing, except for the inclusion of brief quotations in a review.

Publisher: Matthew H. Carleson
Managing Editor: Dan J. Foster
Acquisitions Editor: Deborah F. Abshier
Senior Editor: Kelli Crump
Development Editor: Chris Katsaropoulos
Copy Editor: Hilary Powers
Technical Reviewer: Paul Marchessault
Editorial Assistant: Kevin W. Ferns
Interior Design and Layout: Marian Hartsough
Cover Design: Prima Design Team
Indexer: Emily Glossbrenner

Microsoft and Windows are either registered trademarks or trademarks of Microsoft Corporation.

IMPORTANT: If you have problems installing or running Microsoft Word 97, notify Microsoft Corporation at (206) 635-7056 or on the Web at www.microsoft.com. Prima Publishing cannot provide software support.

Prima Publishing and the author have attempted throughout this book to distinguish proprietary trademarks from descriptive terms by following the capitalization style used by the manufacturer.

Information contained in this book has been obtained by Prima Publishing from sources believed to be reliable. However, because of the possibility of human or mechanical error by our sources, Prima Publishing, or others, the Publisher does not guarantee the accuracy, adequacy, or completeness of any information and is not responsible for any errors or omissions or the results obtained from use of such information. Readers should be particularly aware of the fact that the Internet is an ever-changing entity. Some facts may have changed since this book went to press.

ISBN: 0-7615-1251-9
Library of Congress Catalog Card Number: 97-69042
Printed in the United States of America

97 98 99 DD 10 9 8 7 6 5 4 3 2 1

CONTENTS AT A GLANCE

Introduction x

FRIDAY EVENING
Reviewing the Basics 1

SATURDAY MORNING
Correspondence 81

SATURDAY AFTERNOON
Flyers and Newsletters 147

SATURDAY EVENING
Mail Merge and Tables 217

SUNDAY MORNING
Reports and Long Documents 273

SUNDAY AFTERNOON
Web Pages 341

APPENDIX
Online Resources 397

Index 400

CONTENTS

Introduction x

FRIDAY EVENING
Reviewing the Basics 1
    Finding Your Current Level of Expertise 3
    Starting and Exiting Word 4
    Learning Your Way around Word 5
    Working with Windows 7
    Communicating with Word 11
    Using Dialog Boxes 20
    Changing How the Document Looks Onscreen 24
    Using the Help System 32
    Take a Break 43
    Creating and Editing a Document 43
    Saving Your Work 60
    Closing a Document 65
    Opening a Saved Document 66
    Printing a Word Document 70
    Time-Savers 74

SATURDAY MORNING
Correspondence 81

    What Kinds of Correspondence? 83
    Understanding Templates 84
    Creating a Letter from a Template 85
    Creating a Letter from Scratch 88
    Checking for Errors 106
    Designing Letterhead 112
    Working with Preprinted Stationery 125
    Creating an Envelope 126
    Time-Savers 131

SATURDAY AFTERNOON
Flyers and Newsletters 147

    What Is Desktop Publishing? 149
    Creating a Permission Slip Flyer 150
    Creating a Party Invitation Flyer 155
    Creating a Map 169
    Creating an Advertising Flyer 180
    Take a Break 183
    Creating a Newsletter 184
    Time-Savers 202

SATURDAY EVENING
Mail Merge and Tables 217

    The Basic Mail Merge Process 219
    Assembling Data in a Table 222
    Creating a Merge Letter 229
    Executing a Merge 232
    Save Your Work! 241
    Using Other Kinds of Data Sources 242
    Take a Break 250
    Creating Merged Mailing Labels 251
    Creating Merged Envelopes 254
    Merging a Data Table into a Catalog Listing 257
    Time-Savers 259

SUNDAY MORNING
Reports and Long Documents............................273
- What Makes Longer Documents Different?.............275
- Creating an Outline.....................................276
- Styles Offer Consistency...............................289
- Take a Break..302
- Creating Running Headers and Footers................302
- Creating a Table of Contents..........................315
- Creating an Index.....................................319
- Time-Savers..329

SUNDAY AFTERNOON
Web Pages...341
- A Crash Course in Internet Jargon....................343
- How Web Pages Differ from Other Documents..........346
- Creating a Simple Web Page..........................347
- Creating a Simple Web Site..........................352
- Take a Break..366
- Creating Hyperlinks within a Page....................366
- Creating a Page with Graphical Hyperlinks............369
- Inserting Images on a Page...........................374
- Creating Horizontal Lines on a Web Page.............378
- Publishing the Pages..................................381
- Testing Your Web Pages...............................389
- Getting More Visitors to Your Web Pages.............389
- Editing Your Web Pages...............................390
- Time-Savers..391
- Conclusion..395

APPENDIX
Online Resources......................................397
- Technical Support.....................................398
- Upgrades and Add-Ins.................................398
- Newsgroup Discussions................................399

Index..400

ACKNOWLEDGMENTS

Once again I had a great editorial team at Prima Publishing who helped make this book the product you now hold in your hands. Thanks as always to Debbie Abshier, my favorite Acquisitions Editor in the business, for another opportunity to write for Prima. Chris Katsaropoulos (an old pro in the computer book industry) handled development, with a perfect balance of helpful suggestions and positive feedback. Kelli Crump kept us all on track and always knew where the files were. Thanks, Kelli! Hilary Powers clarified my wording where needed, and Paul Marchessault provided a great tech edit—making sure that all the steps work. Last but not least, Marian Hartsough handled the desktop publishing and made sure that the printer received the manuscript in an attractive form. Thanks everybody!

ABOUT THE AUTHOR

Faithe Wempen (M.A. English) is the owner of Wempen Editorial Services, an Indianapolis-based company that provides writing and editing support to computer book publishers and OEM software developers. Faithe also teaches hardware and software classes, provides one-on-one computer tutoring, and troubleshoots and repairs computers. She has written more than a dozen computer books, including *The Essential Excel 97 Book* from Prima Publishing, and edited over 250 more.

INTRODUCTION

Welcome to a jam-packed weekend of Word! By picking up this book, you're enrolling in an intensive, fast-paced training course that will, in less than 72 hours, teach you more about Word than most books *twice* its size. Amazing but true.

Most books of this size cover only basic skills. They arbitrarily decide what the "easy skills" are in a program, and then they leave out everything else. Unfortunately, real-world word processing doesn't have any respect for such arbitrary divisions, so you end up not getting all the help you need.

Learn Word 97 In a Weekend takes a completely different approach. Instead of dividing things up in the traditional way, first I asked my friends and students this question: "What would you really like to create with Word?" You'll find their answers in the projects in this book.

If a particular project requires you to learn about a feature that some people would consider "advanced," like text frames or running footers, that won't be a barrier; we'll dive right into it. Real life doesn't have tidy categories for what's "basic" and what's not—you just learn what you need to know to get the job done. This is the exact approach this unique book takes.

Who Is This Book For?

Learn Word 97 In a Weekend is for anyone who wants or needs to use Word, but needs some help learning on his or her own. It's for you if you need to:

- Write and save copies of correspondence.
- Make flyers for business or school.
- Create newsletters for businesses, clubs, churches, or schools.
- Design professional-looking reports for work.
- Create a personal Web page on the Internet.

By the end of the book, you will create all these projects, and in the process, you will master almost all the Word features that the average person will ever need to use.

Why Should I Take a Course from a Book?

The first reason is that you can learn at your own pace. I teach classes in Word, so I see firsthand that different people have different "ideal speeds" at which they learn. There is always one speed demon who is bored and tapping a pencil most of the time, and there's always one slower or less experienced student who struggles to keep up with what seems like a dizzying flow of information. I always feel sorry for both these students. If I taught them one-on-one, I would tailor the class just for the individual. With a course-in-a-book, you can take things at your ideal speed.

Another benefit of a book course is it allows you to have a real life. If your sister needs a ride to the airport or your dog gets sick in the middle of the Saturday Afternoon lesson, you can go take care of things and come back right where you left off. No penalty—no forfeited tuition. The chapter titles (Friday Evening, Saturday Morning, and so on) are merely guidelines for those who really want to pack it all into a single weekend.

If your pace turns out to be slower, or you need half-day breaks for real-life projects, feel free to spread the material out to two weekends or even an entire week. You can dedicate five evenings in a typical week, one to each section, and accomplish the same thing. Or use some evening time and some weekend time. The design of the book is flexible, but if you really want to get through it all quickly, start Friday and by Sunday night you'll have finished it all. It's entirely up to you.

Finally, compare the cost of this book to what you would pay at any training center for an all-weekend Word course. In my area, prices for such courses (if you can even find them) start at $200 and go up from there.

What Do I Need to Use This Book?

You need a PC with Microsoft Windows 95 and Word 97 installed. You will also be happier if you have at least a Pentium and 16MB of RAM (32MB or more is even better; I have 64MB and I still run out of memory now and then). *What do I have?*

If you installed Word 97 with the default setup program options, you may want to rerun the setup program to install some components that aren't installed by default, such as the Internet tools and the extra clip art. If you run into a feature at any point in the book that doesn't appear on your copy of Word, the first place to turn is the setup program—you probably just need the custom installation.

For the Sunday Afternoon project (a Web page), you will need Internet access (either through a network or through a modem and a local Internet Service Provider) if you want to publish your page to the Web. Of course, you can create a page without Internet access, just for practice.

TIP If you have Internet access, you should download the Microsoft Office 97 patch from the Microsoft Web site. The patch provides updated Web publishing tools, among other minor improvements to Word 97. See the Time-Savers section at the end of the Friday Evening session for details.

What's Covered in This Book?

Here's a quick tour of what you'll learn as you move through your weekend.

Friday Evening: Reviewing the Basics walks beginners through some basic Word skills, like opening and saving files, printing your work, navigating dialog boxes, using the Help system, and so on. Feel free to skip it if you have already been using Word and feel comfortable with the skills listed in the first few pages of the chapter.

Saturday Morning: Correspondence starts out easy, creating simple letters, and then eases you into changing margins and indents, using different fonts and text sizes, creating and modifying templates, printing envelopes, and spell-checking.

Saturday Afternoon: Flyers and Newsletters helps you turn Word into a desktop publishing system. You'll learn about clip art and other graphics, text boxes, multi-column documents, section breaks, and WordArt.

Saturday Evening: Mail Merge and Tables gets down to business, using Word's table and merge features to set up a mass mailing. You'll also learn how to print mailing labels and batches of envelopes.

Sunday Morning: Reports and Long Documents finds you planning business-like documents such as manuscripts and proposals. You'll learn about outlining and styles, page numbering, running headers and footers, indexes and tables of contents, master documents, and all the other power tools you need to manage a document with many pages.

Sunday Afternoon: Web Pages helps you design your own presence on the Internet. You'll create several simple Web pages, and then graduate to more complex ones containing graphics and special formatting. Finally, you'll learn how to transfer the proper files to an Internet server to make your pages available to the public.

How Can I Prepare for the Weekend Course?

This weekend course will take you through several projects, and you can learn Word nicely by just following the default examples. However, you will get much more out of the weekend if you modify the examples to fit your own needs. For example, on Saturday morning, rather than creating the generic letter shown in the figures, write a real letter that you plan on mailing to someone. This will kill two birds with one stone—you'll learn Word, and you'll take care of some writing jobs that need to be completed anyway.

The other thing to do, if you plan on completing the course in a single weekend, is to clear your schedule. Make sure that all your real-life bases are covered, so you can focus more on the lessons and less on your surroundings.

Introduction XV

Special Elements to Look For

Throughout this book, you'll find several special elements that will help you learn about Word.

 Notes provide extra information that you don't need right at the moment but might like to keep in mind for future reference.

 Tips offer extra "insider" information about a feature, or provide advice and ideas that you can use in your work.

 Cautions warn you about mistakes and pitfalls that inexperienced users often fall into.

Text you type appears in **bold, like this**.

If you can get Word to take action by pressing Alt plus one letter out of a menu name or other command, the letter—called a *hot key*—will show up with an underscore beneath it. For example, you can access the Window menu by pressing Alt+W.

When you really need to know how to use a certain feature that was covered in an earlier session, I'll provide a cross-reference back to where we discussed it; you can skip around if you want, without getting lost.

At the end of each chapter, you'll find a Time-Savers section. In these sections, you'll learn about some extra settings of features in Word that most people don't know about—things that can make it easier to create documents in the future. For example, do you know that if you usually save files in a type other than Word 97, you can set up that file type as a default so Word automatically saves in that format? You'll learn about this trick in the Time-Savers in Friday Evening's session.

I hope you're as excited about this book as I am. Turn to page 1 and get started!

FRIDAY EVENING

Reviewing the Basics

- Starting and exiting Word
- Communicating with Word
- Using the Help system
- Creating and editing a document
- Saving your work

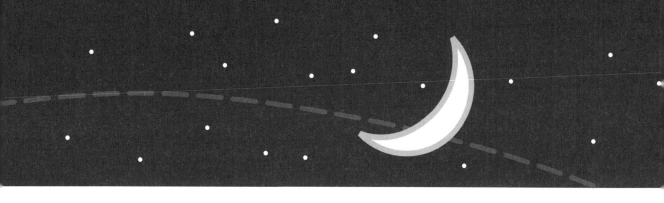

Okay, so maybe Friday evening isn't part of the weekend, strictly speaking, but you'll be so busy on Saturday and Sunday creating real, practical documents that you need to get some of the basics out of the way. So why not tonight?

Finding Your Current Level of Expertise

If you're familiar with Word, you might not even need to complete this session. This evening's instruction is primarily for people new to Word, or who are not confident with basic Word controls and file handling. Take this quick quiz to see where you need to start. Just check the boxes that apply.

I know how to:

- ❏ Start and exit Word on my computer.
- ❏ Use the menus and toolbars.
- ❏ Save my work.
- ❏ Open a saved document.
- ❏ Use the Help system.
- ❏ Move the cursor around in a document.
- ❏ Cut and paste text.
- ❏ Select a block of text for editing.
- ❏ Find and replace strings of text.

If you checked off all the boxes in this list, feel free to skip this session and get some sleep. You can start on the projects early Saturday morning.

If you checked off most of the boxes, you might want to skim this session tonight and pick up the bits of knowledge that you don't know.

If you checked off less than half of the boxes, this Friday Evening session will be perfect for you! You can skip around and pick up the topics you need most if you're pressed for time, but it might be best to start at the beginning and work your way through the whole thing. Now you won't miss anything you'll wish you knew later.

NOTE There is one essential bit in this session that nobody who uses the Office 97 version of Word should miss. It's in the Time-Savers section at the end of this session, and it involves upgrading your copy of Word 97 to the latest version by downloading a patch from the Microsoft Web site. Some of the features you'll learn about in this book will work better with the patch installed, so you'll want to do this before you start the Saturday morning session.

Starting and Exiting Word

There are a lot of ways to start Word. For now, take a look at my favorite way: using the Start menu on the Windows Taskbar.

1. Click on the Start button (bottom left corner of the screen). A menu opens.
2. Point your mouse pointer to the word Programs. (Don't click.) A cascading menu containing program names opens. On my computer, the Programs menu looks like Figure 1.1, but you probably have different programs installed.
3. Point your mouse to Microsoft Word, and click. The program starts.

FRIDAY EVENING Reviewing the Basics   5

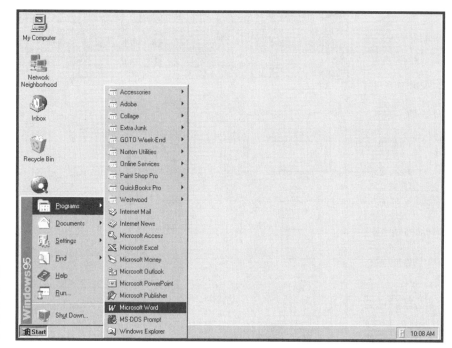

Figure 1.1

An easy way to start Word is to use the Start menu command.

Learning Your Way around Word

So now Word is open, and you're staring at it. First things first: what is all that stuff on the screen? If you already know, feel free to skip this section; but if you don't, hang on tight for a whirlwind tour.

NOTE If this is your first time using Word, the Office Assistant (a paper-clip character) may pop up to ask if you need help. If you see him, click the button labeled "Start Using Word" to continue. The Office Assistant is part of the Help system, which I'll cover a little later this evening.

6 Learn Word 97 In a Weekend

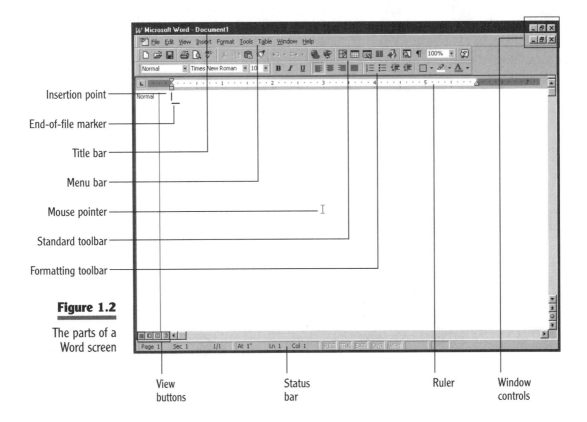

Figure 1.2

The parts of a Word screen

In Figure 1.2, I labeled some of the more important controls in the Word window. Take a quick look at them now, because you'll spend quite a bit of this session learning how to use each of them. The following list describes each control:

- **Window controls.** These let you minimize, maximize, restore, or close the Word window or the document window within it.
- **Insertion point.** This vertical line shows where anything you type will appear. You can move the insertion point with the arrow keys on the keyboard or by clicking with the mouse where you want it.
- **End-of-file marker.** This horizontal line shows the bottom of the

file. When you start out, there is no text, so the end-of-file marker is right next to the insertion point. You can move the end-of-file marker down by pressing Enter.

- **Mouse pointer.** When it's in the work area (as shown in Figure 1.2), it's an I-beam shape. Wherever you click, the insertion point will move to that spot on the screen. If you move the mouse pointer up to a toolbar or menu, it changes to an arrow. You may see other pointer shapes too, depending on what you're doing.
- **Title bar.** This bar across the top of the Word window shows the program name (Microsoft Word) and the document name (Document1). When you save your work under a meaningful name, it appears in the title bar replacing the default name.
- **Menu bar.** This thin gray bar contains the names of the menus you can open. Click on a word to open a menu; then click on a command on the menu to choose it.
- **Standard toolbar.** This toolbar contains a series of shortcut buttons for commonly used menu commands. Click on a button to activate the command. Hold the mouse pointer over a button without clicking to get a ScreenTip which tells what the button is for.
- **Formatting toolbar.** This toolbar is just like the Standard one except its buttons pertain mainly to formatting commands.
- **Ruler.** The ruler shows you where your margins are set and enables you to set and remove tab stops.
- **View buttons.** These buttons are shortcuts for the commands on the View menu that change the way the document is displayed onscreen.

Working with Windows

You may (or may not) have noticed that every program in Windows 95 runs in a window. If you are familiar with the window concept already, feel free to skip this section.

Controlling the Word Window

By default, Word's window is *maximized*, which means it fills the entire screen. You can "unmaximize" it (a.k.a. "restore it") by clicking on the Restore button (the middle of the three buttons in the top right corner). Doing so makes the Word window smaller, so you can see part of the Windows desktop behind it, as shown in Figure 1.3.

You can also minimize a window to get it out of the way. To do this, click the Minimize button (the one with the underline on it). When you minimize a window, it shrinks itself down to a small bar in the Taskbar (see Figure 1.4). To reopen a minimized window, just click on its name on the Taskbar.

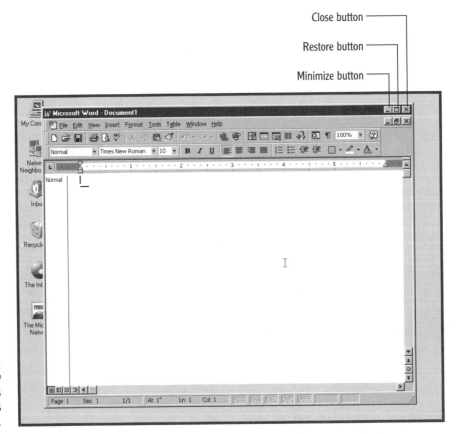

Figure 1.3

This window has been restored to its original size.

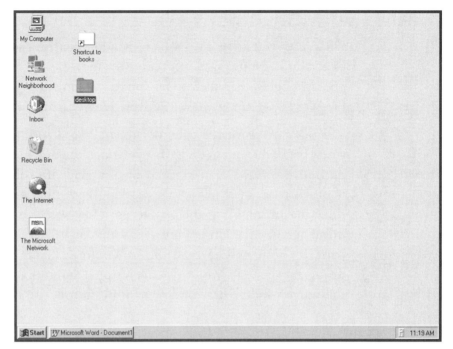

Figure 1.4

The Word window is minimized now.

 NOTE While writing this book, I set my Taskbar in Windows 95 to a setting called "Auto Hide." The Taskbar does not appear unless I move my mouse pointer down to its area. I do this so that more of the Word 97 screen shows in my illustrations. You can Auto Hide your Taskbar; just right-click on the Taskbar, click on Properties, and click to place a check mark in the Auto Hide check box.

The last window control button is the X and it stands for Close. You can close any window (not just minimize it) by clicking on the window's Close button (X). Go ahead and try it, and then reopen Word. If you get a message asking if you want to save your changes, click on No.

Working with Document Windows in Word

Okay, now you know the basics of window controls, so I'll throw a little twist into it. Notice in Word that there are two sets of window controls, one right below the other. So far you've used only the top set, the ones for the Word program window. Can you guess what the other set is for?

The other set is for the open document. Word automatically gives you a new blank document each time you open the program. By default, this document window is maximized (it completely fills the window within which it resides). When you're working with only one document at a time, maximizing it is the way to go. However, if two or more documents are open at once, you may want them restored so you can see parts of both windows at the same time. Figure 1.5 shows three documents open in Word; two are restored and one is minimized. Only the active window has window control buttons. To open a minimized

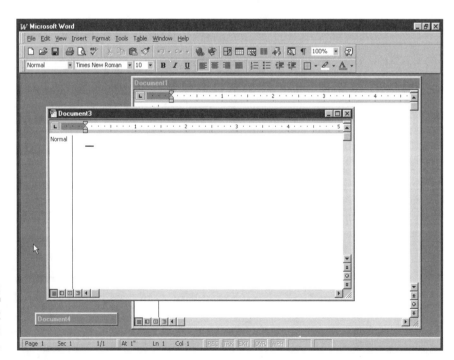

Figure 1.5

Three document windows are open in Word.

window, double-click on its name, or click once on it and then click on the Maximize or Restore button.

To switch among document windows, you can click on any visible part of the window you want to use. If the window isn't visible, open the Window menu and click on the name of the window.

Moving and Resizing a Window

Whenever a window is not maximized, you can resize and move it. To move a window, drag its title bar with the mouse.

TIP You may know this already, but to drag, you click and hold down the left mouse button while moving the mouse; then release the mouse button when the item has moved to where you want.

To resize a window, you can drag any edge of the window. To resize in just one direction, drag a flat side; to resize in two directions at once, drag a corner.

Communicating with Word

Now Word is open on your screen, and the window is just the way you want it. You're ready to start creating something! If you want to jot down some thoughts, start typing. Text appears in the work area (the big white area in the middle).

However, if you want to do more than raw typing, you need to learn how to communicate with Word—to issue commands to indicate your desires (for example, a change in the margins or font size). There are several ways to deliver commands to Word:

- Menu commands
- Shortcut keys

- Toolbar buttons
- Shortcut menus

Using Menu Commands

Using a menu command is the most traditional method. To open a menu, just click on its name on the menu bar. A menu drops down, seemingly out of nowhere. From there, click on the command to select it. For example, in the last section, I wrote that you could switch among open windows by selecting the one you wanted from the Window menu. I've illustrated this in Figure 1.6. Notice the currently active window's name has a check mark by it; I can click on any of the other windows' names to make one of them active instead.

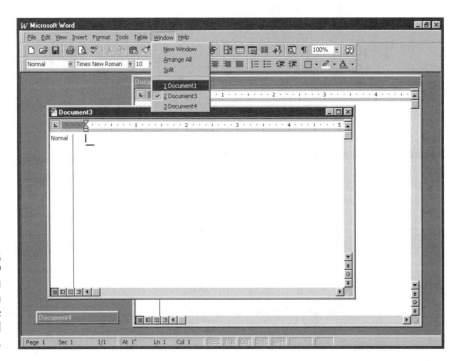

Figure 1.6

The Window menu is open and I can click on the document I want to use.

Menus can contain much more than simple commands like the ones in Figure 1.6. Take a look at Figure 1.7. There are:

- **Cascading menus.** When you see a right-pointing arrow next to a command, it means that if you place the mouse pointer over it, a cascading menu appears, just as on the Start menu you used to start Word from Windows 95.

- **Ellipses (. . .).** When you see an ellipsis next to a command, it means that if you click on the command, a dialog box will appear (more about dialog boxes shortly).

- **Icons.** Some commands have little pictures—often referred to as *icons*—next to them. These pictures match up with a toolbar button on one or more of the toolbars. It's the signal to use the toolbar button in the future as a shortcut to issuing the command.

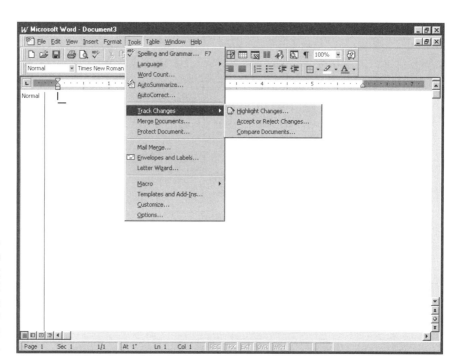

Figure 1.7

This menu has a lot more complicated controls than the simple Window menu you saw in Figure 1.6.

- **Underlined letters.** All commands and menus have an underlined letter in their name. This is for people who prefer to use the keyboard instead of the mouse. An alternative way of opening a menu is to press Alt while you type the underlined letter in the menu name. Once the menu is open, you can select a command by typing the underlined letter in the command's name (you don't have to press Alt once the menu is open).

- **Shortcut keys.** When you see a key (or a combination of keys) listed next to a command on a menu (like F7 or Ctrl+C), it means that next time you can access the command without opening the menu system by simply pressing the key (or combination of keys).

Shortcut keys are not very useful initially because you have to open a menu to see the key(s). However, as you become more experienced, you will begin to remember the shortcut keys, and you may find them quicker than the menu system.

Some commands may not be available at certain times. Unavailable commands are grayed out (they appear in gray letters rather than black). You can't see this in Figure 1.7, but if you open the Edit menu with no text selected, you'll see that the Cut and Copy commands are grayed out along with several others.

Using Toolbar Buttons

As you can see in Figure 1.7, there are two rows of little pictures (icons) across the top of the screen. They are *toolbars*, and each picture is a button. To use a button, just click on it. There is an additional toolbar at the bottom of the screen.

Toolbar buttons are great time-savers for most people. Instead of fumbling through the menu system to try to locate the command you want and choosing the right setting from the dialog box, you can simply click the appropriate toolbar button to issue the same command. For example, to make text bold, select it (I'll explain selecting later tonight), and then choose from the following two options:

- Open the F<u>o</u>rmat menu and click on the <u>F</u>ont command. A dialog box appears. In the dialog box, click on the Bold attribute and then click on the OK button to close the dialog box.
- Click on the Bold button on the Formatting toolbar.

As you can see, toolbar buttons can make things a lot easier. Some toolbar buttons open dialog boxes (like the Open button). Other buttons (like the Bold button) issue commands immediately that are normally buried in a dialog box. Others open drop-down lists from which to choose (see Figure 1.8). Open a list by clicking on the down arrow next to the item you want to change.

A few commands are toggle switches that turn a particular attribute or element on or off (in Figure 1.8, Italic is turned "on"). Some buttons simply perform a function (for example, the Print button), while others, like the Font Color button (the last button on the Formatting toolbar), are combination tools. Click on the button to apply the current setting, or click on the down arrow to open a list of other settings.

TIP The four alignment buttons are mutually exclusive; click on one and the previously selected one becomes unselected.

Figure 1.8

Toolbar buttons vary as to how they operate.

Want to know more about the toolbar buttons? Position the mouse pointer over a button to see a ScreenTip that explains the button's function. To get you started, Tables 1.1 and 1.2 list the default buttons on the Standard and Formatting toolbars.

NOTE Other toolbars may appear, depending on what you're doing. For example, when you're working with a picture, a Picture toolbar appears. You can also create your own toolbars, as you'll learn at the end of the Sunday Morning session.

TABLE 1.1 STANDARD TOOLBAR BUTTONS

Button	Name	Purpose
	New	Starts a new document based on the Normal template.
	Open	Opens the Open dialog box so you can utilize a saved document file.
	Save	Opens the Save dialog box so you can save a document; if the document has been saved previously, this button simply resaves it under the same name.
	Print	Sends the active document to the printer immediately, with no opportunity to set print options.
	Print Preview	Opens the print preview window so you can see how the document will look when printed.
	Spelling and Grammar	Starts a spelling and grammar check.
	Cut	Moves the selected text or objects from the document to the Windows Clipboard.

Table 1.1 Standard Toolbar Buttons (continued)

Button	Name	Purpose
	Copy	Copies the selected text or objects from the document to the Windows Clipboard.
	Paste	Copies the contents of the Windows Clipboard into the document at the insertion point location.
	Format Painter	Copies the formatting of the selected text or object, and then pastes the formatting onto the next selection you make.
	Undo	Reverses the last action. If you open the drop-down list, you can specify a number of actions to reverse.
	Redo	Reverses the last Undo operation. If you open the drop-down list, you can specify a number of actions to redo.
	Insert Hyperlink	Opens the Insert Hyperlink dialog box so you can insert an Internet address into your document.
	Web Toolbar	Displays and hides a special toolbar useful for working with HTML (Internet) documents.
	Tables and Borders	Displays and hides a special toolbar containing controls for creating and formatting tables and adding borders to table cells and paragraphs.
	Insert Table	Opens a drop-down grid of white squares; drag across them with the mouse to indicate the number of rows and columns you want in your new table.
	Insert Microsoft Excel Worksheet	Same as Insert Table, except the object inserted is an Excel worksheet instead of a Word table.

Table 1.1 Standard Toolbar Buttons (continued)

Button	Name	Purpose
	Columns	Opens a drop-down grid of columns; drag across it to indicate the number of columns in which you want your document formatted. Select text first if you want only certain text formatted into columns.
	Drawing	Displays and hides the Drawing toolbar, useful for drawing lines and shapes in your document.
	Document Map	Displays and hides Document Map view, a special view useful for managing large documents.
	Show/Hide ¶	Displays and hides nonprinting characters.
100%	Zoom	Enables you to choose a zoom percentage from a list.
	Office Assistant	Makes the Office Assistant character appear. If it is already visible, Office Assistant asks you what you want help with.

Table 1.2 Formatting Toolbar Buttons

Button	Name	Purpose
Normal	Style	Enables you to choose a style from a list.
Times New Roman	Font	Enables you to choose a font from a list.
10	Font Size	Enables you to choose a font size from a list.

Table 1.2 Formatting Toolbar Buttons (continued)

Button	Name	Purpose
B	Bold	Turns the bold attribute on and off.
I	Italic	Turns the italic attribute on and off.
U	Underline	Turns the underline attribute on and off.
≡	Align Left	Sets paragraphs to align with the left margin.
≡	Center	Sets paragraphs to center alignment.
≡	Align Right	Sets paragraphs to align with the right margin.
≡	Justify	Sets paragraphs to space out so they align with both the left and right margins.
≔	Numbering	Turns the numbered list attribute on and off for a paragraph.
≔	Bullets	Turns the bulleted list attribute on and off for a paragraph.
⇐	Decrease Indent	Moves the paragraph one tab stop toward the left margin each time it's pressed.
⇒	Increase Indent	Moves the paragraph one tab stop toward the right margin each time it's pressed.

Table 1.2 Formatting Toolbar Buttons (continued)

Button	Name	Purpose
	Border	Applies the current border. You can open the drop-down list to choose a different border.
	Highlight	Applies the current highlight. You can open the drop-down list to choose a different highlight color (or no color).
	Font Color	Applies the current color to the font. You can open the drop-down list to choose a different font color.

Shortcut Menus

One of the neat features about Windows 95 programs is that the right mouse button has a purpose. When you right-click on an object (such as text or an icon), a shortcut menu pops up listing the things you can do to the object.

For example, in Figure 1.9, I right-clicked on some text I typed. The shortcut menu lists several commands, including cutting, copying, pasting, changing the font, changing the paragraph attributes, creating a bulleted or numbered list, or drawing a table (you'll learn about all these features later in the book). Once the shortcut menu is open, you can select a command by clicking on it (with the left mouse button), or you can close the menu by left-clicking anywhere outside it or pressing Esc.

Using Dialog Boxes

As you learned earlier in this chapter, some menu commands and toolbar buttons open *dialog boxes*. Dialog boxes are simply requests for more information or opportunities for you to change default settings before

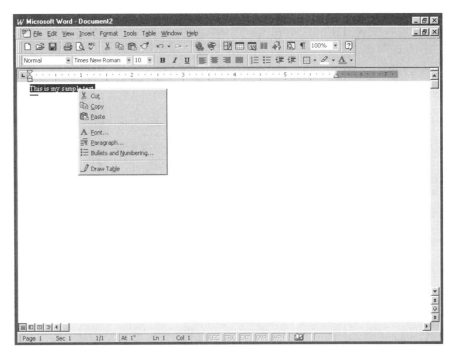

Figure 1.9

Right-click on anything for a shortcut menu.

Word executes a command. Figure 1.10 shows some common dialog box controls you may encounter. Here is a quick summary:

- **Tabs.** Some dialog boxes have multiple pages with tabs because there are too many controls to fit in a single box. Click on a tab to move to that page of the dialog box.

- **Option buttons.** When you must choose one from a group of options, round option buttons appear. Like buttons on a car radio, only one will work at a time. When you click on one, the prior selection becomes deselected.

- **Text boxes.** Just type text into a text box (see Figure 1.11).

- **Increment buttons.** Text boxes in which you're supposed to enter a number often have increment buttons. Click on the up arrow to increase the number by one (from 1 to 2, for example); click on the down arrow to decrease the number by one.

22 Learn Word 97 In a Weekend

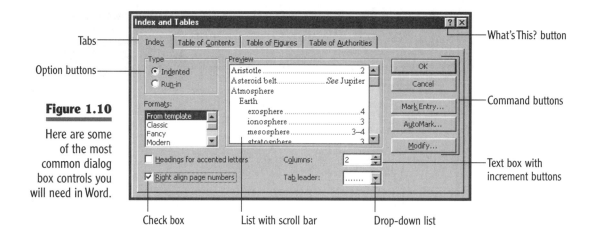

Figure 1.10

Here are some of the most common dialog box controls you will need in Word.

Figure 1.11

On the Sender Info tab, you can type your return address in the text box

- **Check boxes.** Check boxes are on/off switches for certain features. Click the box to place or remove a check mark. An activated feature has a check mark.

- **Command buttons.** Command buttons take you somewhere else. Some buttons, such as the Preview button, take you to an entirely different screen and close the dialog box. Command buttons with ellipses (. . .) open other dialog boxes. Command buttons with >> on them open additional sections of the same dialog box (see Figure 1.12).

- **OK and Cancel buttons.** Almost all dialog boxes have these two buttons. OK accepts your changes and closes the dialog box; Cancel rejects your changes and closes the dialog box.

- **What's This? button.** In some dialog boxes, a ? button appears in the title bar. You can click this button and then click a dialog box control (such as a button or list) to find out how the control is used.

- **Office Assistant button.** Some dialog boxes have an Office Assistant button, which you can click on to open Office Assistant to get help with a procedure. (You can't click on the regular Office Assistant button on the Standard toolbar while a dialog box is open.)

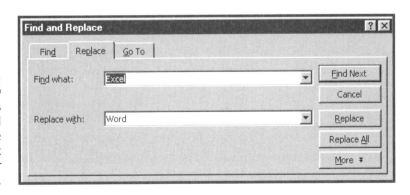

Figure 1.12

Command buttons with arrows expand or collapse the current dialog box to show more or fewer controls.

Changing How the Document Looks Onscreen

One thing that separates Word from lesser word processing programs is its flexibility in viewing. Here's what you can do:

- Zoom in and out
- Switch among Normal, Page Layout, Online Layout, Outline, and Master Document views
- Choose which nonprinting characters you want to see

Let's take a quick look at each of these individually.

Zooming

The zoom function changes the ratio between the on-screen size of your document and its actual size when printed. A 100% view shows the letters onscreen at approximately the same size as they will be when printed (on an average-size monitor). You can zoom in (increase the zoom setting to more than 100%) to see a smaller portion of the document close up. You can also zoom out (decrease the zoom setting to less than 100%) to see more of the page onscreen at once. To move to other areas of the page, drag the scroll boxes in the scroll bars. Figures 1.13 and 1.14 show zoom settings of 40% and 150%, respectively.

The easiest way to change the zoom is to open the Zoom drop-down list on the Standard toolbar (see Figure 1.15). Just click on the down arrow next to the current percentage and then click on a different percentage on the list.

If you need a more precise zoom percentage, open the View menu and choose Zoom. A dialog box opens, as shown in Figure 1.16. You can use the Percent box to specify an exact percentage. Click on the up and down arrows to change the value by one percent at a time, or type a new number directly into the box and press Enter. Click on OK when you're finished with the dialog box.

FRIDAY EVENING Reviewing the Basics

Figure 1.13

At 40%, you can see the entire page at once.

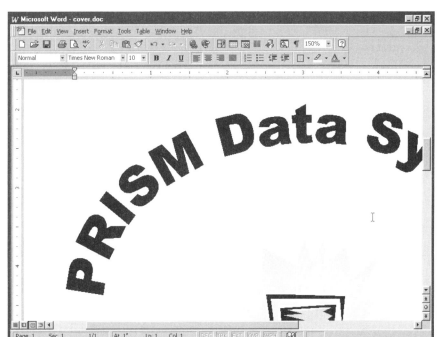

Figure 1.14

At 150%, only a portion of the page is visible, but it is very large and close-up.

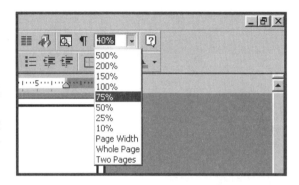

Figure 1.15

Switch quickly to any of the preset zoom percentages from the Zoom drop-down list.

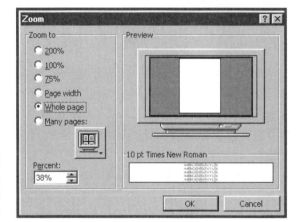

Figure 1.16

Set an exact zoom percentage in the Percent box.

Changing the View

Word comes with several different views, each one good for particular situations.

- **Normal view** is good for general text editing. It takes the least amount of your computer's memory, so major changes (like repagination) appear very quickly. Page breaks are indicated by dotted lines in Normal view (see Figure 1.17). Drawbacks: You can't see your headers and footers, WordArt, or multiple columns.

- **Online Layout view** is good for organizing a document you are going to publish on the World Wide Web, because it shows an outline of the document in a special panel on the left (see

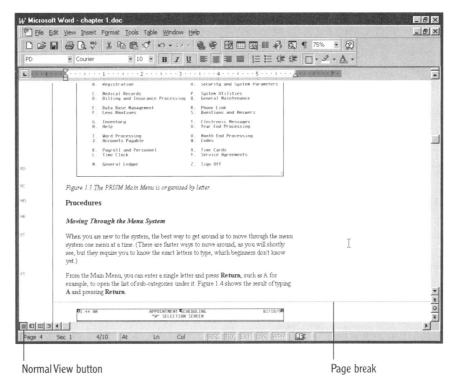

Figure 1.17

A sample document in Normal view

Normal View button   Page break

Figure 1.18). Page breaks do not show because there are no page breaks on a Web page. You'll see this view in action in the Sunday Afternoon session.

○ **Page Layout view** is great when you need to work with a document that contains WordArt, multiple columns, or headers and footers that you want to see while you're working. Page breaks are shown by actual page divisions in this view. You see the document approximately as it will print, as well (see Figure 1.19). Drawbacks: This view eats up your computer's memory, so repagination and other updates occur more slowly. This is especially noticeable on slower and older computers.

○ **Outline view** works well for organizing your thoughts into an outline that you will use to create a large document. When I am

28 Learn Word 97 In a Weekend

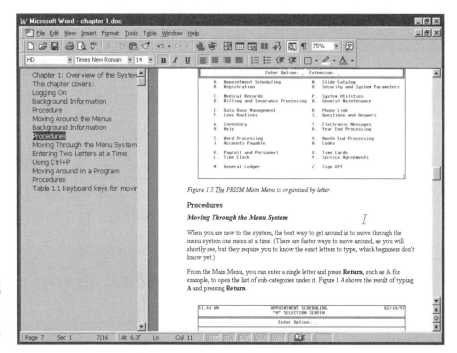

Figure 1.18

A sample document in Online Layout view

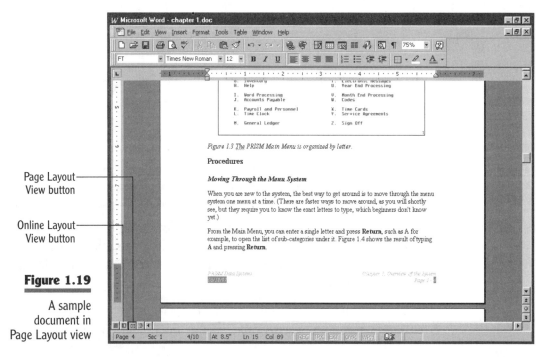

Page Layout View button

Online Layout View button

Figure 1.19

A sample document in Page Layout view

preparing to write a book, I always start in Outline view, as shown in Figure 1.20. In this view, outline levels are denoted by indents and different fonts. Also, a special Outlining toolbar appears.

○ **Master Document view** is useful only if you create a master document that contains subdocuments. Each subdocument is its own section; you can click on a subdocument's name to open it. This view is good to utilize when you are organizing large books with multiple chapters. Notice in Figure 1.21 that a special Master Document toolbar appears in addition to the Outlining toolbar. You'll learn more about Master Document view at the end of the Sunday Morning session.

There are several ways to change the view. The easiest is to click one of the View buttons in the bottom left corner of the screen (these are pointed out in Figures 1.17, 1.19, and 1.20). There is not a button for the Master Document view.

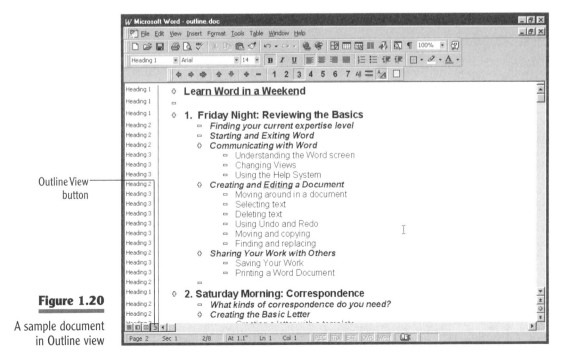

Figure 1.20

A sample document in Outline view

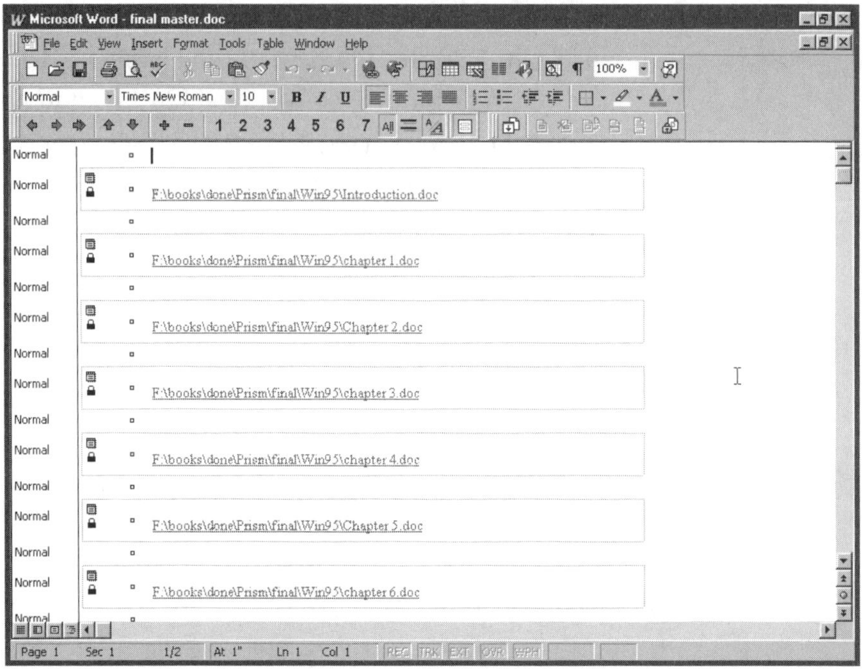

Figure 1.21

A sample document in Master Document view

The other way to change the view is to open the View menu and click on the name of the view you want (this is the method you use for the Master Document view).

Throughout the rest of this book, I'll assume that you'll switch to whatever view you find most helpful at the moment. Preferences vary: some people prefer to work in Page Layout view all the time. Personally, I like working primarily in Normal view and switching to the other views only when needed.

Displaying or Hiding Nonprinting Characters

Nonprinting characters are symbols like tab stops, spaces, and end-of-paragraph markers. Some people find that it helps to see these onscreen as they work so they can orient themselves within a document. Other people think it just clutters things up.

If you want to display or hide all the nonprinting characters, click the Show/Hide ¶ button on the Standard toolbar. Figure 1.22 shows a document with all the nonprinting characters displayed. Dots between words indicate spaces.

If you want to choose which nonprinting characters you want to see, choose Tools, Options (open the Tools menu and click on the Options command). Click on the View tab. Halfway down, you'll see a section called Nonprinting Characters, with a check box next to each type (see Figure 1.23). Click to select or deselect each type, and then click on OK.

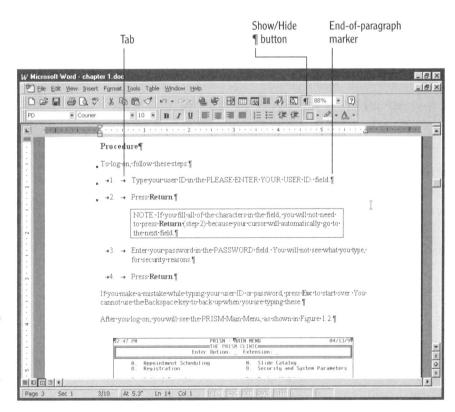

Figure 1.22

Some people find it useful to see nonprinting characters like these.

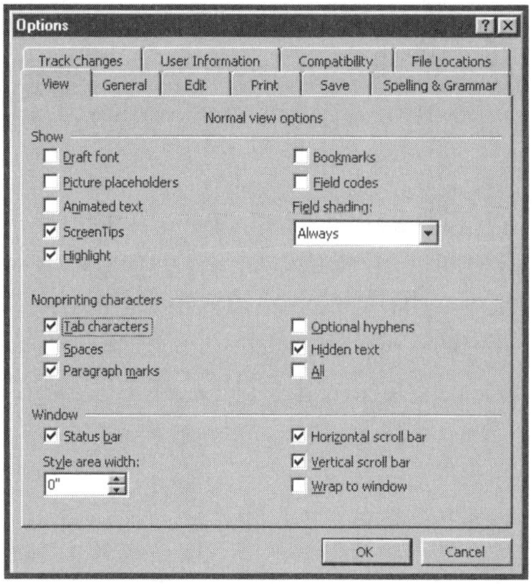

Figure 1.23

You can specify exactly which nonprinting characters you prefer to see onscreen in the Options dialog box.

Using the Help System

Word's Help system is a complete user manual, and it's better than a printed copy because you can jump quickly from section to section without looking up a single page number.

Since every person is different, Word offers many ways to get help with the program. Some of these Help methods will be familiar to experienced Windows users; others are brand-new for Office 97 products. You can do the following:

- Ask Office Assistant for help.
- Choose what you're interested in learning about from a series of Help topics.
- Get help on a particular element onscreen with the What's This? tool.
- If you are connected to the Internet, access the Microsoft on the Web feature to view Web pages containing Help information.

Office Assistant

Office Assistant is the little paper clip character that popped up the first time you started Word. It may look silly, but behind it is a powerful Help system.

 Office Assistant has replaced the Answer Wizard feature from Word for Windows 95.

By default, Office Assistant starts whenever you start Word and sits in a little box on top of whatever you're working on, as shown in Figure 1.24. You can turn it off by clicking on the Close button (X) in its top right corner. To turn Office Assistant on again, click the Office Assistant button in the Standard toolbar or choose Help, Microsoft Word Help.

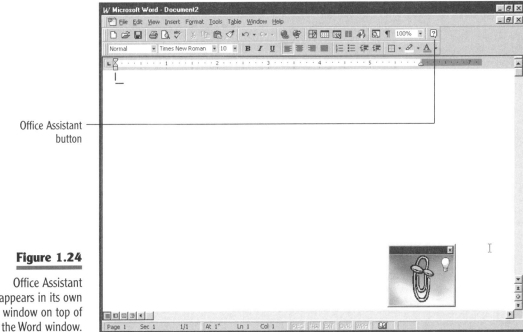

Figure 1.24

Office Assistant appears in its own window on top of the Word window.

TIP

If you don't like the paper clip, choose one of the other Office Assistants. Right-click on Office Assistant and click on Choose Assistant from the shortcut menu. Then click the Back and Next buttons to find an assistant that you prefer, and click on OK to change the character. If you get a message telling you that the file cannot be located, put your installation CD in your drive and try again.

When you open or click on Office Assistant, a bubble appears next to (or above) its box asking what kind of help you want (see Figure 1.25). You can do any of the following:

- Type a question in the text box to tell Office Assistant what kind of help you need and then click on Search.
- Select one of Office Assistant's guesses about what you need help with, if any appear.

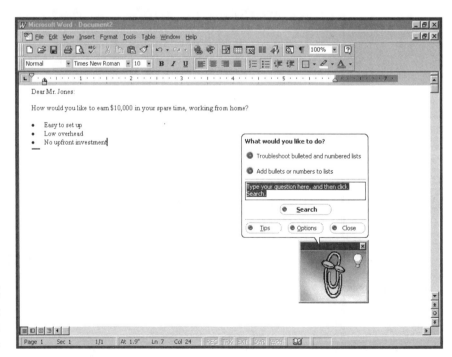

Figure 1.25

Office Assistant asks what you need help with.

- Click on the <u>T</u>ips button to get any tips that Office Assistant can provide for the task you're performing.
- Click on the <u>O</u>ptions button to customize the way Office Assistant works.
- Right-click in the Office Assistant window to select options from a shortcut menu.
- Click on Close (the word *Close,* not the X button) to close the bubble (but leave Office Assistant onscreen).

If you close the Help bubble, you can reopen it at any time by clicking on the Office Assistant button on the Standard toolbar; pressing F1; choosing <u>H</u>elp, Microsoft Word <u>H</u>elp; or clicking on the Office Assistant window.

TIP If a light bulb appears next to Office Assistant, it means that Office Assistant has a suggestion for you. To get the suggestion, click on the light bulb. Click on the Close button when you're finished reading the suggestion.

If you need help on a particular topic, simply type a question into the text box shown in Figure 1.26.

1. If Office Assistant's Help bubble isn't onscreen, click on the Office Assistant button on the Standard toolbar or click on the Office Assistant window.
2. Type a question into the text box. For example, you might type **How do I save?** to get help saving your work.
3. Click on the <u>S</u>earch button or press Enter. Office Assistant provides some topics that might match what you're looking for. For example, Figure 1.26 shows Office Assistant's responses to the question "How do I save?"
4. Click on the option that best describes what you're trying to do. For example, I chose "Save a document." A Help window appears

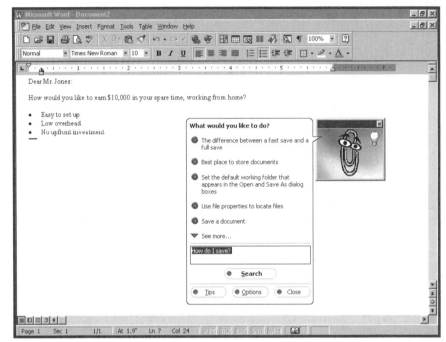

Figure 1.26

Office Assistant attempts to narrow down exactly what you are trying to accomplish.

with instructions for the specified task. If none of the options describe what you want, click on the See More arrow to view more options, or type in a different question in the text box.

The Help window that appears containing the task instructions is part of the same Help system that you can access with the Help, Contents and Index command. See "Working with Help Information" later in this session for information about navigating this window.

Help Topics

If you want a more conventional way to get help, try choosing the Contents and Index command on the Help menu. When you open the Word Help system in this way, you move through the topics listed to find the topic in which you're interested.

The Help system has several tabs, each one offering a different way to use Help. Click on a tab to display its options.

- **Contents** lets you browse the Help system as you would a reference book.
- **Index** lets you look up Help topics alphabetically.
- **Find** lets you search for a certain word among all the topics in the system.

Complete the steps in the following sections to use the Contents, Index, or Find methods of getting help.

Contents

The Contents tab of the Help system is a series of "books" you can open. Each book has one or more Help topics in it. Some books even contain other subbooks! It's like pulling a real book off the shelf and browsing through it for the topic in which you're interested. Figure 1.27 shows a Contents screen. To select a Help topic from the Contents screen, follow these steps:

1. Choose Help, Contents and Index.
2. Click on the Contents tab.
3. Find the book that describes, in broad terms, what you want help with and double-click on it. A list of Help topics appears below the book, as shown in Figure 1.27.
4. Double-click on a Help topic to display it.
5. When you finish reading a topic, click on the Help Topics button to go back to the main Help screen, or click on the Help window's Close button (X) to exit Help.

Index

The Index is an alphabetical listing of all the Help topics available. It works well if you know the exact term you want to look up, like saving or printing, for example. Use it as you would use the index in a real book.

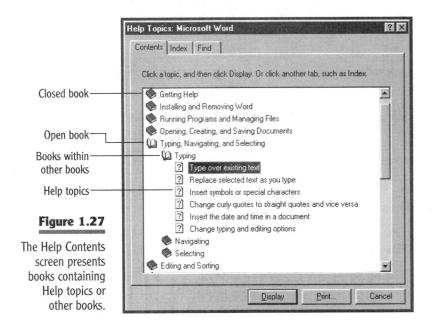

Figure 1.27

The Help Contents screen presents books containing Help topics or other books.

1. Choose Help, Contents and Index.
2. Click on the Index tab.
3. Type the first few letters of the topic you want help with. The index list jumps quickly to that spot (see Figure 1.28).
4. Double-click on the topic you want to see. You may see information, or you may see another list. If you see a list, double-click on a list item to get to specific information.
5. Read the information. See the section "Working with Help Information" for details.
6. When you finish reading a topic, click on the Help Topics button to go back to the main Help screen, or click on the Help window's Close button (X) to exit Help.

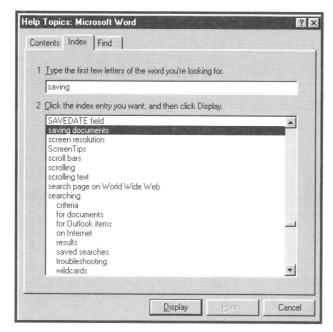

Figure 1.28

The Index tab enables you to browse alphabetically instead of by category.

Find

What if you're not sure of the name of the feature for which you're looking? Find works best in these situations. Find searches not only the titles of Help topics, but also their contents, and retrieves all the topics in which the text you typed appears.

1. Choose Help, Contents and Index.
2. Click on the Find tab. The first time you use Find, it asks you to build the Find index. Click on Next and then click on Finish to create the list.
3. Type the topic you're looking for in the top box (1).
4. If more than one line appears in the middle box (2), click on the one that most closely matches your interest. Find considers uppercase and lowercase versions of a word to be different. For example, in Figure 1.29 there are separate entries for "Save" and "save," as well as for other forms of the word ("saves" and "saved").

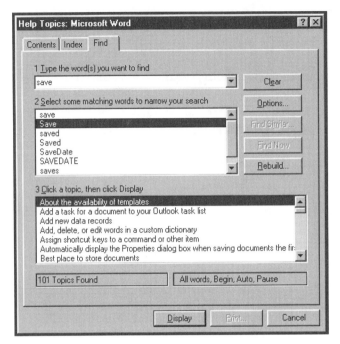

Figure 1.29

Use Find to locate all the Help topics that deal with a certain subject.

5. Browse the topics that appear at the bottom (3), and click on the one that matches the help you need (see Figure 1.29).

6. Click on the Display button or press Enter to display the Help information.

7. When you finish reading a topic, click on the Help Topics button to go back to the main Help screen, or click on the Help window's Close button (X) to exit Help.

Working with Help Information

After you locate the Help topic you need—then what? Read it, of course. All the methods of getting Help end up at the same place—only the journey is different. For example, you could locate the "Save a Document to an FTP Site" information by any of the four methods I told you about and get the same information shown in Figure 1.30.

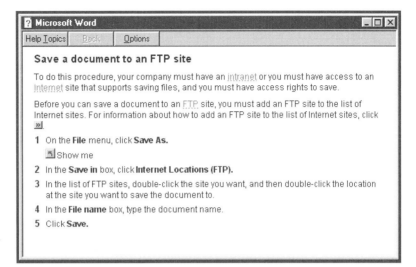

Figure 1.30

After you arrive at the information you need, you can read it onscreen, print it, or move to another Help topic.

When a Help topic is onscreen, here's what you can do with it:

○ Click on an underlined word to see a definition of it (for example, "intranet" in Figure 1.30).

○ Click on a button to jump to another Help screen. In Figure 1.30, a >> button is available to take you to a screen of related information.

○ Print a hard copy of the information by clicking on the Options button and then choosing Print Topic.

○ Copy the text to the Clipboard (for pasting to files in Microsoft Word or any other Windows-based program) by clicking on the Options button and then choosing Copy.

○ Return to the main Help topic that brought you to this subtopic by clicking on the Back button. The Back button is not available if you are viewing a topic that you arrived at directly from Office Assistant, Contents, Index, or Find.

○ Return to the main Help Topics screen by clicking on the Help Topics button.

○ Close the Help window by clicking on the Close button (X).

What's This? Help

Sometimes all the words and topics in the world can't help you. How do you look up a toolbar button when all you know is that it looks like a paintbrush, or a globe with a piece of chain on it?

The answer is the What's This? feature. You can point to an object onscreen and Word will tell you what that object's purpose is. Here's how it works:

1. Press Shift+F1 or choose <u>H</u>elp, What's <u>T</u>his? Your mouse pointer turns into a big arrow with a question mark next to it.
2. Click on an object. A box of information pops up telling you about it. For example, Figure 1.31 shows the information I received when I clicked on the ruler.

 TIP What's This? works well for screen elements in Word, but it also works for text onscreen and controls in dialog boxes. Try it any time and see what information you get!

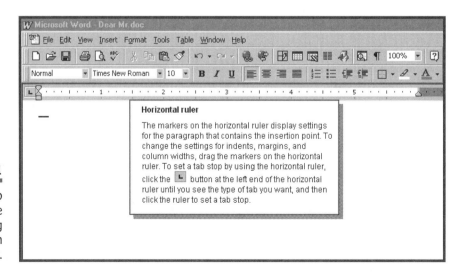

Figure 1.31

What's This? Help spares you the trouble of figuring out the name of an on-screen element.

Take a Break

Congratulations! You made it through half of the Friday Evening session. Stand up, have a stretch, and give your eyes a rest. This is a great time to go get a snack from the fridge. When you get back, you'll start working with text.

Creating and Editing a Document

When you start Word, you get a blank document automatically. You can use it, or you can create a new document based on a template. A *template* is a group of timesaving preprogrammed settings suitable for a particular type of document, such as a letter or a report. (You'll get a chance to use a template first thing tomorrow morning, so don't worry about it right now.)

For now, let's just stick with the blank document that is already on your screen. Go ahead and type several paragraphs right now. If you don't know what to type, type the text that appears in Figure 1.32. When you get to the end of a line, just keep typing; Word automatically wraps the text to the next line. To start a new paragraph, press Enter twice.

NOTE   You're pressing Enter once to start a new paragraph and once more to put a blank line between it and the next one. Tomorrow morning you'll learn how to adjust the spacing between paragraphs so it won't be necessary to place blank lines between them by hand.

Moving Around in a Document

Now that several paragraphs are onscreen, perhaps you want to move the insertion point back into the text you typed. For example, if you typed the text in Figure 1.32, try inserting a middle name for Manual between his first and last name. To do this, you need to position the insertion point, and then type additional text.

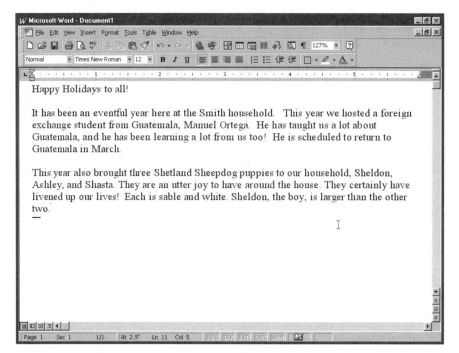

Figure 1.32

Here's the sample text I typed into Word.

 TIP Since Word is, by default, in Insert mode, the existing text moves over to make room for the text you're inserting. If you prefer, you can set Word to overwrite existing text with new text. Choose Tools, Options, and click on the Edit tab. Click to place a check mark in the Overtype mode check box, and then click on OK. Or, you can just press the Insert key on the keyboard.

There are several ways of moving the insertion point. One of the easiest is to press the arrow keys on the keyboard, moving the insertion point precisely where you want it. Beginners like this method because it doesn't require any dexterity with the mouse.

Another easy way is to position the mouse pointer (which changes to an I-beam over text) at the spot where you want the insertion point to go, and then click. Experienced users use this method because it is very fast, but sometimes beginners have a hard time positioning the mouse pointer in exactly the right spot.

If you can't see the spot where you want to place the insertion point (for example, if your document is longer than one screenful), use the scroll bars to move the display (see Figure 1.33). You can click on the up or down arrows to move the display up or down one line at a time. Also, you can drag the scroll box to move quickly through a long document, or click above or below the scroll box to move one screenful at a time.

Word also offers a variety of shortcut keys for moving around in a document (see Table 1.3). You won't need them just to make the simple edit of adding Manuel's middle name, but you might put a sticky note on this page so you can refer to it later, when you're working with longer documents.

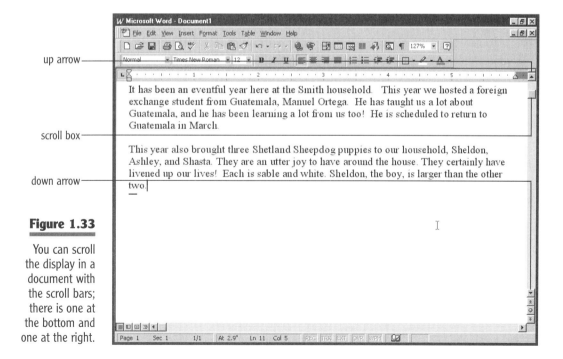

Figure 1.33

You can scroll the display in a document with the scroll bars; there is one at the bottom and one at the right.

Table 1.3 Shortcut Keys for Moving the Insertion Point

To Move	Press
One word to the left	Ctrl+Left Arrow
One word to the right	Ctrl+Right Arrow
One paragraph up	Ctrl+Up Arrow
One paragraph down	Ctrl+Down Arrow
One cell to the left (in a table)	Shift+Tab
One cell to the right (in a table)	Tab
To the end of a line	End
To the beginning of a line	Home
To the top of the window	Alt+Ctrl+Page Up
To the end of the window	Alt+Ctrl+Page Down
Up one screen (scrolling)	Page Up
Down one screen (scrolling)	Page Down
To the top of the next page	Ctrl+Page Down
To the top of the previous page	Ctrl+Page Up
To the end of a document	Ctrl+End
To the beginning of a document	Ctrl+Home

FRIDAY EVENING Reviewing the Basics

Selecting Text

It's very important to get the hang of selecting text, because this is something you'll need to do over and over in the upcoming sessions. When you select text, you're telling Word: "The next command that I give you should apply to the selected text." After you select text, you can issue almost any command—you can change the text's font, copy or cut it, make it into a different number of columns than the rest of the document, and so on.

When text is selected, it appears in *reverse video*, which means that if it was formerly black text on a white background, it appears as white text on a black background. Figure 1.34 shows some selected text.

The simplest way to select text is to drag the mouse across it. In other words:

1. Position the mouse pointer at the beginning of the text you want to select.

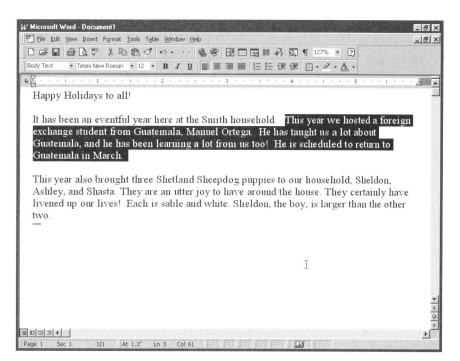

Figure 1.34

Here, I selected part of a paragraph.

2. Hold down the left mouse button while you move the pointer to the end of the text.

   3. Release the mouse button. The text remains selected, as shown in Figure 1.34.

Some beginners find it difficult to select text with the mouse because it requires them to precisely position and move the mouse. An alternative way to select is to:

   1. Position the insertion point where you want the selection to start.

   2. Press Shift.

   3. With the Shift key still pressed, use the arrow keys to extend the selection.

   4. When the area you want is selected, release the Shift key. The text remains selected, just as if you had used the mouse.

There are also some shortcuts for selecting, both with the keyboard and the mouse. Table 1.4 tells you about the mouse methods, and Table 1.5, the keyboard ones.

Deleting Text

You can delete text in either of two ways: you can delete one character at a time, or you can select a group of characters and delete them all at once. To delete one character at a time:

- Position the insertion point to the right of the character you want to delete, and then press Backspace. This action is great for simple typing errors that you catch on the spot; just Backspace over your mistake and retype.

- Position the insertion point to the left of the character you want to delete, and then press Delete. If you press and hold Delete, it deletes characters continuously until you release it.

There are also several equally good ways to delete blocks of text. The tricky part is selecting the text to be deleted. If you can select text easily,

TABLE 1.4 SELECTING WITH THE MOUSE

To Select	Do This
A word	Double-click on the word.
A graphic	Click on the graphic.
A line of text	Move the pointer to the left of the line until it changes to a right-slanting arrow, and then click.
Multiple lines of text	Move the pointer to the left of the lines until it changes to a right-pointing arrow, and then drag up or down.
A sentence	Press and hold Ctrl, and then click anywhere in the sentence.
A paragraph	Triple-click anywhere in the paragraph.
Multiple paragraphs	Move the pointer to the left of the paragraphs until it changes to a right-pointing arrow, and then double-click and drag up or down.
A large block of text	Click at the start of the selection, scroll to the end of the selection, and then press and hold Shift and click.
An entire document	Move the pointer to the left of any document text until it changes to a right-pointing arrow, and then triple-click.
A vertical block of text (except within a table cell)	Press and hold Alt, and then drag.

deleting should not be a problem. Select text to delete, and then take any of the following actions:

- Press Delete.
- Choose Edit, Clear.
- Choose Edit, Cut.

Table 1.5 Shortcut Keys for Selecting

To Extend a Selection	Press
To the end of a word	Ctrl+Shift+Right Arrow
To the beginning of a word	Ctrl+Shift+Left Arrow
To the end of a line	Shift+End
To the beginning of a line	Shift+Home
To the end of a paragraph	Ctrl+Shift+Down Arrow
To the beginning of a paragraph	Ctrl+Shift+Up Arrow
One screen down	Shift+Page Down
One screen up	Shift+Page Up
To the end of a window	Alt+Ctrl+Page Down
To the beginning of a document	Ctrl+Shift+Home
To include the entire document	Ctrl+A
To a vertical block of text	Ctrl+Shift+F8, and then use the arrow keys; press Esc to cancel the selection mode.

- Press Ctrl+X.
- Click on the Cut button on the Standard toolbar.
- Right-click on the selected text and choose Cut from the shortcut menu that appears.

Go ahead and experiment with deleting bits of the sample text you typed.

NOTE More experienced users may have noticed that I mixed up two different commands in the preceding list of deletion methods: clearing (true deleting) and cutting (moving to the Clipboard). I'll explain the Clipboard later in this session, in the "Moving and Copying" section, but for now, suffice to say that if you cut something and never paste it, it's functionally equivalent to deleting it. Some people find cutting easier than clearing, so I included all the ways to cut as options for deleting.

Using Undo and Redo

Now that you have deleted big chunks of your sample, it's time to learn about a real lifesaver of a feature: Undo. Undo allows you to reverse past multiple actions. You can use it, for example, to reverse all the deletions you made to your sample.

The easiest way to undo a single action is to click on the Undo button on the Standard toolbar. You can click on it as many times as you like; each time, it undoes one action. (If you don't like using the toolbar button, you can use its equivalent menu command: Edit, Undo.)

You can undo multiple actions all at once by opening the Undo button's drop-down list, as shown in Figure 1.35. Just drag the mouse across the actions to undo (you don't need to hold down the mouse button). Then click when the desired actions are selected, and presto, they are all reversed.

Redo is the opposite of Undo. If you make a mistake with the Undo button, you can fix the problem by clicking on the Redo button. Like the Undo button, it has a drop-down list, so you can redo multiple actions at once. If you haven't used the Undo feature in your last action, the Redo button will not be available.

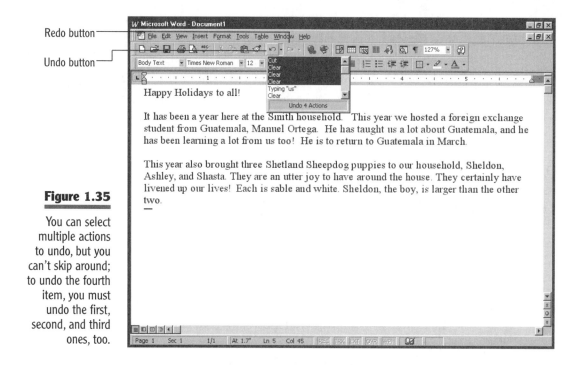

Figure 1.35

You can select multiple actions to undo, but you can't skip around; to undo the fourth item, you must undo the first, second, and third ones, too.

 TIP There is no menu equivalent to the Redo command unless the very last action you complete involves the Undo button. Why? Well, there's a command right underneath Undo at the top of the Edit menu that lets you repeat your last action. For example, if you're typing, Word repeats what you typed since you last selected a command: just choose Edit, Repeat Typing. You can press Ctrl+Y to get the same effect. However, if the last task you finish is an Undo, this command changes to Redo, and it works just like clicking on the Redo button. Yes, it's confusing. I'm sorry.

Moving and Copying

Now comes the fun part! You're going to learn how to move and copy selections from your document to other locations. (See, I told you selecting was an important skill.) You can move things around within the same document (like rearranging paragraphs or words), or you can move or copy them to other documents or even files in other programs! The sky's the limit.

What most confuses beginners is there are so many different methods for moving and copying! It's really mind-boggling. Word provides a lot of ways because everybody has their own ideas about what's easy, and Microsoft apparently wanted to please everybody at once.

To make it simple, here are the two main categories: Cut, Copy, and Paste (methods that involve the Windows Clipboard), and Drag-and-Drop (a method that involves dragging selections with the mouse).

Cut, Copy, and Paste

Take a moment and ponder this thing called the Windows Clipboard. Think of it as a holding tank, floating somewhere out there in Windowsland. Nearly all Windows-based programs have access to the Clipboard.

When you use the Cut command in any Windows program, the program takes whatever you select and moves it to the Clipboard. It disappears from the document on which you are working. In contrast, when you use the Copy command, the program makes a copy of the selection and moves the copy to the Clipboard. The original remains in the document.

Now you're ready to use the material on the Clipboard. You position your insertion point where you want the material to go, and then issue the Paste command. Since all Windows programs share the same Clipboard, you can issue that Paste command from any Windows program, effectively sharing data from one program with another. Whatever is on the Clipboard remains there until one of these things happens:

- You cut or copy something else to the Clipboard (from any program).
- You shut down Windows 95 (or the power goes off).

Because the material stays in the Clipboard, you can paste it multiple times. For example, if you want your name pasted in five different spots in a document, you can copy it once to the Clipboard, then move the insertion point to the right spots, and issue the Paste command five times.

Got that? Good. Now you're ready to try it out.

1. Select text in your sample document. (It doesn't matter how much or how little for this exercise.)
2. Click on the Cut button on the Standard toolbar.
3. Reposition the insertion point somewhere in the document.
4. Click on the Paste button on the Standard toolbar.
5. Click on the Paste button a few more times to see additional copies pasted.
6. Repeat the steps using the Copy button in Step 2 instead of Cut.

Remember how I said there were so many different ways do to it?

To cut, you can:

- Click on the Cut button on the Standard toolbar.
- Choose Edit, Cut.
- Right-click on the selection and choose Cut from the shortcut menu.
- Press Ctrl+X.

To copy, you can:

- Click on the Copy button on the Standard toolbar.
- Choose Edit, Copy.
- Right-click on the selection and choose Copy from the shortcut menu.
- Press Ctrl+C.

To paste, position the insertion point where you want the text to go, and then:

- Click on the Paste button on the Standard toolbar.
- Choose Edit, Paste.
- Right-click on the insertion point and choose Paste from the shortcut menu.
- Press Ctrl+V.

Drag-and-Drop Editing

People who are comfortable using a mouse usually love drag-and-drop. People who can't quite get coordinated with the mouse avoid drag-and-drop, and with good reason: it can be tricky getting the mouse pointer positioned just right.

Drag-and-drop involves dragging selected text to a new location, the same way that you drag icons around in Windows 95 (or drag the cards in the Solitaire game).

1. Select text.
2. Position the mouse pointer over the selection so that the pointer turns into an arrow (rather than an I-beam).
3. Hold down the left mouse button and move the mouse to drag the text to the desired location. The mouse pointer turns into an arrow with a rectangle around it to show that it's dragging your selection.

CAUTION Drag-and-drop works best if the desired location is also visible on the screen; if it's not, you have to drag all the way up or down the screen to make it scroll, and it sometimes scrolls faster than you would like. If possible, try to scroll the display so that both the old and new locations are visible before you start the drag-and-drop process.

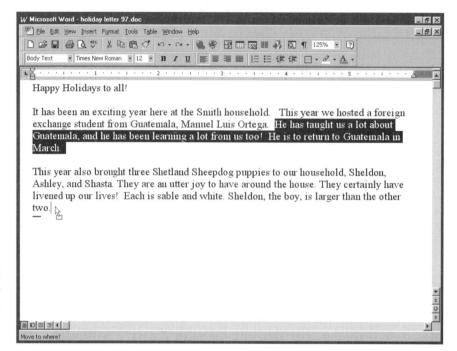

Figure 1.36

The mouse pointer shows you where you are dragging the text.

4. Point the mouse pointer at the spot where you want to drop the selection (see Figure 1.36). A dotted vertical line shows where the selection will be dropped. Release the mouse button.

You can also use drag-and-drop for copying; just press and hold Ctrl before you press the mouse button down, and don't release the key until you release the mouse button. When you're copying, your mouse pointer has a little plus sign next to it.

Finding and Replacing

In short documents like the sample you typed, there is no need for the Find feature because you can see all the text onscreen. When you get into longer documents, it becomes very handy.

Suppose I want to find all the instances of "he" in my sample (see Figure 1.32). (Not a very imaginative example, I know, but the sample is so short that there aren't very many repeated words. Bear with me, eh?)

1. Choose Edit, Find or press Ctrl+F. The Find and Replace dialog box opens.
2. In the Find what text box, type **he** (or the word you want to find if your sample is different).
3. Click on the Find Next button. The first instance of the word after the insertion point is highlighted (see Figure 1.37).
4. To find the next instance, click on Find Next again.
5. Keep clicking and finding until you get a message that Word has finished searching the document. Click on OK to close the message.

Okay, what's the first thing you noticed about this task? Word not only found the word "he," but also words that contained it, like "here" and

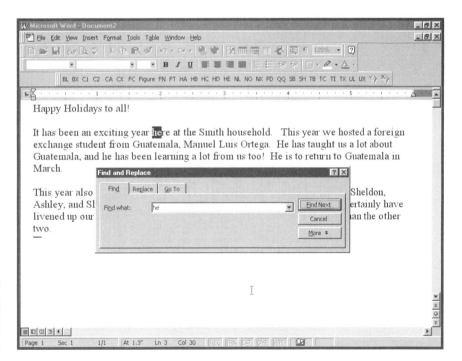

Figure 1.37

Word highlights one instance of the found text at a time.

"Shetland." You probably didn't expect or want these results. To prevent this, use Find again, but with some modification:

1. Choose Edit, Find or press Ctrl+F again. Your word to find should already be in the Find what text box.
2. Click on the More button to open up the additional controls.
3. Click to place a check mark in the Find whole words only check box (see Figure 1.38).
4. Click on Find Next. This time Word finds only the word "he."
5. Now that you've seen how this option works, click on Cancel to close the dialog box.

There are a lot more Find options than just the one option you tried in this task. Some of them are self-explanatory, like Match Case, but others can be a little tricky. I'll provide more information about the options in the Time-Savers section at the end of this session.

Replace is like Find with a bonus. You can find something and then replace it with a different string of text.

1. If the Find and Replace dialog box is already open, click on the Replace tab. If it's not, choose Edit, Replace or press Ctrl+H.

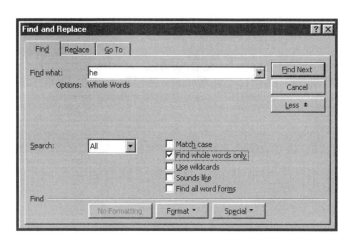

Figure 1.38

More controls are available for finding and replacing when you click on the More button.

2. If needed, change the word in the Find what text box.
3. Type the replacement text string in the Replace with text box.
4. If you need to set special options, click on the More button and choose what you need. For example, in Figure 1.39, I replaced every "he" with "she" when "he" is a whole word.
5. Click on the Find Next button to find the next instance.
6. If the text string should be replaced, click on Replace. Word goes on and finds the next instance automatically. If the text string should be left alone, click on Find Next to skip it.
7. When you get the message that Word has finished searching the document, click on OK.

If you are sure you want to replace a certain word every time it appears, you can do all the words at once by clicking on Replace All. Be careful: there may be cases you have not thought about. For example, suppose your editor told you that you should say "for example" instead of "for instance." A global replace of "instance" with "example" would also change sentences like "This is the third instance of this phenomenon" and make them incorrect.

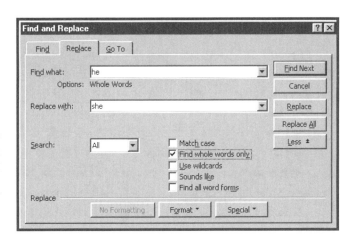

Figure 1.39

Replace works just like Find except you can substitute one word for another as you use the feature.

Saving Your Work

Skip ahead a moment and pretend you have created something worthy of saving. After you enter something you want to preserve, you need to save it to disk.

Each successive new document you open has the generic name Document1, Document2, and so on. Word assigns these names to prevent you from getting confused when there is more than one unsaved document open at once. When you save a document, give it a descriptive name that will help you remember its purpose.

Names can be up to 255 characters and can include spaces. For practical purposes, however, you should keep the names reasonably short, such as Smith 8-97 or Henson Report. You can include spaces and symbols (except / \ : * ? " < > or |) in your filenames. As long as the Save as type text box says "Word Document," there is no need to type .doc at the end of the name because Word adds that automatically. (If the Save as type text box shows anything else, you need to open its drop-down

> ### WHAT HAPPENS WHEN YOU SAVE?
>
> **You can think of your computer's memory as the top of your desk and your hard disk as a drawer in the desk. When you work in Word, you're working on the top of the desk, just as you are when you write a letter or add numbers by hand. When you exit Word or turn off your computer, it's like a janitor coming in and scooping everything from your desk surface into the garbage. Everything in memory is wiped out. If you want to preserve a work-in-progress, you need to copy it to the hard disk so it's safely stashed away in a drawer where the janitor can't get to it. Copying it to the hard disk is called *saving*.**

list and choose Word document unless you really want to save in a different format.)

After you save a document, there is a copy on your hard disk; you'll learn how to get to it later in this session. The copy stays on your hard disk until you delete it. Each time you make changes to a document, you must save it again to include the changes in the copy on your hard disk.

Save Vs. Save As

There are two procedures for saving: Save and Save As. If you have never saved the document before, they are identical: they both ask for a name and location for the file. After you save the document, Save resaves the document with the same name and location that you initially entered, whereas Save As gives you the opportunity to save the document with a different name and location.

The first time you save a document, you assign it a name and a location so you can retrieve it later.

1. Do any of the following to open the Save As dialog box:
   - Click on the Save button on the Standard toolbar.
   - Press Ctrl+S.
   - Choose File, Save or File, Save As. (They work the same if you have not saved this document previously.)
2. In the Save As dialog box (see Figure 1.40), enter a name for the document in the File name text box. (Just type over the name that's there.)
3. (Optional) To save the document in a different folder, use the navigation buttons in the dialog box to change the folder or drive (see the following section for help with this). The default folder is the My Documents folder on the same drive on which Windows 95 is installed.
4. Click on the Save button in the dialog box. The document is saved to disk, and the new name appears in the title bar.

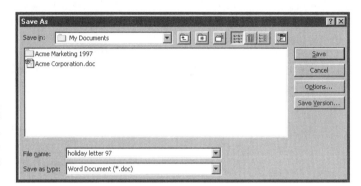

Figure 1.40

Use the Save As dialog box to specify a filename and location.

Changing the Folder or Drive

If you have not used many Windows 95 programs, the file navigation system may seem foreign at first. You must use it whenever you need to change the drive or folder in a dialog box that saves or opens files. You'll encounter it in the Save As dialog box (see Figure 1.40) and also in the Open dialog box covered later in the session.

To change to a different drive, you must open the Save in or Look in drop-down list. (The name changes depending on whether you're saving or opening a file.) Figure 1.41 shows this drop-down list in the Save As dialog box. From it, choose the drive on which you want to save the file.

Next, you must select the folder where you want to save the file (or open it). When you select the drive, a list of the folders on that drive appears. Double-click on the folder you want to select.

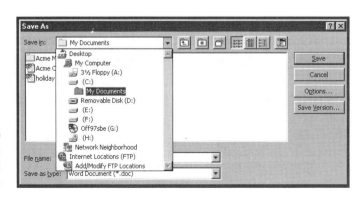

Figure 1.41

Use this drop-down list to choose a different drive.

Table 1.6 explains the buttons and other controls you see in the Save As and Open dialog boxes, as well as in other Windows 95 dialog boxes you may encounter.

TABLE 1.6   BUTTONS FOR CHANGING DRIVES AND FOLDERS IN WINDOWS 95 DIALOG BOXES

Button	Name	Purpose
	Up One Level	Moves to the folder above the one shown in the Save in box.
	Look in Favorites	Shows the C:\WINDOWS\FAVORITES folder, no matter which folder was displayed before.
	Create New Folder	Creates a new folder (Save As dialog box only).
	List	Shows the folders and files of the folder currently displayed in a list.
	Details	Shows details about each file and folder.
	Properties	Shows the properties of each file and folder.
	Preview	Shows a preview of the current file (Open dialog box only).
	Commands and Settings	Opens a dialog box of settings you can change that affect the dialog box.
	Search the Web	Enables you to search the Internet for documents to open (Open dialog box only).
	Add to Favorites	Adds a shortcut to the folder currently displayed to the Favorites list (Open dialog box only).

TIP Notice in Figure 1.41 that you can select Internet Locations to save a file from the Save in drop-down list. If you are connected to an Internet FTP site, you can save the file directly to that server's disk drive rather than your own hard disk. You'll learn more about this on Sunday afternoon.

Saving a Document Subsequent Times

After a document has been saved, you can resave it using the same filename and location by doing any of the following:

- Click on the Save button on the Standard toolbar.
- Press Ctrl+S.
- Choose File, Save.

If you need to reopen the Save As dialog box—to specify a different name or location, for example—choose File, Save As and then save the file as you did the first time.

Saving in Other Formats

You may have noticed in the Save As dialog box the Save as type drop-down list. It enables you to save your Word document in a variety of foreign formats for use with other programs. For example, suppose a co-worker uses only WordPerfect. You can export your document in WordPerfect so that your co-worker can use it. You can export to more than a dozen formats, including various versions of Word, WordPerfect, Works, Write, .rtf, and plain text.

TIP Earlier versions of Word can't read the Word 97 format, so you need to save in the earlier version's format to exchange work with someone who has not yet upgraded.

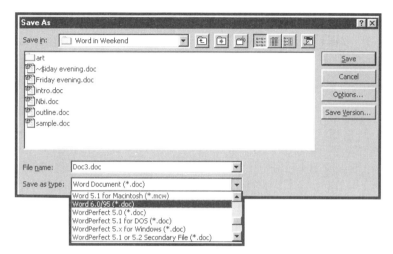

Figure 1.42

You can save your work in other formats for compatibility with other programs.

To save in another format, save the file normally using the Save As dialog box. Before you click on <u>S</u>ave, open the Save as <u>t</u>ype drop-down list and select a different type, as shown in Figure 1.42. Finally, click on <u>S</u>ave.

If you consistently need to save in another format, you can save time by setting up Word to use the other format by default. To do this, choose Tools, Options, and click on the Save tab. In the Save <u>W</u>ord files as drop-down list, choose the preferred format and then click on OK.

Closing a Document

When you save a document, it remains onscreen so that you can continue to work on it. When you finish working with the document, you can close it in one of two ways:

- You can exit Word. The document closes when Word closes.
- You can close the document and keep working in other Word documents.

To quit Word, close its program window. You can choose File, Exit, or click on the Word window's Close button (X). To close a document and leave Word open, do any of the following:

- Click on the document window's Close button (X). If the document window is maximized, the correct Close button is the X closest to the Standard toolbar. If the document window is not maximized, the X is at the right end of the document window's title bar.
- Choose File, Close.
- Press Ctrl+W.

When you close a document that you have made changes to since your last save, you'll be asked if you want to save your work. Click on Yes or No, depending on what you want. If you click on Yes and the document has not yet been saved, the Save As dialog box opens.

Opening a Saved Document

There's no point in saving your documents to your hard disk unless you are going to open them again. When you open a file, you redisplay it onscreen, where you can modify it further. To open a saved Word file, follow these steps:

1. Do one of the following to open the Open dialog box shown in Figure 1.43:
   - Click on the Open button on the Standard toolbar.
   - Choose File, Open.
   - Press Ctrl+O.
2. If the file you want to open appears, click on it. Otherwise, change the drive and folder displayed to find it. (Refer to "Changing the Folder or Drive" earlier in this session for help.)
3. Click on the Open button, or double-click on the document file. The document opens onscreen.

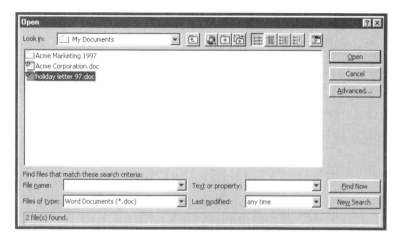

Figure 1.43

Choose the saved file you want to open and then click on the Open button.

Opening Files from Other Programs

Opening files in other formats can be easy if the format is similar to Word's. For example, opening a file from another word processing program, such as WordPerfect, is nearly automatic.

1. If it is not open already, open the Open dialog box (choose File, Open).
2. Open the Files of type drop-down list and choose the type of file you want to open.
3. If needed, change the drive or folder to the one where the file to be opened resides.
4. Double-click on the file to open, or click on it once and then click on Open.

The files listed when you choose a particular file type from the Files of type list are based wholly on their extensions. For example, when you choose Text Files (.txt), Word does not check each file to see whether it actually is a text file; it merely lists all the files with .txt extensions. If a file is misnamed with the wrong extension, it does not appear in the list. To rename a file, find it in the Windows Explorer, click on it, press F2, and type a new name.

Finding a Document to Open

If you're having trouble locating your document, Word can help you look. Perhaps you forgot which folder you saved it in, or you moved it in Windows 95 since you saved it. No matter what the reason, Word's Find feature can rescue you.

1. Open the Open dialog box.
2. In the File name box at the bottom of the dialog box, type the name of the file for which you're looking (see Figure 1.44).

TIP You can use wildcards if you don't know the entire name of a file. The asterisk (*) wildcard character stands in for any character or set of characters, and the question mark (?) wildcard character stands in for any single character. For example, if you know the file begins with "P," you could type **P*.doc**, as shown in Figure 1.44, to find all Word files that begin with "P."

3. (Optional) Enter other search criteria:
   - If you're looking for a different file type, choose it from the Files of type drop-down list.

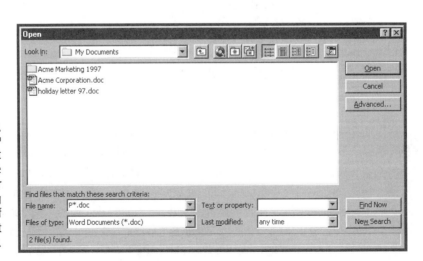

Figure 1.44

If you aren't sure where a file resides, search for it by entering the portion of the name that you know.

- If you're looking for a file containing certain text, type that text in the Te*x*t or property box.
- If you know when you last modified the file, choose the time interval from the Last *m*odified drop-down list.

4. Click the *A*dvanced button. The Advanced Find dialog box appears (see Figure 1.45).

5. In the Look *i*n section at the bottom of the Advanced Find dialog box, narrow the search area as much as possible using these techniques:
   - If you are sure that the file is in a certain folder, type that folder's path (such as C:\WINDOWS) in the Look *i*n box.
   - If you are sure that the file is on a certain drive, select that drive from the Look *i*n drop-down list.
   - If you don't know which drive contains the file, select My Computer from the Look *i*n drop-down list.

6. Make sure that the Searc*h* subfolders check box is marked. If it isn't, click on it.

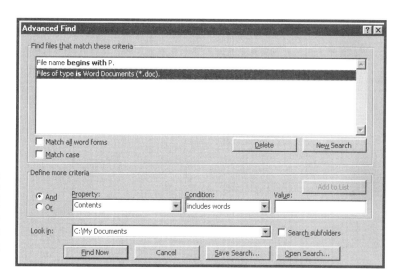

Figure 1.45

Use the Advanced Find dialog box to select the folders and drives you want to search.

7. Click on the Add to List button to add your criteria to the search list.
8. Click on the F̲ind Now button. The Open dialog box reappears and displays the files that match your search criteria.
9. Double-click on the desired file to open it.

NOTE As you may have noticed in Figure 1.45, more complex search options are available. See Word online help for more details.

Printing a Word Document

The easiest way to print is to click on the Print button on the Standard toolbar. It doesn't get much simpler than that. When you click on this button, the active document prints one copy of the entire document on the default printer.

TIP How do you tell which printer is the default? Point the mouse at the Print button on the toolbar and a ScreenTip pops up. It tells you the button is the Print button and which printer is the default. If you have more than one printer, you can change the default printer in the Print dialog box, which you'll learn about in the following section.

The default print options work well if you want only the default settings, but many times you will want more than one copy, selected pages, or some other special settings when you print. To set your print options, use the Print dialog box:

1. Choose F̲ile, P̲rint or press Ctrl+P. The Print dialog box appears (see Figure 1.46).
2. Set any options in the Print dialog box (how many copies, which printer to use, what range to print, and so on) that you want to use.
3. Click on OK to print.

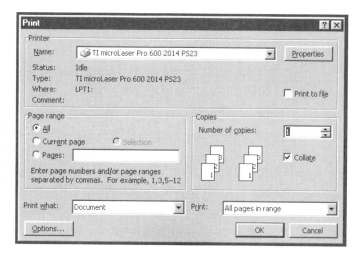

Figure 1.46

The Print dialog box enables you to choose nonstandard print settings, including different amounts of copies or pages.

Selecting a Printer

The first thing to do in the Print dialog box is check whether the printer you want to use appears in the Na<u>m</u>e text box. If it doesn't, open the drop-down list and select it.

 NOTE If the printer you want to use doesn't appear on the drop-down list, it has not been set up in Windows 95, and you will need to set it up through the Control Panel before you can use it in any Windows program.

The Settings button next to the printer enables you to access the printer's Properties dialog box. Generally you shouldn't have to use it so I recommend leaving it alone unless problems arise. If you do have problems, you might want to check the dialog box to make sure all the settings are normal.

Choosing a Page Range

The Page Range area of the Print dialog box enables you to specify a certain number of pages to print from your document, if the document contains enough text to fill more than one page. The default is A<u>l</u>l, which prints everything in the document. You can enter a range of pages in the From and To boxes.

I use this feature most often after I print an entire document once. Inevitably, I find a misspelling or error on one page and need to reprint that page after I make the correction. Setting the Page range to include only the page I corrected saves me paper.

TIP There is also a selection option in the Page range area. It's unavailable unless you have some text selected when you open the Print dialog box. You can use it to select only a certain block of text to print. This option is useful if what you want to print is partly on one page and partly on another.

Setting the Number of Copies

The Copies options are pretty straightforward. How many copies do you want? One is the default. What's a little less direct is the Collate check box underneath. This feature is applicable only if both of the following are true:

- You are printing more than one copy.
- The document you are printing has more than one page.

Collating means printing the copies so that they're ready to distribute, like this: copy 1 page 1, copy 1 page 2; copy 2 page 1, and copy 2 page 2. If you deselect this check box, all the copies of each page will print in a row, like this: copy 1 page 1, copy 2 page 1; copy 1 page 2, and copy 2 page 2.

Portrait or Landscape?

You may know about page orientation already. Here's a quick review: Portrait (the default) means the text is printed parallel with the short edge of the paper. Landscape (the alternative) means the text is printed parallel with the long edge.

An easy way to remember these is to think of a portrait of a person. It's almost always taller than it is wide. In contrast, a landscape painting is usually wider than it is long.

Even though choosing a page orientation is a printing-related choice, you don't set it up from the Print dialog box. Instead, you do the following:

1. Choose File, Page Setup. The Page Setup dialog box appears.
2. Click on the Paper Size tab (see Figure 1.47).
3. In the Orientation section, click on the Portrait or Landscape button.
4. Click on OK to accept your settings.

Even though you can specify Landscape in your printer's Properties dialog box, I don't recommend it. The settings you make there affect all your Windows programs, so you will have to change it back the next time you want to print something in Portrait. It is better to set the orientation for just the specific document in the Page Setup dialog box in Word.

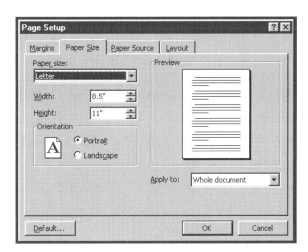

Figure 1.47

The Page Setup options enable you to enhance the look of the printed page.

Time-Savers

In each session, I'll end with a section like this one, called Time-Savers. This material is not essential, and if you're tired, you can skip it and read it later at your leisure (maybe next weekend). Time-Savers are alternative ways of doing things or ideas for expending a little extra effort now to save yourself time in the long run.

Other Ways to Start Word

Everyone has his or her own idea about the easiest way to start Word. Here are some alternative methods that you might find easier than the Start button method we covered at the beginning of this session.

- Find the Word program in Windows Explorer or My Computer and double-click on it.
- If you use the Microsoft Office shortcut bar, click on the Word icon there.
- Drag the Word program icon onto your Windows 95 desktop from Windows Explorer or My Computer, creating a shortcut. Then double-click on the shortcut to open Word.
- On the Microsoft Office shortcut bar, click on the New Document button and use the dialog box that appears to start Word. Choose Blank Document as the template to use.
- If you have a New Document command at the top of your Start menu, use it to start Word. Choose Blank Document as the template to use.

You can also start Word and open an existing document at the same time, using any of these methods:

- On the Microsoft Office shortcut bar, click on the Open document button and use the dialog box that appears to open an existing document while you are starting Word.

- If you have an Open Document command at the top of your Start menu, use it to start a new document or open an existing one while you are starting Word.
- Find a Word document in Windows Explorer or My Computer, and double-click on it to open Word and the document at the same time.
- Drag a Word document onto your Windows 95 desktop from Windows Explorer or My Computer, and then double-click on that shortcut to open Word and the document at the same time.

Checking Out Microsoft's Web Site

All Microsoft Office 97 applications, including Word, are tightly connected to the Internet. Simply put, Microsoft has made additional Help resources for Word available at its Web site on the Internet. To access it, just choose Help, Microsoft on the Web, and the document you want to see. (You may need to dial up your Internet Service Provider's computer first, unless you are already connected or you access the Internet through a LAN.) Your Web browser opens and the document appears. Figure 1.48 shows the result of selecting the Frequently Asked Questions document.

NOTE When you access the Web page, it may look different from what you see in Figure 1.48 because these pages are updated periodically with new information. Ah, the beauty of Internet-provided help—always the latest information.

Microsoft has a patch for Office 97 available for download on their Free Stuff page that you should install as soon as possible if you are using the Office 97 version of Word. To get to the page, go to Word and choose Help, Microsoft on the Web, Microsoft Office Home Page. Your Web browser opens and shows a page of Microsoft Office news. Find and click on the Office 97 Service Release link, and follow the instructions to

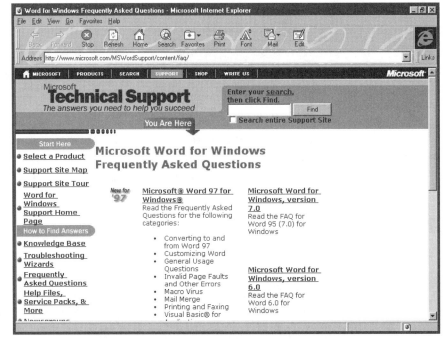

Figure 1.48

One of the many Help documents for Word available at the Microsoft Web site.

download and install the patch. This patch updates some of the other Office applications as well, but it does install the Web Publishing Wizard, which you'll use in the Sunday Afternoon session.

More Find and Replace Options

When using the Edit, Find or Edit, Replace feature that you learned about in this session, you can click on the More button to access a series of check boxes and drop-down lists. Here's a summary of the options you'll find there.

- **Match case.** This check box makes Word find only instances with the same capitalization as you typed. For example, "he" would not find "He."

- **Use wildcards.** When this check box is marked, you can use * to stand for a string of characters or ? to stand for a single character. For example, sh* would find *Shetland, Sheepdog, she, shelter*—any word beginning with "sh." The string *nd would find all words ending with "nd" like *end, friend,* and *band.* The string sh? would find all words that are 3 letters long and begin with "sh," like *she* and *shy,* but not *show.*
- **Sounds like.** Use this check box to search by sound. For example, if you were looking for "Luis" but you didn't know how it was spelled, you might search for "Louise" with this check box marked to find it.
- **Find all word forms.** This check box helps you look for words that are similar but may not be spelled similarly, such as "be," "is," and "are."
- **Search.** This drop-down list specifies the direction from the insertion point you want to search. Your choices are Down (from the insertion point to the end), Up (from the insertion point to the beginning), or All (from the insertion point down, and then wrapping around to the top until the insertion point is reached again). All is the default.
- **Format.** This is a drop-down list from which you can specify certain formatting to be part of the Find criteria. For example, if you know that the word you want to find appears in italic, you can click on the Format button, choose Font, select Italic from the dialog box that appears, and click on OK. If you decide not to make formatting part of the criteria, click on the No Formatting button to clear it.
- **Special.** This drop-down list enables you to search for special characters that you can't type into the Find what text box, such as a tab stop, a paragraph break, or a graphic.

TIP After I have set my options in the Find dialog box, I like to click on the Less button to shrink the dialog back down to a smaller size before I click on Find Next to begin finding. When the dialog box is expanded, it often obscures the text being found. You can move the dialog box around onscreen by dragging its title bar, but it's easier if it doesn't get in the way in the first place.

Changing the Default Save Location

If you find yourself changing the location for saving your files each time, perhaps you should make a different folder the default folder where Word saves. Normally it's My Documents, but you can change it to any folder. For example, I set mine to a folder I created called "Books" because the Word files I work with are used in the books that I write.

To change the default file location, choose Tools, Options, and click on the File Locations tab. Click on the Documents line and then click on the Modify button. In the Modify Location dialog box, browse to the new folder you want to use (using the same controls as in the Save As dialog box) and click on OK. Then click on OK again to close the Options dialog box.

Previewing Your Print Job

Print Preview is a great feature because it helps you save paper. You can try out your print and page setup settings onscreen before you set your printer into action.

You can enter Print Preview (see Figure 1.49) in several ways: from the Print Preview button in the Print dialog boxes, by choosing File, Print Preview, or by clicking on the Print Preview button on the toolbar.

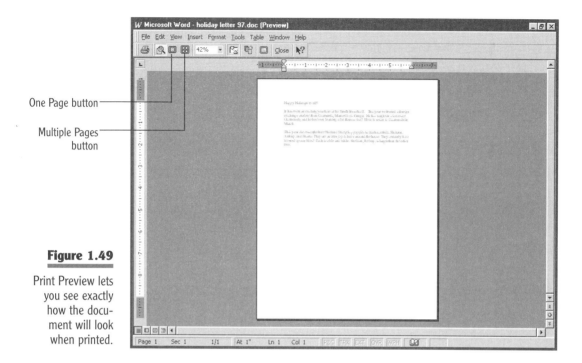

Figure 1.49

Print Preview lets you see exactly how the document will look when printed.

Print Preview starts out in Full Page mode, as shown in Figure 1.49. You can see one entire page in this view. To zoom in to examine a part of the page more closely, click on that part of the page. Notice that the mouse pointer looks like a magnifying glass, signaling that you can zoom by clicking. When you want to zoom back out again, click again on the sheet. You can also switch between these two zoom levels by clicking on the Zoom button at the top of the screen.

You can also zoom out to see several pages at once, if your document has more than one page. Just click on the Multiple Pages button and drag to select a number of pages. To get back to a single page, click on the One Page button. If there are more pages than are currently visible, you can use the scroll bar or the Page Up and Page Down keys to move among pages.

When you're done with Print Preview, you need a way out. There are two ways to close Print Preview:

- Click on the <u>P</u>rint button to enter the Print dialog box and then click on OK to print.
- Click on the <u>C</u>lose button to leave Print Preview without printing (for example, if you realize that you need to do more editing before you print).

SATURDAY MORNING
Correspondence

- ✿ Understanding templates
- ✿ Creating a letter from scratch
- ✿ Checking for errors
- ✿ Designing letterhead
- ✿ Working with preprinted stationery

Many people still use their word processors only to write letters. You may find yourself in this group of computer users who haven't quite made the jump to using Word for its many other applications. If this is the case, read on, because this morning's session will provide you with all the ins and outs to creating the professional or personal letters that suit your needs. So butter your bagel, put a little more sugar in your coffee, and get ready to immerse yourself in the new age of correspondence.

What Kinds of Correspondence?

Before you dive in, take a minute to think about the kinds of letters you need to write. See how many of these apply to you.

I would like to write letters:

- ❏ To relatives, informing them of my activities.
- ❏ To businesses I buy products or services from, complaining or expressing satisfaction.
- ❏ To old friends I haven't seen in a while.
- ❏ To utility companies, inquiring about my bill.
- ❏ To people who may want to buy something that I have for sale.
- ❏ To fellow employees, explaining the status of a project.

❏ To potential employers, asking to be considered for a job.

❏ To businesses that have requested references for someone who has worked for me.

The key to writing a good letter is to keep your audience firmly in mind at all times. Your audience—and your purpose in writing to them—will dictate the type of letterhead you want, the words you choose, and even how you sign your name.

There are two ways to create a letter with Word. You can start from scratch, or you can start with a template. Word provides lots of templates to help you get started with the most common documents, and several letter templates are available. Some people find that these templates are a great help, while others think they're merely annoying. I'll show you both methods and you can take it from there.

Understanding Templates

Whenever you start a new document, you begin with a template. A template is a predefined group of settings, such as margins, fonts, styles, tab stops, and so on. You may not realize it, but even the blank document that you see when you first start Word is based on a template: Blank Document. Every time you click on the New button on the Standard toolbar, you start another new document based on Blank Document. Blank Document gives you these settings:

- Top and bottom margins of 1" and right and left margins of 1.25"
- Styles of Heading 1, Heading 2, Heading 3, Normal, and Default Paragraph Font
- Typeface of 10-point Times New Roman

You can create a letter from scratch using the Blank Document template, but Word also provides some special templates that create fancy letters without much fuss. These are designed primarily for business use, but you can use them to create personal letters, too.

- **Contemporary letter.** A gray globe and graphics in the background, 10-point Times New Roman font, and a date and signature line at the left margin.
- **Elegant letter.** The return address and company name in all caps, 10-point Garamond font throughout, and a date and signature line indented to the middle.
- **Professional letter.** The company name in bold, 10-point Arial font, and a date and signature line at the left margin.

NOTE Besides the letter templates, Word also provides a special feature called the Letter Wizard, which walks you through the process of creating and formatting a letter with a series of dialog boxes. You'll learn about the Letter Wizard in the Time-Savers section at the end of this session.

Creating a Letter from a Template

Let's try out my favorite of the three letter templates, the Contemporary one. Follow these steps:

1. Choose File, New. The New dialog box opens. You may have fewer tabs than the dialog box in Figure 2.1 shows, depending on whether you have all the templates installed.
2. Click on the Letters & Faxes tab, if it is not already on top.

TIP If you do not have the Contemporary Letter template installed or you do not see a Letters & Faxes tab, you can rerun the Word 97 (or Office 97) setup program to install the templates you need. Just click on Add/Remove, then on Microsoft Word. Click on the Change Option button. Click on Wizards and Templates, and then the Change Option button again. Click on the Select All button, click on OK twice, and then Continue. When you see the message that setup has completed successfully, click on OK. Now reopen Word and you should have additional templates in the New dialog box.

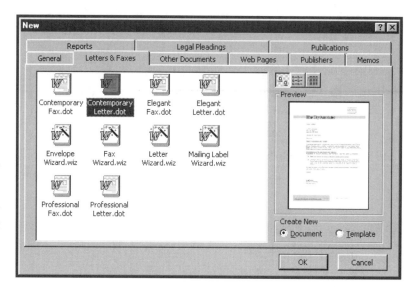

Figure 2.1

You can start a document based on a template other than the default (Blank Document) with the New dialog box.

3. Click on the Contemporary Letter icon, and then on OK. A new document opens based on that template. The fields you need to fill in are gray, as shown in Figure 2.2.

4. Start with the top gray box and follow the directions in it—in other words, click in it and type your return address. You can press Enter to start a new line. Don't forget to include your phone number.

5. Select the words "Company Name Here" and then type your own company's name to replace them.

6. Continue customizing the letter by following the instructions in the gray boxes. You will need to enter:

    ✪ The mailing address of the recipient

    ✪ The salutation (for example, "Dear Susan:")

    ✪ Your company's motto at the bottom of the letter

7. Select the entire paragraph that begins "Type your letter here" and press Delete to remove it. Type your own letter text to replace it.

8. Click on the Print Preview button on the Standard toolbar and

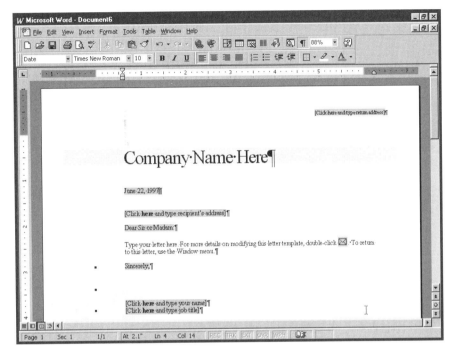

Figure 2.2

Word creates the letter outline automatically, but you must fill in the details yourself.

take a look at the letter. If it is too high on the page, click on Close to return to the letter and add some blank spaces between the date and the return address.

9. When you are satisfied with your letter, click on the Print button on the Standard toolbar to print the letter.

My finished letter appears in Figure 2.3. Yours, of course, will be different because it's customized. Don't forget to sign your letter before you mail it!

If you don't like any of the letter templates Word provides, don't fret. You can easily create your own letter template using letterhead you design for yourself. In fact, later this morning I'll show you how to do just that. But before we get too deep into designing letterhead, let's type a basic, no-frills letter, to get your feet wet with Word's formatting and page layout features.

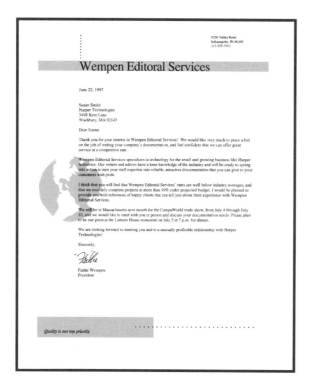

Figure 2.3

My finished letter using the Contemporary Letter template.

Creating a Letter from Scratch

Did you ever take a typing class in high school? I did. I can still remember Miss Bundy making me type and retype the same letter, over and over, until I produced a copy that was free of typos. (There was no spell-checker, and I typed everything in triplicate with carbon paper.)

Back in those days, business letters were plain and serious. Even in today's office world of fancy fonts and graphics, the style hasn't changed much. Businessmen and women still communicate on paper differently than in e-mail, and a nice-looking official letter with a signature conveys a completely different message than anything on the monitor. There is definitely still room for a simple, straightforward business letter "like Grandma used to type" and you'll work on that type of letter first, to make sure your basic Word skills are up to par.

Typing the Letter Text

Some Word users write and format at the same time, but beginners will find it easier to write first and format later. First, get some text into the computer:

1. Start a new document based on the Blank Document template. (Remember, an easy way to do this is to click on the New button on the Standard toolbar.)
2. Type your return address at the top, pressing Enter to start each new line. Then press Enter two times to leave some space.
3. Type today's date, and then press Enter two times.
4. Type the recipient's name and address, and leave two lines of space beneath these items.
5. Type the salutation (for example, **Dear Sherry,**). So far, your letter should look something like what's shown in Figure 2.4.
6. Type the body of the letter. (Just make something up if you're not really writing to someone right now.)
7. When you finish the last paragraph, press Enter twice and type your closing. (**Sincerely yours,** will do just fine.)
8. Press Enter five times (to leave space for your signature) and type your name. Now you're finished with the letter text. Mine appears in Figure 2.5.

Setting the Margins and Page Alignment

Our first stop on the formatting trail is to make sure the margins are appropriate and the letter is centered vertically on the page. You can check this easily by using Print Preview:

1. Click on the Print Preview button on the Standard toolbar or choose File, Print Preview. Your letter appears exactly as it will print. (See Figure 2.6 for mine.)

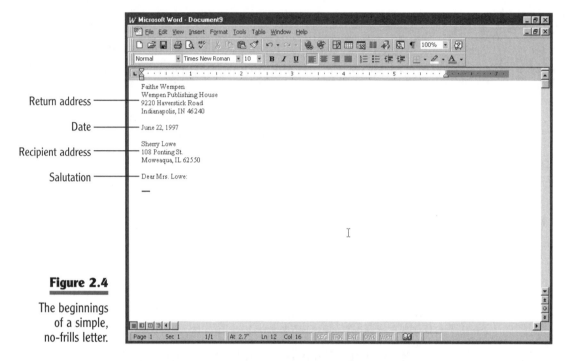

Figure 2.4

The beginnings of a simple, no-frills letter.

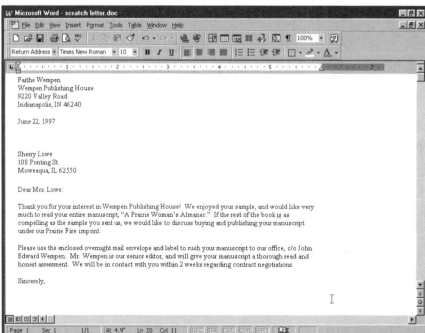

Figure 2.5

The unformatted completed letter.

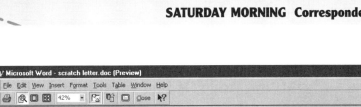

SATURDAY MORNING Correspondence   91

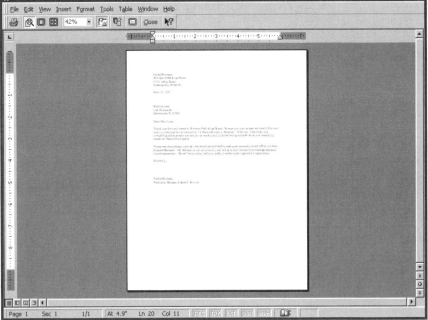

Figure 2.6

In Print Preview, you can immediately see your letter's appearance.

2. Decide what's wrong with the overall appearance. For example, in Figure 2.6, you can see that:

- The letter is not centered vertically on the page.
- Because my letter is fairly short, it looks like I could add some additional blank lines between the date and the recipient's address to make the letter look more balanced.
- The left and right margins look large enough, but I might want to increase them a little to give the illusion that there is more text in the letter body.

3. Click on the Close button on the Print Preview toolbar to exit Print Preview.

4. Choose File, Page Setup. The Page Setup dialog box opens.

5. Click on the Margins tab to display the margin controls (see Figure 2.7).

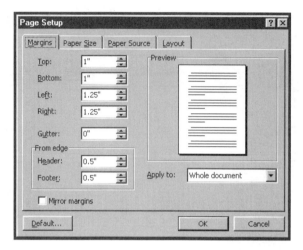

Figure 2.7

You can change each of the four margins individually.

6. If you think your letter needs it, increase or decrease the left and right margin settings.
7. Click on the Layout tab (see Figure 2.8).
8. Open the Vertical Alignment drop-down list and choose Center.
9. Click on OK to close the dialog box.

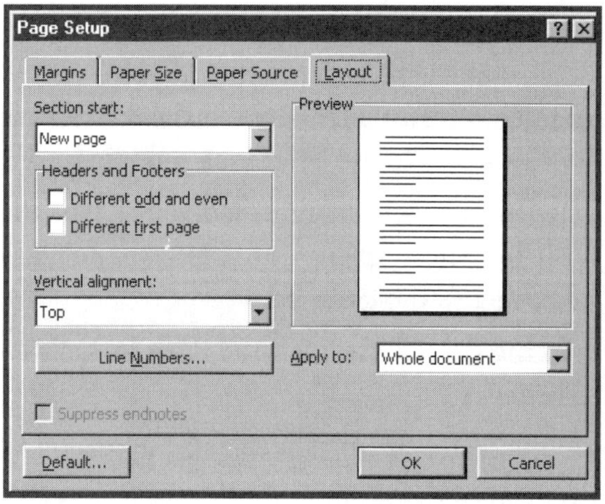

Figure 2.8

On the Layout tab, you can set the vertical alignment to Center, vertically centering the letter on the page.

SATURDAY MORNING Correspondence 93

10. Back in your letter, click on the line beneath the date to place the insertion point.
11. Press Enter a few times to add some extra blank lines.
12. Now go back into Print Preview and check your results. Your letter should look better now! Mine does, as you can see in Figure 2.9.

TIP In typing class, your teacher probably taught you to vertically center a letter by adding blank lines before your return address at the top of the letter. This works fine in Word, but if you add more paragraphs to the letter, you must go back and remove the blank lines to make everything balanced again. Setting the Vertical Alignment to Center in the Page Layout dialog box is better because it centers the text automatically when you add or delete material from a letter.

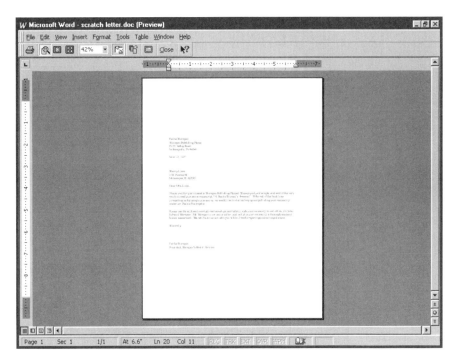

Figure 2.9

The letter is shaping up nicely now that it's vertically centered and not so crowded-looking.

Choosing the Font and Size

Next, we need to choose a font for the letter. The default is 10-point Times New Roman, which is fine if your letter is long enough to make the page look reasonably full. But if your letter is shorter, like mine, you may want to increase the font size to 11 or even 12 points. Depending on your own personal style and preference, you may also want to choose a different font, too.

1. Select the entire document. You can do this by dragging your mouse across all the text, but an easier way is to press Ctrl+A.
2. Choose Format, Font. The Font dialog box opens (see Figure 2.10).

NOTE You can also change the font and font size from the drop-down lists on the Formatting toolbar. However, if you don't know which font you want, choosing one by name can be a frustrating hit-or-miss exercise. With the Font dialog box, you can see a sample of a font before you commit to it.

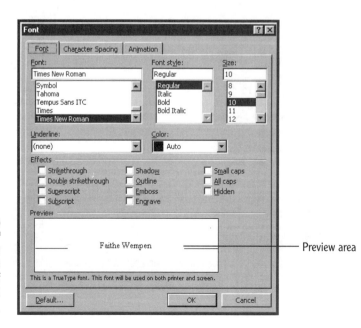

Figure 2.10

The Font dialog box controls the characteristics of the individual letters.

Preview area

SATURDAY MORNING Correspondence

3. In the Font list, click on a different font, and then check out the Preview area to see how it's going to look. If you don't like it, try another font. For this example, I chose Arial.

TIP For business letters, stick with conservative, formal fonts like Times New Roman and Arial. For all letters, avoid fonts that are ornate or highly stylized, because they can be difficult to read.

4. In the Size list, you can increase or decrease the size of your letter. For long letters, 10 point is good; for short ones, try 12 point. Not sure? 11 point is a good compromise.

5. Click on OK.

6. Go back to Print Preview and check out the effect of the changes. (Remember, you can zoom in by left-clicking on the document in Print Preview, and zoom out by right-clicking.) Then click on Close to return to the letter.

Setting Tabs and Indents

Now you have a basic letter that you need not be ashamed to send. Go ahead and print a copy of it—click on the Print button on the Standard toolbar.

It's a bit plain and conservative, isn't it? Why don't you see what you can do to add a bit of variety to it? Start by turning it into a Semi-Block letter. Then set a tab stop in the middle of the ruler, and set indents for the letter's body paragraphs.

NOTE Semi-Block? Don't bother to get out your secretarial handbook; I can tell you what it means. The letter style with which you've been working is called Full Block. In Full Block, everything starts at the left margin. In Semi-Block, each paragraph is indented five spaces and the return address, date, closing, and signature line all start in the middle of the line.

1. Select the entire document again. (Remember, the easy way is to press Ctrl+A.)
2. If the ruler is not showing, choose View, Ruler so you can see it.
3. Locate the midpoint of the white area on the ruler (it's at the 3 mark on mine) and click on it. This places a tab stop for all the selected paragraphs (the entire letter). It looks like a capital "L."
4. Now click away from the selected text to deselect it.
5. Position the insertion point at the beginning of the first return address line, and press Tab to move the line to the tab stop.
6. Repeat Step 5 for all the lines of the return address, the date, the closing line, and the signature line. When you're done, your letter should look something like Figure 2.11.
7. Select the body paragraphs of the letter.

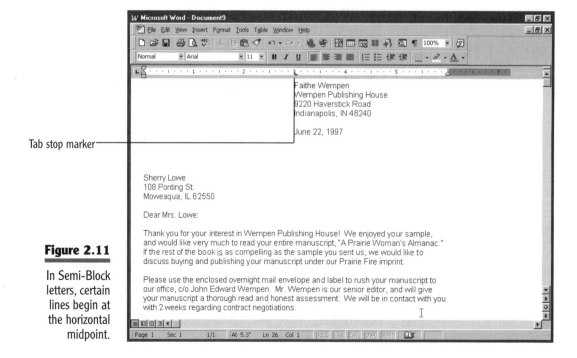

Tab stop marker

Figure 2.11

In Semi-Block letters, certain lines begin at the horizontal midpoint.

8. Choose Format, Paragraph. The Paragraph dialog box appears.
9. If the Indents and Spacing tab is not on top, click on it (see Figure 2.12).
10. Open the Special drop-down list and choose First Line.
11. In the By text box, change the number to .5".
12. Click on OK. Now each of your body paragraphs have indented first lines, as shown in Figure 2.13.

When you finish, print out another copy. Now your letter is formatted in perfect Semi-Block style. Your typing teacher would be proud.

NOTE There is another letter style recognized by secretaries' handbooks everywhere: Modified Block. Basically, it's Semi-Block without the first-line indent on the body paragraphs. Now you know, in case anyone ever asks.

Notice there are two buttons on the Formatting toolbar that deal with indents: Increase Indent and Decrease Indent. You didn't use them for the

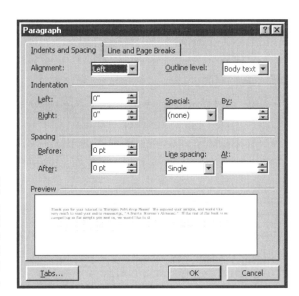

Figure 2.12

You can specify a first-line indent for each of the body paragraphs in the Paragraph dialog box.

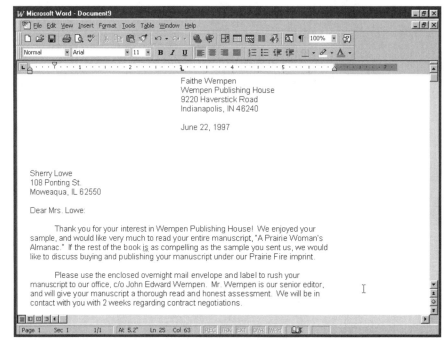

Figure 2.13

Indented first lines can make paragraphs easier to read for some people.

preceding exercise because they indent or "outdent" the entire paragraph, not just the first line. You'll find a use for them in a later session.

Adjusting Line Spacing

Until now, I have told you to press Enter twice between paragraphs, creating some extra space between them. If you are an experienced typewriter user, you probably accepted this without question. But word processing is a different ball game, and there's a better way to place space between paragraphs than "extra Enters."

The key is to set the line spacing. *Line spacing* refers to two kinds of vertical spacing: spacing between paragraphs and spacing between the lines of a paragraph. Line spacing can do wonders for a letter, and you can make such fine adjustments that nobody notices. Is your letter too long, making the page look crowded? Decrease the vertical space between paragraphs to ½ of a line, instead of a full line. Is your letter too short? Add just a smidgen of extra vertical space (called *leading*) between the paragraph lines. As you practice with Word, you'll find all kinds of ways to use line spacing to create illusions.

1. Click on the Show/Hide ¶ button on the Standard toolbar to turn on the hidden characters, so you can see where your paragraph breaks are located.

2. Delete all the extra lines between paragraphs. Exception: if you added extra lines between the date and the recipient's address, leave them alone. Your letter will look all scrunched up, as shown in Figure 2.14.

3. Click anywhere in the last line of the return address.

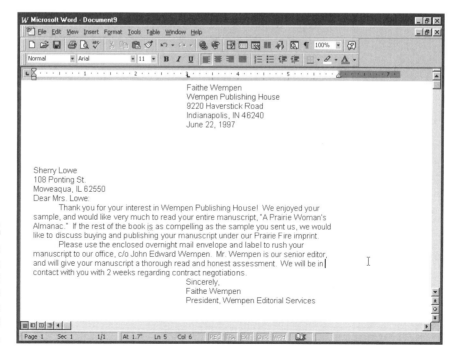

Figure 2.14

You need to remove the extra lines so you can create space between paragraphs with Word.

4. Choose Format, Paragraph. The Paragraph dialog box appears.

5. In the Spacing area, change the number in the After text box to whatever size font you are using (probably 10, 11, or 12). Spacing is measured in points, and if you want one line of space, you have to know the number of points in a line.

6. Click on OK. There seems to be a blank line between the return address and the date! But it is not really a line—it is 10, 11, or 12 points of space.

7. Now select a block of text, starting with the last line of the recipient's address and ending with the last body paragraph of the letter. You'll format these lines all at once.

8. Repeat Steps 4 through 6 to add spacing between the paragraphs.

9. Now you need to do the closing line. It is different because you need more space after it—enough for you to sign your name. Repeat Steps 4 through 6, but use a large number of points. Four lines' worth is good; that would be 40, 44, and 48 points, respectively, for 10, 11, and 12 point fonts.

NOTE Why do you set spacing After instead of Before? No compelling reason; you can go either way. For example, in two paragraphs, you get the exact same effect if you add spacing before paragraph 2 as you do if you add spacing after paragraph 1. I always stick with After so I don't get confused and end up with too much spacing. Spacing is cumulative, so if I set 12 points of spacing before and after each paragraph, I have 24 points of spacing between two paragraphs.

When you finish, your letter should have the spacing it had before. So why did you bother, if you're back where you started? Well, mainly you did it as an exercise. But now that you understand how to add space between paragraphs, try the more advanced exercise in the next steps—it is something you couldn't accomplish with extra Enters!

Maybe your letter is too short and you want to space things out a little, but you don't want it to be too noticeable. (You can also use these tricks with term papers to make them appear longer!)

1. Select the block again from the last line of the recipient's address down to the last paragraph of the letter body.
2. Choose Format, Paragraph to reopen the Paragraph dialog box.
3. Increase the number in the After field by 2. This adds two additional points to the spacing, which is a subtle change that most people will not notice.
4. Now open the Line spacing drop-down list and choose At Least.
5. In the At text box, the current font size appears. Increase it by 2.
6. Click on OK.

Your letter still looks normal, but a bit more spacious. It fills the page a little better. Mine appears in Figure 2.15. Try *that* on a typewriter!

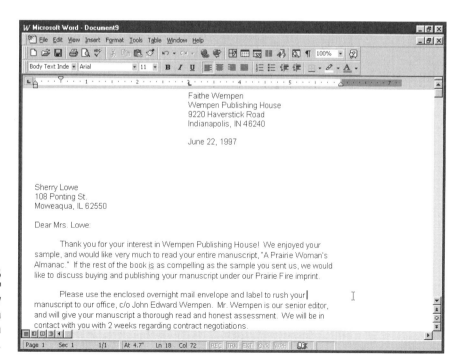

Figure 2.15

The letter now has a bit of extra line spacing in strategic spots.

NOTE Did you notice some of your other choices in the Line spacing drop-down list? There are Single, 1.5 Lines, and Double, among others. Keep this in mind if you ever need to double-space a term paper or report. (And keep in mind that you can fudge the spacing by one or two points in either direction to make it shorter or longer as needed!)

Creating Bulleted Lists

Sometimes you might want to include a list in a letter. For example, I had a client recently who wanted monthly reports so I typed up the status of various phases of the project in a letter, outlining each phase in a bulleted paragraph (see Figure 2.16).

If the letter you typed doesn't have any paragraphs suitable for bullet points, don't worry. Mine doesn't either. But for the sake of the exercise,

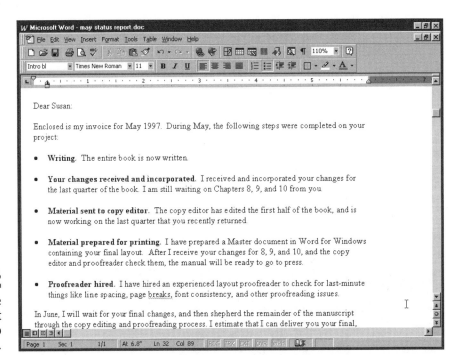

Figure 2.16

Here's a real-life letter I wrote that used bullets to convey facts.

SATURDAY MORNING Correspondence

I typed some dummy bullet points into it, which I will remove later. Follow these steps to use bullets:

1. First, save your previous work. (Refer to the Friday Evening session if you need to refresh your memory.)
2. Position your insertion point at the end of the first body paragraph in your letter, and press Enter. This creates a new paragraph for you to type in (see Figure 2.17).
3. Click on the Bullets button on the Standard toolbar to turn the bullet attribute on.
4. Type the following, pressing Enter between lines, so your bulleted list looks like Figure 2.18: **Quality**, **Customer Service**, and **Reliability**.

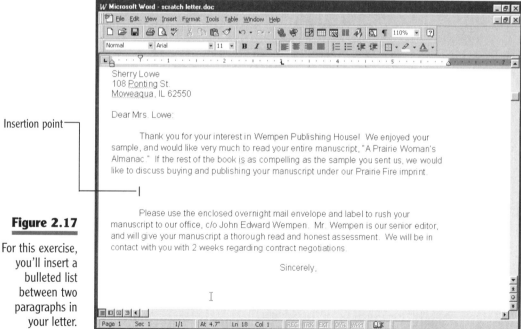

Figure 2.17

For this exercise, you'll insert a bulleted list between two paragraphs in your letter.

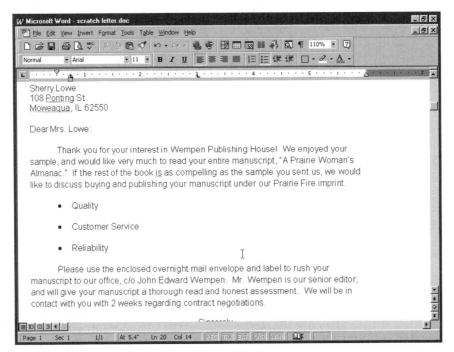

Figure 2.18

Now your letter contains a simple bulleted list.

But what happens if the paragraph is more than one line long? Follow these steps to find out:

1. Position your insertion point after the word "Quality" and type a period.
2. Press the spacebar twice and then type the following (without pressing Enter):

   Our products have been rated number one in initial quality by independent testing laboratories for three years in a row.

Notice that the extra text of the bulleted paragraph wraps neatly under the first line.

Now that there is a whole sentence in the bulleted paragraph, "Quality" no longer stands out the way it should. So make it bold:

1. Select "Quality" and the period that follows it.

2. Click on the Bold button on the Formatting toolbar or press Ctrl+B.

When you finish, your bulleted paragraph should look like the one in Figure 2.19.

Okay, the exercise is over. Now you need to get rid of those bulleted paragraphs, since they probably don't fit too well in your letter. You can do it in one of these ways:

- Select the bulleted paragraphs and press Delete.
- Close your file (<u>F</u>ile, <u>C</u>lose) and do not save your changes; then reopen the file (<u>F</u>ile, <u>O</u>pen).

TIP A quick way to reopen a recently used file is to open the File menu and choose the filename from the list at the bottom of the menu. This lets you bypass the Open dialog box.

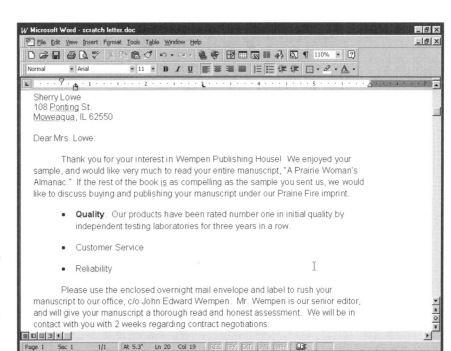

Figure 2.19

When you have a multiline bulleted paragraph, bolding the important first words can be a nice touch.

Checking for Errors

Whether you used a template to create your letter or you hammered one out from scratch, it may contain spelling errors. So take the time right now to check spelling and grammar.

Spell-Checking Individual Words

Do you see any words in your letter that are underlined in red? That's Word's way of telling you that a word is not in its dictionary and may be misspelled. If you don't have any red-underlined words, congratulations! However, for the sake of this exercise, you are going to need at least one misspelling, so add some spelling mistakes for Word to find. (Changing "the" to "th" is always a good one, as is changing "one" to "oen.") Then follow these steps:

1. Right-click on a red-underlined word. A list of spelling suggestions appears, as shown in Figure 2.20.

Figure 2.20

Word red-underlines words that don't appear in its dictionary.

2. Do one of the following:

- If the word is truly misspelled—and the correct spelling appears on the shortcut menu—click on the correct spelling. The word is corrected.

- If the spelling is okay now but you want Word to notify you when it appears in other Word sessions in the future, choose Ignore All. The word will not be marked as misspelled until you restart Word.

- If the word is correct and will always be correct in future documents, choose Add to add it to the dictionary.

- If you want Word to correct this misspelling automatically for you in the future, choose AutoCorrect and pick the correct spelling from the submenu that appears.

- If you want to type your own correction for the word, or tell Word to change every instance of it in this document, click on Spelling. Refer to the section "Checking the Entire Letter for Spelling and Grammar" for additional assistance.

- If you want to leave this particular instance of the word alone, simply press Esc or right-click on another red-underlined word

Grammar-Checking Individual Words and Phrases

Okay, so if the red squiggly underlines are possible spelling errors, what are the squiggly green lines? They're possible grammar problems. If you don't have any green underlines in your letter, good for you! Add a couple in for this exercise. Here are some good grammatically impaired sentences you could add:

The dog were delighted to see us.

The business which gets the job will be very rich.

NOTE If you don't see any red or green squiggly lines, either your document is totally correct or someone has turned off your display of them. To check, choose Tools, Options, and click the Spelling and Grammar tab. Make sure that the Check spelling as you type and Check grammar as you type check boxes are marked. Incidentally, this is where you can go to turn off the spelling and/or grammar check in the future if it ever bothers you.

Don't worry if the sentences don't make any sense in your letter; you can delete them when you're done with this exercise. When you are ready to check a green-underlined word or phrase, follow these steps:

1. Right-click on the green-underlined text. A shortcut menu appears listing what Word thinks would be good revisions, as shown in Figure 2.21.

2. Perform one of the following actions, as appropriate:
   - If one of the revisions seems correct, click on it.
   - If the sentence is okay as written, or you want to go back and adjust it by hand instead of using the grammar-checker's suggestions, click on Ignore Sentence.
   - If the sentence needs changing but none of the suggestions on the shortcut menu are correct, and you're not sure what to do about it, click on Grammar.

Checking the Entire Letter for Spelling and Grammar

If your letter is long, it may be tiresome to right-click individually on each red- or green-underlined word or phrase. In such cases, it's easiest to use the full-blown spell-check feature in Word. It checks all the words and sentences for both spelling and grammar.

To begin the spelling check of your worksheet, click on the Spelling button on the Standard toolbar; or choose Tools, Spelling and Grammar; or press F7. If you have no misspelled words, Word presents a dialog box telling you that your spell-check is complete. Click on OK to close the dialog box.

SATURDAY MORNING Correspondence

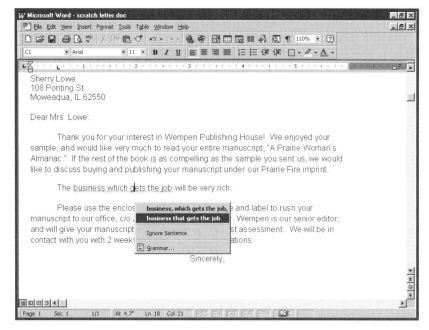

Figure 2.21

Right-click on green-underlined text to get some correction suggestions.

If, on the other hand, Word finds a misspelled word, as it did in Figure 2.22, you can choose from the following options:

- **Ignore.** Skips over this occurrence of the word.
- **Ignore All.** Skips over all occurrences of the word in this Word session.
- **Suggestio<u>n</u>s.** Lists words close to the spelling of the word you actually typed. Choose the correct one by clicking on it.
- **Not in Dictionary.** Shows the word in its context. You can double-click on the misspelled word and type a correction if none of the words in the Suggestions box are correct.
- **<u>C</u>hange.** Changes the word in the cell to the word highlighted in the Suggestions box. (Don't click on this button until you choose the correct word in the Suggestions box or type a correction in the Not in Dictionary box.)

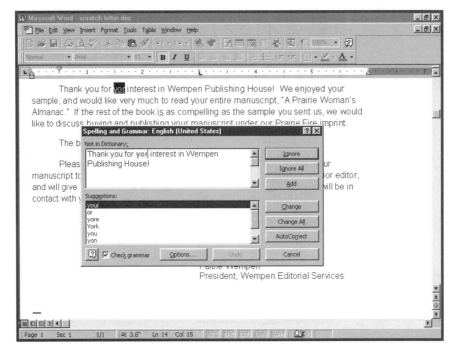

Figure 2.22

If Word finds a word that is not in its dictionary, this dialog box asks you what to do about it.

- **Change All.** Changes all occurrences of the word in the entire document to the word highlighted in the Suggestions text box.
- **Add.** Adds the word to Word's dictionary so that it will recognize it in the future.
- **AutoCorrect.** Adds the word to the AutoCorrect list so that if you misspell it the same way in the future, Word automatically corrects it as you type.

◆◆◆◆◆◆◆◆◆◆◆◆◆◆◆◆◆◆◆◆◆◆◆◆◆◆◆◆◆◆◆◆◆◆◆◆◆◆◆

Don't click on the AutoCorrect button for misspellings that you may sometimes want to change to some other word, or you may introduce embarrassing mistakes into your presentation. For example, if you often type "pian" instead of "pain," but sometimes you accidentally type "pian" instead of "piano," don't tell Word to always AutoCorrect to "pain," or you may find that Word has corrected your attempt at typing piano and made it a pain!

◆◆◆◆◆◆◆◆◆◆◆◆◆◆◆◆◆◆◆◆◆◆◆◆◆◆◆◆◆◆◆◆◆◆◆◆◆◆◆

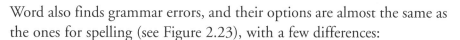

SATURDAY MORNING Correspondence   111

Word also finds grammar errors, and their options are almost the same as the ones for spelling (see Figure 2.23), with a few differences:

- There is a Next Sentence button that enables you to skip the entire sentence Word has found and move on to checking the next one.
- There is no Add button. You can't add a particular grammar construct to the dictionary.
- There is no Change All button. You must evaluate each grammar situation individually.
- There is no AutoCorrect button. You cannot AutoCorrect grammar.

When the spelling and grammar check is over, Word displays a dialog box. Click on OK.

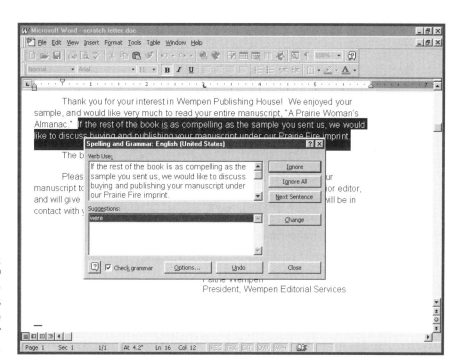

Figure 2.23

Word's grammar-checker has controls similar to those for misspellings.

CAUTION Don't take Word's grammar opinion as the gospel truth. It is frequently wrong. For example, in Figure 2.23, it has pointed out a possible grammar error that, in fact, is correct as it stands. Making the change would turn the sentence into the subjunctive tense, and the sentence's meaning would change to something not intended. Use your own brain as the ultimate authority! You can turn off grammar checking completely by deselecting the Check Grammar check box.

Take a Break

Now that you understand how to format a letter and correct errors in it, you'll work on applying your skills to creating letterhead. So take a breather and maybe a walk around the block, because this next section will require even more of your creative juices.

Designing Letterhead

So far, you have learned to type a very basic return address block in your letter. But letterhead opens up a whole new world in making your letter attractive.

When I talk about *letterhead,* I mean the standard text and the top (and possibly, bottom) of the letter that stays the same in every letter you write. If you flip back to Figure 2.3 (the letter created with the Contemporary Letter template), for example, the letterhead would be everything in and above the gray box at the top, and everything in and below the gray box at the bottom.

Your letterhead should reflect your business or personal style. Some people like to keep their letterhead very simple; others jazz it up with special fonts and logos. Figures 2.24 through 2.26 show some examples of letterhead to help you think about what style you might want to apply.

Figure 2.24 shows a simple letterhead within the reach of any beginning Word user. On the other hand, I used some fairly advanced features to

SATURDAY MORNING Correspondence   113

Figure 2.24

Here's a simple but effective personal letterhead.

Figure 2.25

This business letterhead uses some of Word's clip art to dress it up.

Figure 2.26

This business letterhead uses Word's WordArt feature to create vertical text.

put together the latter two letterhead examples. First go through the process of creating the letterhead from Figure 2.24, and then I'll show you briefly how to use some advanced features to create the other two.

Creating a New Template File

Once you spend a lot of time creating letterhead, you will want to use it over and over again. Therefore, you need to create a specially formatted Word document, a Document Template, in which to store your creation.

1. Choose File, New. The New dialog box opens.
2. If it's not already on top, click on the General tab.
3. If it's not already selected, click once on the Blank Document icon.
4. In the bottom right corner of the dialog box, click on the Template option button.

5. Click on OK. A new blank document opens with the name "Template1" in the title bar.

Setting Your Defaults

One nice thing about a template is that you can specify exact margin and font settings.

1. Choose File, Page Setup. The Page Setup dialog box appears.
2. Change any margins, as you learned earlier in this session. For most letters, the default margins will be fine. (I did not change mine for this template.)
3. Click on OK.
4. Choose Format, Font. The Font dialog box appears.
5. Choose a font and font size for your letter. (I like Times New Roman 11 point for letters.)
6. Click on the Default button. A warning box appears asking if you want to change the default font for this template.
7. Click on Yes.

Typing the Text

For your letterhead, you'll want your own name, address, and phone number. Go ahead and type it all in now—all on one line, as shown in Figure 2.24. Don't worry about the symbols separating the text; you'll add those in a moment.

While you're at it, add some blank lines below the letterhead. You'll need them later. (Trust me.)

Inserting the Symbols

Notice in Figure 2.24 that the information normally on separate lines is on one, and symbols separate the groupings. This is a very simple, compact way to put your return address on letterhead without taking up too much space. You can use any symbol on your keyboard, like an asterisk (*), but it looks fancier if you use a symbol that a typewriter can't produce.

In the following exercise, you can use any symbol you want. You will probably be pleasantly surprised at the wide variety of symbols available!

1. Position the insertion point where you want the symbol to appear. For example, position it between your name and street address.
2. Choose Insert, Symbol. The Symbol dialog box opens.
3. Open the Font drop-down list in the dialog box and choose a font. The Symbol font is the one shown in Figure 2.27, but any of the Wingdings fonts are also very good.
4. When you find a symbol you like, click on it. Its box expands so you can see it more clearly. If you don't want that symbol, click on another. You can change the font, too, if none of the current font's symbols please you.
5. When your symbol is selected, click on the Insert button.
6. Behind the dialog box should be your line of text. Click in the line of text to make it active (the dialog box is still open). Drag the dialog box's title bar to move it out of the way, if needed.

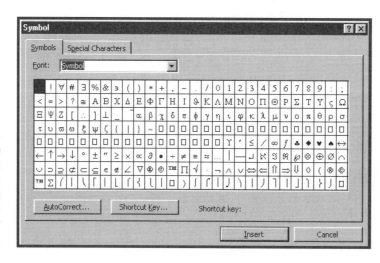

Figure 2.27

Use the Symbol dialog box to choose and insert symbols that are not found on your keyboard.

SATURDAY MORNING Correspondence 117

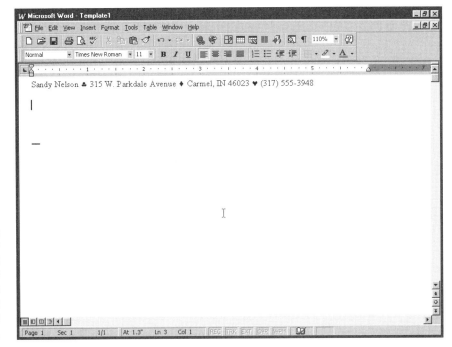

Figure 2.28

The letterhead is looking better, now that the groupings of information are separated by symbols.

7. In the line of text, click to position your insertion point where you want the next symbol.

8. Repeat Steps 3 through 5 to choose and insert the desired symbol.

9. Repeat Steps 6 through 8, as needed, until you have inserted all the symbols you need.

10. Click on Close. Now your letterhead should have all the symbols it needs, in the right places, as shown in Figure 2.28. If the symbols need to be moved, move them (as you learned in the Friday Evening session).

Add the Bottom Border

Glance back at Figure 2.24, and you'll see that next you need to add a border beneath the letterhead line. In the figure, it's a double border (two thin lines very close together), but yours can be anything.

NOTE You might think that a simple double-underline format would do, but you'd be mistaken: underlining is a character format that you use to underline individual words and letters, like this. What we want is a solid line beneath the entire line that the paragraph is on, from margin to margin. The difference? Underline is a character format (affecting individual characters—including spaces, unless you tell Word otherwise), while a border is a paragraph format (affecting the entire paragraph).

To create a border, follow these steps:

1. Click to move the insertion point anywhere within the letterhead line. (Because a border is a paragraph feature, it will automatically apply to the entire paragraph in which the insertion point lies; you don't have to select it.)
2. Choose Format, Borders and Shading. The Borders and Shading dialog box opens.
3. If it is not already on top, click on the Borders tab (see Figure 2.29).

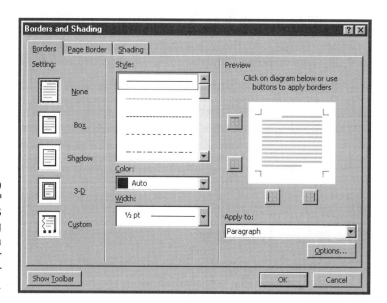

Figure 2.29

Use the Borders and Shading dialog box to place a bottom border under your letterhead line.

 NOTE There is also a Border button on the Formatting toolbar, but you're not using it here because you want a custom border (a double line) rather than a standard one. You may want to play with it a bit to see the kinds of effects it will give you.

4. Scroll through the Style list and click on the line style that you want to use.

5. Click on the Custom button, removing the border from all sides of the sample in the Preview area and clearing the way for our bottom border to be added.

6. (Optional) If you want a different line thickness from the one in the default, choose it from the Width drop-down list.

7. In the Preview area, click at the bottom of the sample paragraph, placing a bottom border on the sample.

8. (Optional) If you want a bit of extra spacing between the bottom of your text and the top of the line, click on the Options button. The Border and Shading Options dialog box appears (Figure 2.30). Increase the number in the Bottom text box a bit (for example, to 5 points), and click on OK.

9. Click on OK to apply the line to the text, as shown in Figure 2.31.

Making Your Name Bold

This step is easy. Just select your name (both first and last, and middle, too, if you typed one), and click on the Bold button on the Formatting toolbar or press Ctrl+B.

Adding Extra Spaces

The final formatting task is to make the words in the letterhead appear evenly centered between the right and left margins. In other words, you want this line to be fully justified. However, due to a "feature" of Word, you can't simply apply Full Justify alignment to the paragraph. Why?

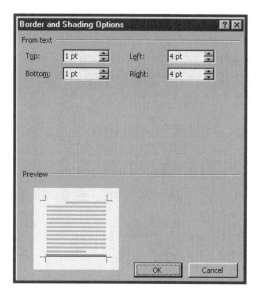

Figure 2.30

You can adjust the amount of white space here.

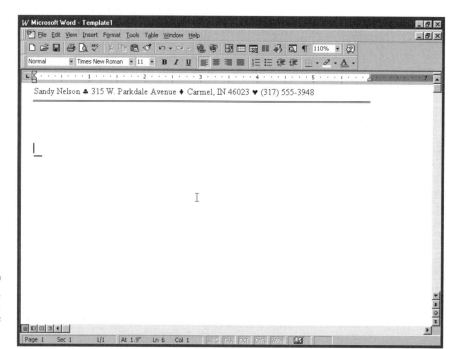

Figure 2.31

The letterhead is really shaping up with the addition of the bottom border.

SATURDAY MORNING Correspondence

When you Full Justify a paragraph, it makes all the lines in the paragraph except the last one align perfectly between the margins. But your paragraph has only one line, which is (by definition) the last line. So no go.

What you need to do is add individual spaces (with the spacebar) evenly on both sides of each symbol inserted.

 TIP You may want to display the non-printing characters (including spaces) by clicking the Show/Hide ¶ button on the Standard toolbar. Seeing the spaces will make it easier to complete this exercise.

1. To make sure you are starting out with even spacing, remove all the spaces on both sides of each symbol, as shown in Figure 2.32.
2. Add one space to both sides of each symbol.

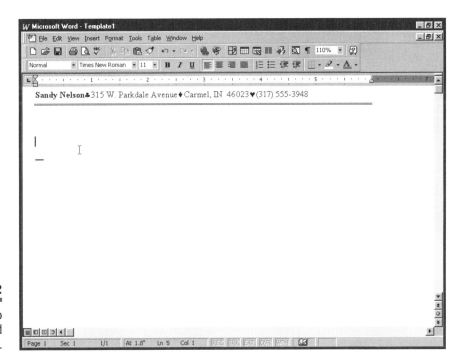

Figure 2.32

Start with no spaces around the symbols.

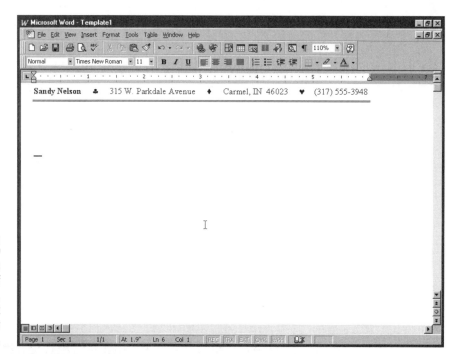

Figure 2.33

I added five spaces to both sides of each symbol, except for the last spot that only received four.

3. Evaluate the line. Does the text come all the way to the edge of the bottom border on the right? If not, repeat Step 2.

4. You probably will "go over" at some point: you'll add too much space, and the letterhead will wrap to a second line. When this happens, remove one space at a time until the line stretches the entire length of the bottom border (see Figure 2.33).

Inserting a Date Code

Here's a great trick that you'll never see on a typewriter. You can insert a code that will pull in the date from your computer's clock every time you use the template, so you will always have the current date in place.

1. Position your insertion point six lines down from your letterhead. Press Enter a couple more times if needed to create the extra blank lines in the file.

CAUTION Now you know why I initially told you to press Enter a few times after typing the text for your letterhead. If you didn't do it, you are now in somewhat of a pickle. When you position your insertion point at the end of the letterhead line and press Enter to create blank lines, the bottom border moves down. To salvage the situation, select the entire document (Ctrl+A). Then click on the down arrow next to the Border button on the Formatting toolbar, and click on the picture that has no border. Add those extra blank lines after your letterhead. Position the insertion point once again in the letterhead line. Then reopen the Border button's drop-down list and choose the picture that looks like the bottom border.

2. When your insertion point is where you want the date to be, choose Insert, Date and Time. The Date and Time dialog box appears (see Figure 2.34).
3. Choose the date format you want to use from the list.
4. Make sure the Update automatically check box is check marked.
5. Click on OK. Now you have a date code in your template that will always show the correct date. You can tell that it's a code because it appears in gray, but it will appear normal in a document.

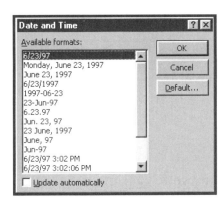

Figure 2.34

Choose the date format you want from the available formats.

Save Your Template

Now it's time to save the template so you can reuse it. Templates are saved in a special folder: Program Files\Microsoft Office\Templates. The subfolders within this folder determine the tabs you see in the New dialog box. Because this template is for a letter, you will want to save it in the Letters & Faxes subfolder.

1. Click on the Save button on the Standard toolbar. The Save As dialog box appears.
2. Double-click on the Letters & Faxes folder to move to that folder.
3. In the File name list box, replace the current name (which is the first few words of the file) with a descriptive name you will remember. For example, you might call it "Simple Letterhead" (see Figure 2.35). Notice that you cannot change the file type, Document Template.
4. Click on OK. Your template is saved.

Using the New Template

Now you can use your template in much the same way you used the Contemporary Letter template at the beginning of this session. It's not quite as fancy (for example, it doesn't have gray boxes with dummy information

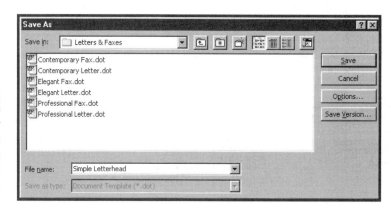

Figure 2.35

Save your letterhead as a template so you can use it over and over again.

already entered), but it will do nicely for most purposes. Follow these steps to use your template:

1. Choose File, New. The New dialog box appears.
2. Click on the Letters & Faxes tab.
3. Double-click on your template to start a new document with it. A new document appears, with your template's text and formatting already included.
4. Type your letter just as you did when typing a letter from scratch, except omit the return address.

Your "simple" letterhead is complete. A lot of work for something that was supposed to be simple, wasn't it? All your hard work will make you appreciate the fact that, by saving your work as a template, you will never do the same work again.

NOTE If you are interested in the other two sample letterheads that I showed you back in Figures 2.25 and 2.26, check out the steps at the end of this session for recreating them.

Working with Preprinted Stationery

Lots of companies use preprinted stationery with their company name, return address, and maybe even a motto or slogan. If you're lucky enough to have such stationery at your disposal, creating the letterhead portion of your template is easy; all you have to do is leave the appropriate amount of space for the preprinted info. If this is your situation, here's what to do:

1. Measure with a ruler the space between the top of the letterhead paper and the point where you want the date of your letter to print. For most letterhead, this is two to two and a half inches, but it never hurts to measure.

2. If your letterhead has preprinted text at the bottom of the page, measure the distance between the bottom of the page and the lowest point where your letter text should run. Two inches is average.

3. Write these measurements down and make the changes to the margin settings, as you learned earlier in this session (File, Page Setup).

Creating an Envelope

Almost every letter you send needs an envelope printed for it. Printed envelopes look neater and more professional than hand-written ones, and they can also include postal bar codes that speed the mail delivery.

Be aware that not every printer can print an envelope well. Some laser printers crush or wrinkle envelopes, or their heat melts the sticky stuff on the flap. Some dot matrix printers bend each envelope around the platen, causing a permanent warp in the paper. On average, Inkjet printers seem to do better than the other kinds with envelopes. If you find that your printer consistently ruins envelopes, try buying labels to feed into your printer, and then stick the labels on the envelopes. You'll learn about labels for mass mailings this evening.

Word makes it possible for you to create an envelope to go with each letter you type, and it saves the envelope information with the letter as a separate section in the document. (Section? What's a section? It's a divider of sorts; you'll learn about it this afternoon.)

Setting Up the Envelope

Start with the letter you created onscreen. It should be ready to go, and should contain the recipient's address, so Word can transfer the information to the envelope automatically for you.

SATURDAY MORNING Correspondence

CAUTION Make sure it's the letter, not the template, that's open. If the title bar says "Simple Letterhead," the template is open. Close it (File, Close), and start a new document based on the template (File, New) to type your letter.

1. Choose Tools, Envelopes and Labels.
2. Click on the Envelope tab. Notice that Word has transferred the addresses from your letter to the dialog box (see Figure 2.36).
3. Check the address in the Delivery address field to make sure Word transferred it correctly. Make any changes as needed.
4. If the envelope you are using has the return address pre-printed, click on the Omit check box and skip to Step 6.
5. If your letter had your return address typed in it, it appears in the Return address box; check it to confirm. If, on the other hand, you used letterhead for your letter, Word cannot detect your return address, so the box is blank. If this is the case, type it in now.
6. Word uses the dimensions for a #10 envelope by default (a standard long business envelope). If you need to print on another size

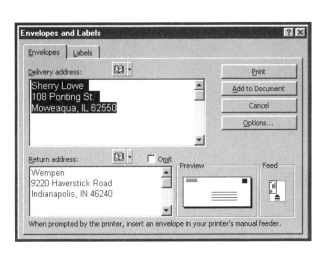

Figure 2.36

Word makes creating an envelope very easy; it even transfers addresses from the letter.

envelope, click on the Options button and choose a different type in the Envelope Options dialog box (see Figure 2.37). Click on OK to return to the Envelope dialog box.

7. Click on the Add to Document button. The box closes, and you see the envelope onscreen. It looks different depending on the view you're using, but Figure 2.38 shows how it looks in Page Layout view when zoomed to about 40%.

Testing Your Printer's Envelope Orientation

Dot matrix printer users can skip this section. It's just for inkjet and laser printer owners, to help you figure out how to put the envelope into the printer to get the results you want—and it only needs to be done once for each printer.

1. Go to your printer and take a piece of paper out of the paper tray. Draw a big arrow pointing to the top of the paper on one side.

2. Feed the sheet of paper into your printer's manual feed if it's different from your regular paper tray. If you don't have a manual feed slot, put the paper back in the tray face up, with the arrow pointing toward the printer.

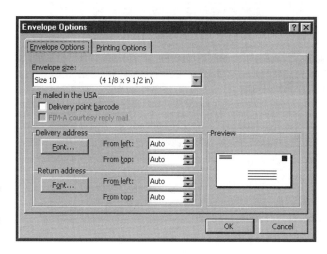

Figure 2.37

You can choose a different envelope size here.

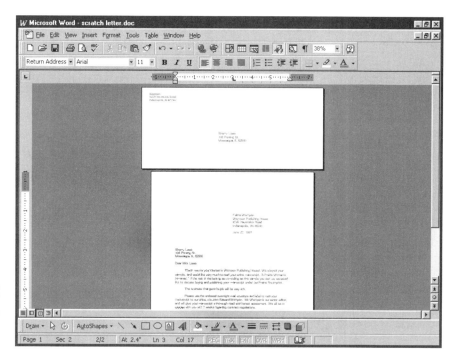

Figure 2.38

The envelope is now part of the document.

Even if you think you know how paper should be positioned in the paper tray to print on the right side, you should do the test anyway, especially if you have a manual-feed slot that is separate. The manual-feed slot sometimes works differently from the paper tray. For example, on my printer (a Texas Instruments MicroLaser Pro 600), I put paper in the paper tray face up, but I feed paper in the manual feed face down.

3. Choose Tools, Envelopes and Labels again to reopen the dialog box, and click on Print to print a test copy of the envelope.

4. Retrieve your printout from the printer and compare the location of the envelope lettering with the arrow you drew. From that, you should be able to figure out how you need to feed an envelope into the printer.

5. To help yourself remember the setting, choose Tools, Envelopes and Labels again, click on the Options button, and click on the Printing Options tab (see Figure 2.39).

6. Click on the picture that matches the way you need to feed the envelope in, and click on OK.

7. Now take another piece of paper from your paper tray and draw small X's where you think the return address and mailing address should appear on the paper. Then insert the paper into your manual feed.

8. Click on Print. The envelope text prints on your paper.

9. If the text printed where you placed the X's, you're ready to print the envelope! If not, repeat these steps.

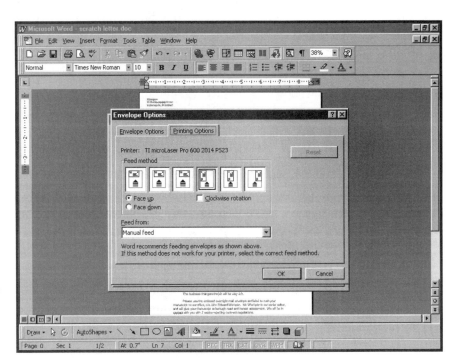

Figure 2.39

On this tab you can set your printer's correct envelope orientation.

Printing the Envelope

After all the testing and preparation, printing the actual envelope is a snap:

1. Choose Tools, Envelopes and Labels.
2. Insert the envelope into the printer according to the diagram in the bottom right corner of the dialog box. (Remember, you chose this illustration yourself in the preceding steps, so you know it's reliable.) Dot matrix printer users can simply feed the envelope in like a single sheet of paper, according to their printer documentation.
3. Click on Print. The envelope prints.

Time-Savers

That's it for the basic letter, letterhead, and envelope scoop. If you still have some time left in your morning, try some of these Time-Savers procedures to learn a little bit more about Word.

Using the Letter Wizard

The Letter Wizard is a combination of a template and a dialog box. It creates a custom template for you that combines elements of all three of the letter templates to your precise specifications. Try it out!

1. Start a new document based on the Blank Document template.
2. Choose Tools, Letter Wizard. The Letter Wizard dialog box opens (see Figure 2.40). It has four tabs, and you must fill out all the options on all four.
3. Click on the Date line check box, and choose a date format from the drop-down list next to it.
4. Under Choose a page design, open the drop-down list and choose the letter template on which to base the letter.

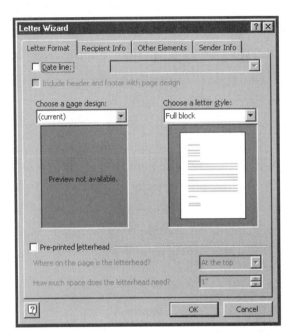

Figure 2.40

Fill out the Letter Wizard dialog box's settings on all four tabs, starting with this one.

 TIP The Letter Wizard works best if you choose one of the three letter templates that come with Word instead of one you created from scratch.

5. Under Choose a letter style, choose one of the paragraph alignments (Full block, Semi-block, or Modified block).

6. If you are using preprinted letterhead paper, click on that check box and specify the location and amount of space that the letterhead requires.

7. Ready to move on? Click on the Recipient Info tab (see Figure 2.41).

8. Enter the recipient's name in the Recipient's name box, and his or her address in the Delivery address box.

9. In the Salutation area, click on the option button that best describes your relationship with the person: Informal, Formal, Business, or Other. (Other lets you fill in your own salutation.)

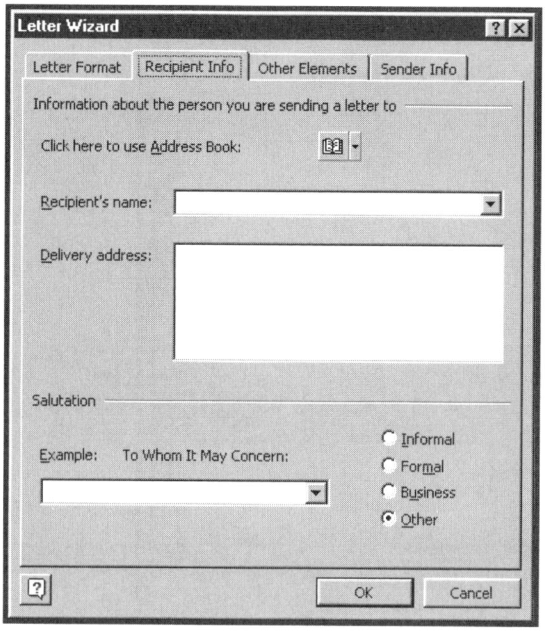

SATURDAY MORNING Correspondence   133

Figure 2.41

Enter the recipient's name and address here.

10. Click on the Other Elements tab (see Figure 2.42).

11. In the Include section, mark any of the check boxes for lines that you need, and then choose the wording for the line from the drop-down list across from the check box.

12. If anyone else needs to receive a copy of the letter, enter the name and address in the Cc: field.

TIP You may have noticed the Address Book button above several of the address fields. If you have names and addresses set up in Microsoft Outlook, Mail, Exchange, or Schedule+, you can pull them from your profile into Word by clicking on the button.

13. Click on the Sender Info tab (see Figure 2.43).

14. Enter your name and address in the Sender's name and Return address fields, respectively. If you are using preprinted letterhead,

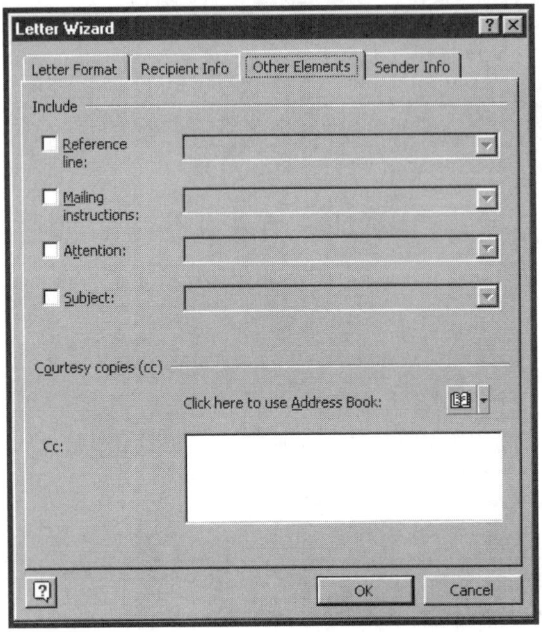

Figure 2.42

Choose any special enclosure or reference lines that should appear in the letter.

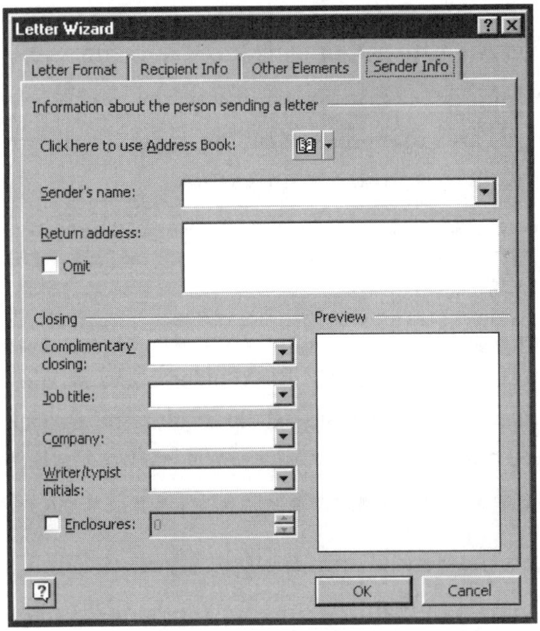

Figure 2.43

On the final tab, enter information about yourself.

click on the <u>O</u>mit check box to leave the return address off the letter.

15. In the Closing area, type the wording you want in any of the text boxes, or open the drop-down lists and choose previously used or common wordings.

16. If you are going to have enclosures, click on the <u>E</u>nclosures check box and enter the amount in the text box.

17. Click on OK. Your letter template is generated.

18. Fill in the gaps and holes, as you did with the letter templates you used at the beginning of this session.

Inserting Boilerplate Text with AutoText

Do you struggle for the right wording when writing a letter? You're not alone. Unless you've taken a business or secretarial course in the last few years, you probably don't remember the standardized wording used in business for various situations. Luckily, Word can help.

1. Position the insertion point where you want the phrase to appear.

2. Choose <u>I</u>nsert, <u>A</u>utoText. A submenu appears with the various categories of AutoText available.

3. Point your mouse at one of the categories to see a list of available text, as shown in Figure 2.44.

4. Click on the phrase you want to insert into the document.

You can also create your own AutoText entry.

1. Choose <u>I</u>nsert, <u>A</u>utoText, AutoTe<u>x</u>t. The AutoCorrect dialog box opens with the AutoText tab on top (see Figure 2.45).

2. Do any of the following:

    ✪ To delete an existing entry, click on it on the list and then click on <u>D</u>elete.

Learn Word 97 In a Weekend

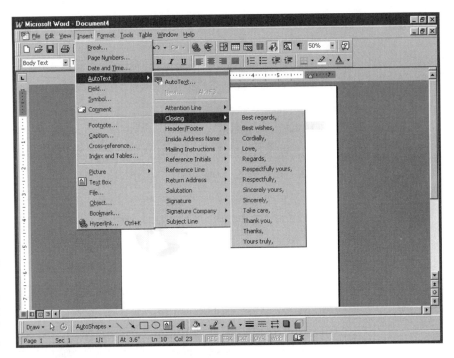

Figure 2.44

Word comes with dozens of commonly used business terms and phrases in AutoText for various situations.

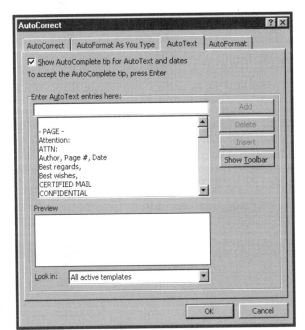

Figure 2.45

You can edit the AutoText library and add your own entries here.

SATURDAY MORNING Correspondence

- To edit an entry, click on it and then make your corrections in the text box.
- To add an entry, type it in the text box and then click on Add.
- To insert text into your document, click on it on the list and then click on Insert.

3. Click on OK to close the dialog box, if needed.

Notice in Figure 2.45 that there is also a Show Toolbar button. You can click on it to include the AutoText toolbar at the top of the Word window, along with the other toolbars. From it, you can open a drop-down list to choose AutoText entries to insert. If you decide you don't like it onscreen, right-click on any toolbar and click to remove the check mark next to AutoText.

Setting Custom Grammar Checking Rules

As you were checking grammar earlier this morning, you may have wondered "Where did all those grammar rules come from, anyway?" Actually, there is not one definitive set of grammar rules; grammar that is acceptable in some situations is unacceptable in others.

Word enables you to choose the level of formality you want in your grammar, and it even lets you pick and choose among the individual grammar rules, for those who understand them.

1. When you're in the Spelling and Grammar window (Tools, Spelling and Grammar), click on the Options button. The Spelling and Grammar Options dialog box opens (see Figure 2.46).

2. Open the Writing style drop-down list and choose a level of formality. (The default is Standard, but for business letters, I like to use Formal.)

3. (Optional) To choose the individual grammar rules, click on the Settings button to open the Grammar Settings dialog box (see Figure 2.47).

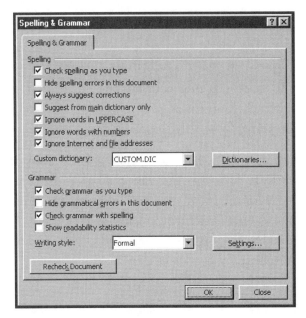

Figure 2.46

You can change the formality level and customize how the spelling and grammar check operates here.

4. Place or remove check marks next to the various types of grammar tests to use or ignore. Then click on OK to return to the Spelling and Grammar Options dialog box.

5. Click on Recheck Document to rerun the spelling and grammar

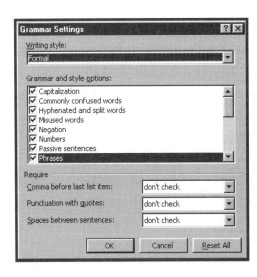

Figure 2.47

Grammar gurus can choose their own grammar tests that Word should perform on a document.

check based on your new rules. A confirmation box appears; click on Yes.

6. Click on OK to return to the spelling and grammar check.

Using AutoCorrect to Fix Common Typing Errors

With AutoCorrect, Word can correct certain common misspellings automatically as you type. One way to put a word on the AutoCorrect list is to click on the AutoCorrect button in the spell-checker. Another way is to directly access the AutoCorrect feature.

To access AutoCorrect, choose Tools, AutoCorrect. The AutoCorrect dialog box appears, as shown in Figure 2.48.

At the top of the dialog box is a series of check boxes that help you fine-tune some other corrections that AutoCorrect makes:

- **Correct TWo INitial Capitals.** If you accidentally hold down Shift too long and get two capital letters in a row, such as in the word *MIcrosoft*, Word corrects this if you leave this check box marked.

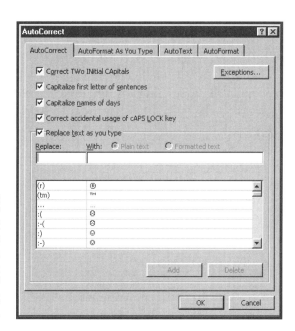

Figure 2.48

The AutoCorrect dialog box enables you to automatically edit the list of corrections that Word makes.

- **Capitalize first letter of sentence.** Leave this check box marked to let Word capitalize the first letter of the word that follows a sentence-ending punctuation mark or begins a new paragraph.
- **Capitalize names of days.** Leave this check box marked to make sure the names of days—Sunday, Monday, and so on—are capitalized.
- **Correct accidental use of cAPS LOCK key.** If you leave Caps Lock on, Word can sometimes detect it and fix the problem. For example, if you type a sentence like "hE WAS GLAD TO SEE US," Word concludes that Caps Lock is inappropriately on and turns it off for you.
- **Replace text as you type.** This check box enables the main portion of AutoCorrect: the word list. You must leave this check box on if you want AutoCorrect to correct the words on the list.

On the list in this dialog box, you'll see a number of word pairs. To the left is the common misspelling, and to the right is the word that Word substitutes in its place. Scroll through this list to get a feel for the corrections that Word makes.

If Word insists on making a correction that you do not want, you can delete it from the list. Simply select it on the list and click on the Delete button. For example, my editors like me to code certain headings with (c) in front of them, so the first thing I do in any Office program is remove the AutoCorrect entry that specifies that (c) must be converted to a copyright symbol (©).

To add your own entries to the list, type the misspelling in the Replace text box and the correction in the With text box, and then click on the Add button. When you are finished, click on OK to close the AutoCorrect dialog box.

Creating Fancier Letterheads

Earlier in this session, I created some fancier letterhead samples, which are shown in Figures 2.25 and 2.26. Now it's your turn to learn some of

the more advanced techniques involved in putting together an aesthetically pleasing composition.

 If you are a beginner at Word, skip these advanced letterhead sections! They involve using several advanced features that will only confuse you at this point. Wait until this afternoon, when you learn about these features in detail, before you attempt these letterheads.

Creating the "Happy Chef" Letterhead

This letterhead has both a top and bottom design. The top, as shown in Figure 2.49, is made up of a piece of clip art and two text boxes. I started a new template based on the Blank Document template, and switched to Page Layout view (View, Page Layout). Then:

1. I placed the clip art (Insert, Picture, Clip Art). I then dragged a corner to resize it, and dragged the middle to move it into position. (This particular piece of clip art came from the People At Work category of pictures; you'll learn about clip art this afternoon.)

2. Next, I drew a text box next to the artwork (Insert, Text Box). In the text box, I typed the two lines, pressing Enter between them. The first line I formatted in 18-point Arial Bold, and the second line I formatted in 12-point Times New Roman Italic. (You'll get to text boxes this afternoon, too.) Then I centered both lines (by clicking on the Center button on the Formatting toolbar).

3. Finally, I drew another text box over in the right corner, and entered the return address and phone number. I formatted the lines in 10-point Arial and aligned them with the right margin (by clicking on the Align Right button on the Formatting toolbar).

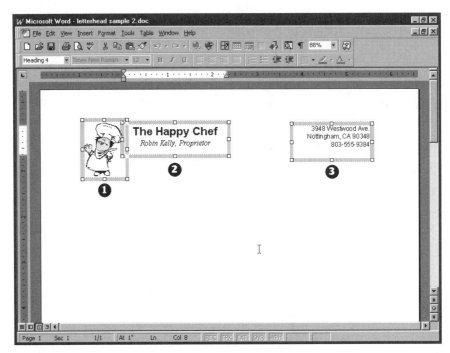

Figure 2.49

Here's how I made the top part.

Then it was time to create the bottom part of the letterhead. Here's how that went:

4. I created another text box and added some text in Times New Roman 14-point italics. I right-aligned the text.

5. Then I used the Clip Gallery again to place another piece of clip art. (This piece also came from the People at Work category.) I resized it and moved it into the position you see in Figure 2.50.

Creating the Colvin Pottery Letterhead

The Colvin Pottery letterhead (which you saw back in Figure 2.26) looks simple, but quite a bit of work went into it. The following steps explain the basic process:

1. I started with a new template based on the Blank Document template. I switched to Page Layout view (<u>V</u>iew, Page Layout), and set

SATURDAY MORNING Correspondence

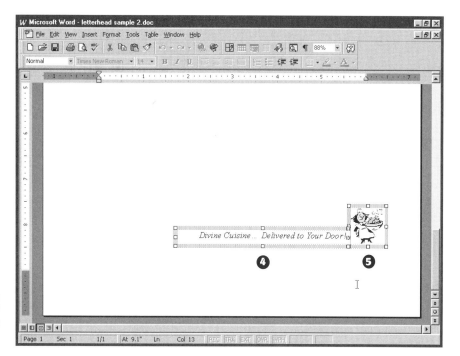

Figure 2.50

And here's the bottom part!

the Zoom to Whole Page (from the Zoom drop-down list on the Standard toolbar) so I could see the whole page.

2. I opened up WordArt (Insert, Picture, WordArt) and chose the design in the top right corner. Then in the Edit WordArt Text dialog box, I typed COLVIN POTTERY in all caps. After I clicked on OK, the screen looked like Figure 2.51.

3. I clicked on the WordArt Vertical Text button to make the text run left to right. Then I turned on the Drawing toolbar (by right-clicking on one of the other toolbars and choosing Drawing).

4. On the Drawing toolbar, I opened the Draw menu and chose Rotate or Flip and then Rotate Left. Then I dragged the WordArt to the left edge of the page and resized it (by dragging the corner) to fill the tall edge of the paper, as shown in Figure 2.52.

5. Next, I made the letters a little more squat by dragging the handle

Drawing button

WordArt Vertical Text button

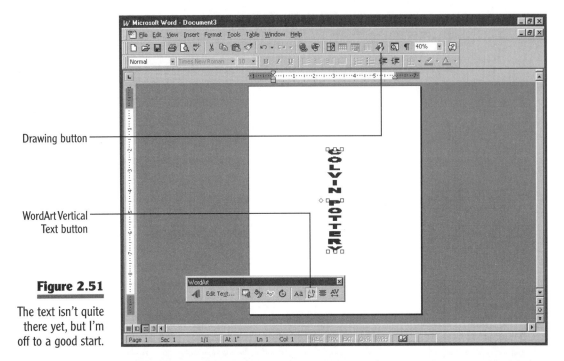

Figure 2.51

The text isn't quite there yet, but I'm off to a good start.

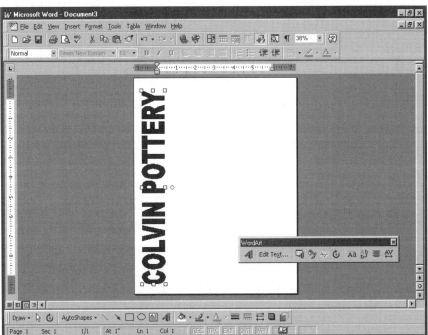

Figure 2.52

The WordArt is in the right direction and the appropriate height.

on the long side of the WordArt a bit to the left. Then I right-clicked on the WordArt and chose Format WordArt, and set the Fill to a light gray and the Line setting to None.

6. I placed a text box in the bottom right corner (Insert, Text Box) and typed the return address there. I formatted the text in 10-point Arial.

7. Finally, I inserted an appropriate piece of clip art (Insert, Picture, Clip Art), and moved and resized it so it accented the return address attractively, as shown in Figure 2.53.

8. One last thing: the company name took up a lot of room at the left margin, so I adjusted the document margins to account for it (File, Page Setup). I set the left margin to 2".

That's exactly how I created the letterhead you saw back in Figure 2.26, and exactly how you can do your own, at least once you've completed your weekend training and have a little Word experience under your belt.

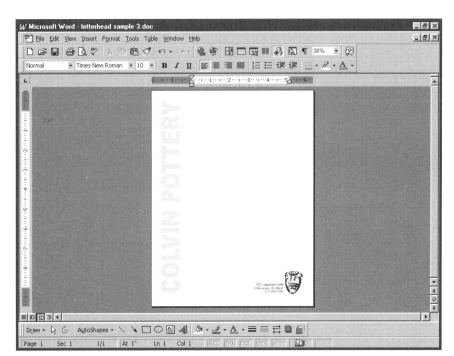

Figure 2.53

The letterhead is almost finished.

SATURDAY AFTERNOON

Flyers and Newsletters

- ✿ Creating a permission slip flyer
- ✿ Designing a party invitation flyer
- ✿ Drawing a map
- ✿ Making a newsletter
- ✿ Reusing your newsletter

This morning's session may have seemed a bit serious to you, but the instructions I've offered to this point are necessary to master the basics of Word 97. Now it's time to let your hair down and boogie to the beat of flyers and newsletters. This afternoon, you'll learn to create effective flyers customized to your audience. Later, you'll apply what you've learned to a basic newsletter and be on your way to desktop publishing nirvana.

What Is Desktop Publishing?

The kind of work you'll wade through this afternoon falls under a loosely constructed definition of desktop publishing. Back in the "olden days" of computer technology (10 to 20 years ago), people who wanted to create documents with photos, fancy fonts, and other extras could not do the job themselves. They turned to a publisher with the right equipment to generate such things, or they created a pasteup by hand (literally by cutting and pasting with scissors and glue) and took it to a photocopying center.

In the last 10 years, however, word processing and page layout programs have advanced to such a degree (and are so much cheaper) that almost anyone with a computer can afford to do his or her own publishing, right at the desk at home. Thus, we have the term "desktop publishing."

Professional desktop publishing people prefer to use high-end, expensive programs like PageMaker or QuarkXpress. However, average folks like you and me can get by nicely with a powerful word processor like Word. You will be surprised at how much you can do!

Creating a Permission Slip Flyer

You'll start with a really simple flyer, one that anybody involved in children's activities can benefit from: the permission slip. I consider these in the "flyers" category because they're typically one-page affairs directed to a large group of people. Figure 3.1 shows a sample.

Creating the Basic Text

First of all, type your text into the computer. You'll want a heading at the top, explanatory paragraphs next, and then the area that the parent is supposed to fill out. If you don't have your own text to type, use the text in Figure 3.1.

Eagle Valley Little League

1997 SUMMER TOURNAMENT

The Eagle Valley Little League summer program participants are invited to attend a tournament for little league members ages 8 to 13 in Little Rock, Arkansas on **August 8** from 8:00 AM to 4:00 PM. The trip will be chaperoned by coaches and parents.

Transportation:
A bus will be leaving from Park County Grade School at **7:00 AM**, providing transportation to and from the site for any league participants and their parents who do not want to drive to the tournament. The cost will be $1 per passenger. The bus is limited to the first 60 people to arrive and pay their fee that morning.

What to Wear/Bring:
Players should be dressed in their team uniforms, including hats. Each player and parent should bring a sack lunch with his or her name clearly marked on the outside, and 50 cents for a beverage.

What is the Permission Slip For?
A permission slip is required for each player who participates in the tournament and/or rides the bus. No players will be allowed to board the bus unless a permission slip is on file or is provided at bus-boarding time. Parents driving players to the game themselves may turn in permission slips at the tournament site. Players with their own transportation to the site must turn in their permission slips before they will be allowed to play.

Parents with more than one child participating must turn in a separate slip for each child.

Who is Collecting the Permission Slips?
Permission slips can be turned in at any time to Coach Lewis (555-4983). You can call him to ask any questions you may have.

Tear here and keep the top part for reference

PLEASE PRINT!

I give my permission for my child ______________________ to attend the Eagle Valley Little League tournament, (circle one) including/excluding bus transportation. With this signature I release the Eagle Valley Athletic Association from any liability in the event of delays or accidents related to the trip.

Name (print): ______________________

Signed: ______________________ Date: ____________

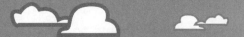

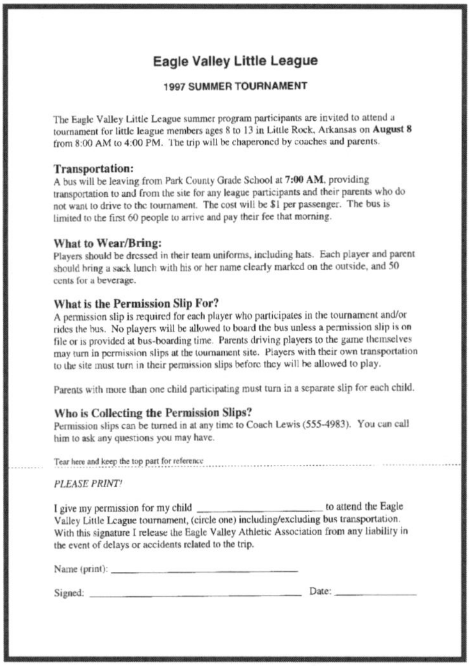

Figure 3.1

If you're a parent, you have probably filled out dozens of flyers in your lifetime.

Formatting the Text

The next step is to format the text so it looks attractive and the important parts stand out.

1. If you did not leave blank lines between paragraphs, select the entire document (Ctrl+A) and then add 12 points of space after each paragraph (Format, Paragraph). Remember, you learned this in the Saturday Morning session.
2. Select the title and format it as 16-point Arial bold.
3. Select the subtitle (1997 SUMMER TOURNAMENT, in the sample) and format it as 12-point Arial bold.
4. Select the title and subtitle lines from Steps 2 and 3, and click on the Center button on the Formatting toolbar to center them.
5. Select the remainder of the document and format it as 12 point. (It is already Times New Roman, which is the font we want.)
6. Select each of the headings in the document (for example, Transportation) and format them as 14-point Times New Roman bold.
7. Select the date of the event in the first paragraph (for example, August 8) and press Ctrl+B to make it bold.
8. Select the time that the bus is leaving (for example, 7:00 AM) and make it bold, too.
9. Select the words "PLEASE PRINT!" and press Ctrl+I to make them italic.
10. Select the paragraph that starts "Tear here" and format the entire paragraph as 10 point.

Good job! You made it through the text formatting.

Adding the Tear-Off Line

Now it's time to create the dotted line at which the parents should tear. In the preceding session, you learned how to create a bottom border for a paragraph, and that's basically what we're going to do here. However, notice in Figure 3.1 that the dotted line goes almost all the way to the edge of the paper. So after you create the bottom border for the paragraph, you'll need to extend the paragraph's margins.

1. Switch to Page Layout view.
2. Open the Zoom drop-down list and choose Page Width.
3. Click on the "Tear here" line.
4. Choose F̲ormat, B̲orders and Shading. The Borders and Shading dialog box appears.
5. Click on the B̲orders tab, if it is not already on top.
6. On the St̲yle list, locate and click on a plain dashed line.
7. In the Setting area, click on the N̲one button, clearing the border from the Preview area.
8. Click on the bottom of the sample in the Preview area, placing a dotted border under the sample, as shown in Figure 3.2.
9. Click on OK. Your paragraph now has a dotted border beneath it, as shown in Figure 3.3.
10. If the ruler is not onscreen (see Figure 3.3), choose V̲iew, R̲uler to make it appear.

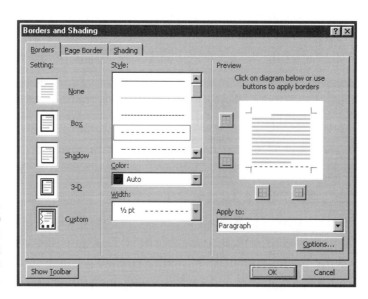

Figure 3.2

Your Borders and Shading dialog box should look like this after Step 6.

SATURDAY AFTERNOON Flyers and Newsletters 153

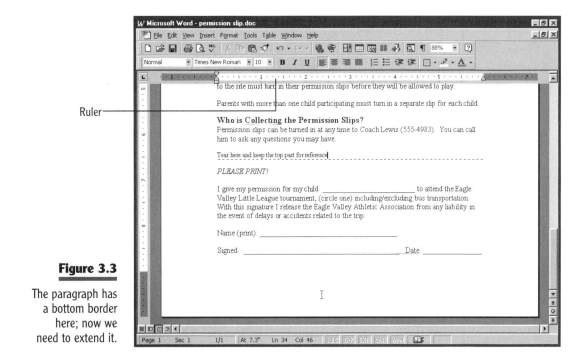

Figure 3.3

The paragraph has a bottom border here; now we need to extend it.

11. On the ruler, position the mouse pointer on the little rectangle at the left margin, and wait until the words "Left Indent" pop up as a ScreenTip. This lets you know that you're in the right spot.

12. Drag the rectangle to the left until it stops.

13. Now drag the triangle at the right margin to the right until it, too, is as far toward the edge of the paper as it can go. Your screen should look like Figure 3.4 when you finish.

TIP Why a rectangle at one end and a triangle at the other? On the left, the rectangle controls the entire paragraph's left margin; the two triangles at the left control the paragraph's first lines and subsequent lines. (Some paragraphs need a different indent on the first line than on the others.) At the right margin, this is not an issue, so there is only one simple marker.

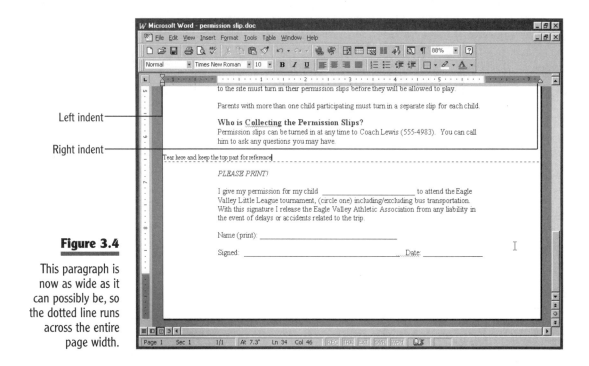

Figure 3.4

This paragraph is now as wide as it can possibly be, so the dotted line runs across the entire page width.

14. The last step is to realign the "Tear here" text. To do so, click on the beginning of the sentence to place the insertion point there.

15. Click on the ruler to set a tab stop at the normal left margin for the rest of the document. (Hint: it's at the spot on the ruler where the gray and white areas meet.)

 TIP If you try to place the tab stop directly over the spot where gray and white meet, your mouse pointer changes to a left and right pointing arrow and you can't place the tab stop. Word thinks you want to change the margin. To get around this, place the tab stop slightly to the right of the spot you want, and then drag it into the correct position.

16. Press Tab, moving the text into alignment with the text in the rest of the flyer.

That's it! Now your flyer should resemble the one in Figure 3.1.

SATURDAY AFTERNOON Flyers and Newsletters

Creating a Party Invitation Flyer

Whether you're holding an office party (perhaps your boss is retiring) or a New Year's Eve bash at your home, creating a flyer for a party can make it more successful.

After all, what's the whole idea of party invitations? To convince people it's going to be a fun event so they will come to it. With a flyer created in Word, you can add festive clip art and page borders, making the party look like a well-planned bash. You can put directions to the party site on it and print it on brightly colored paper so everyone can find those directions at the last minute. Isn't this better than one of the fill-in-the-blanks cards that you buy at the local card shop? And you don't have to do all the work of filling out each invitation by hand! In the following sections, you'll be creating a party flyer like the one shown in Figure 3.5.

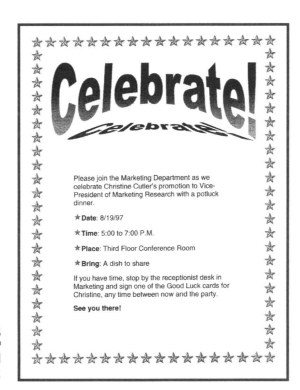

Figure 3.5

Here's my finished party flyer.

Placing a Page Border

"Cool, groovy, and totally awesome" were my exact words the first time I found Word 97's Page Border feature. Check it out:

1. Start a new document based on the Blank Document template.
2. Choose Format, Borders and Shading.
3. Click on the Page Border tab.
4. Open the Art drop-down list and choose a picture or design for the border. I chose stars, but you can pick anything you like (see Figure 3.6).
5. Click on OK. The page border is applied to your document, as shown in Figure 3.7.

TIP You can't see it in Figure 3.7 because this book is printed in black and white, but the border I chose is yellow. Try to choose colored borders and clip art if you have a color printer. If you have a black-and-white printer, you can choose any art you want, and Word will convert it to grayscale when you print it.

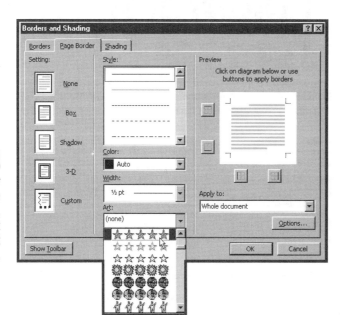

Figure 3.6

The Page Border tab looks much like the Border tab, except that it contains this Art drop-down list.

SATURDAY AFTERNOON Flyers and Newsletters

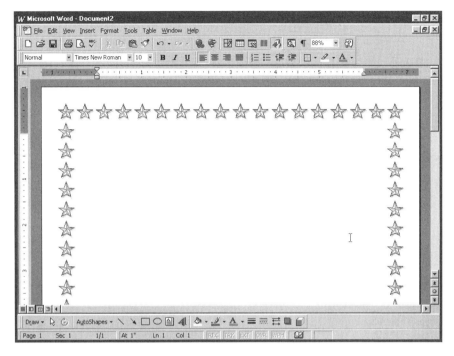

Figure 3.7

Start by placing a festive border around the page.

Creating a WordArt Title

Next you'll add a title to the flyer. But not just any ordinary text will do for such a festive occasion, so use WordArt.

Microsoft WordArt is a text manipulation program within Word. It enables you to type short bits of text and mold, twist, and reshape it to look more interesting. Figure 3.8 shows some examples of WordArt. Ready to try your hand at it?

1. If it is not already displayed, display the Drawing toolbar at the bottom of the screen by clicking on the Drawing button on the Standard toolbar.

2. On the Drawing toolbar, click on the WordArt button. (It's pointed out in Figure 3.8.) The WordArt Gallery dialog box appears.

3. Click on one of the samples similar to what you want. (You can

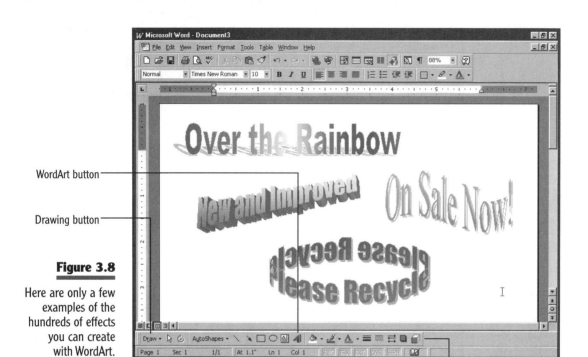

Figure 3.8

Here are only a few examples of the hundreds of effects you can create with WordArt.

change the design later, so don't sweat the decision.) For this example, I chose the third from the left in the fourth row, as shown in Figure 3.9.

4. Click on OK. The Edit WordArt Text dialog box appears.

5. Type the text you want in the title, replacing "Your Text Here" (see Figure 3.10).

Try to keep it short because WordArt looks best when it is not cluttered. If you use more than two or three words, it often ruins the effect.

6. (Optional) If you want a different font, font size, or attribute, change it by using the controls at the top of the Edit WordArt Text dialog box. I usually leave them set at the defaults.

SATURDAY AFTERNOON Flyers and Newsletters 159

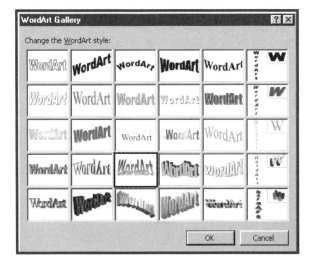

Figure 3.9

Choose a basic WordArt design.

Figure 3.10

Type your text here.

7. Click on OK. Your text appears as WordArt in the document, and the WordArt toolbar appears, as shown in Figure 3.11. The white squares are handles.

But wait! You aren't finished yet. You need to reposition and resize the WordArt. Move it up to the top left corner, to give yourself plenty of room to make it larger.

8. Position the mouse pointer over the middle of the WordArt, so the

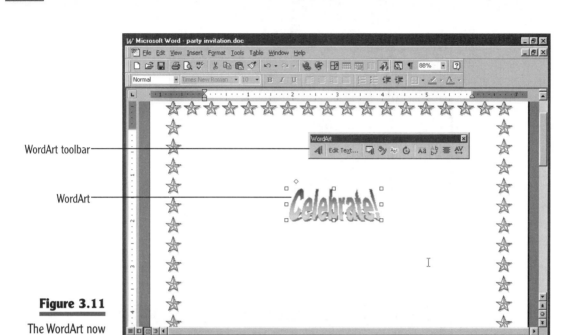

Figure 3.11

The WordArt now appears in the document.

mouse pointer turns into a four-headed arrow, and drag the WordArt into the top left corner (inside the border), as shown in Figure 3.12. Dotted lines show where the WordArt will be located.

9. Now make it large enough to fill the width of the flyer. To do so, drag the bottom right corner. When you're done, it should look something like Figure 3.13.

10. Click on the WordArt Shape button on the WordArt toolbar to change the shape of your WordArt. A group of buttons appears showing the different shapes you can use.

11. Click on the shape you want.

TIP You can repeat Steps 10 and 11 over and over, trying out different shapes, until you find the best one for your flyer.

SATURDAY AFTERNOON Flyers and Newsletters 161

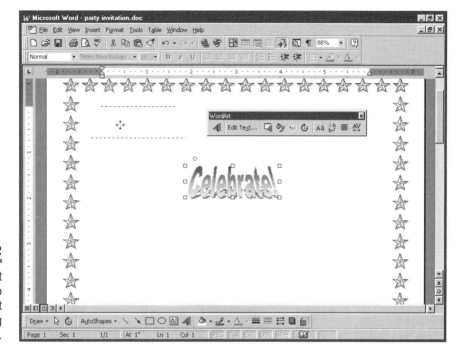

Figure 3.12

Move the WordArt into the corner so you can resize it without running out of room.

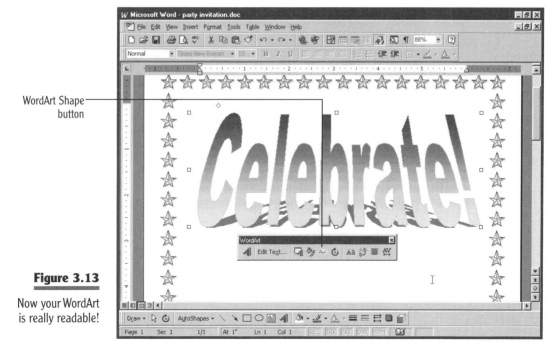

Figure 3.13

Now your WordArt is really readable!

Figure 3.14

Choose a WordArt shape for your text.

Looks pretty good, eh? The finished product appears in Figure 3.14 with the shape I selected. There is more you can do with WordArt, but I won't bog you down with it here. I'll come back to it in the Time-Savers section at the end of this session.

Adding Text and a Bulleted List

Now that you have a title for your flyer, you'll need to inform partygoers what to wear, what to bring, where to go, and what time to arrive. To do so, you'll create a text box and fill it with the information.

1. Make sure you're still in Page Layout view, and set the Zoom to Whole Page.
2. On the Drawing toolbar, click on the Text Box button, and draw a

Figure 3.15

Placing a text box ensures that the text you type will not overlap or interfere with your WordArt.

text box on the page that fills the area where you want to put your text (see Figure 3.15).

3. Set the Zoom to Page Width again, so you can see more clearly the area where you'll be typing, and use the scroll bars to display the top of the text box.

4. Type the introductory text for the flyer. I used the following text, but you can use whatever you like:

   Please join the Marketing Department as we celebrate Christine Cutler's promotion to Vice-President of Marketing Research with a potluck dinner.

5. Press Ctrl+A to select all the text, and format it as 16-point Arial.

6. Now add the details. I used the following lines; substitute your own

information as needed. (Don't add extra space between lines; you'll fix the spacing momentarily.)

Date: 8/19/97

Time: 5:00 to 7:00 P.M.

Place: Third Floor Conference Room

Bring: A dish to share

7. Now set between-paragraph spacing. Select the whole thing again (Ctrl+A) and choose F*o*rmat, *P*aragraph. Set the Aft*e*r spacing to 16 point and click on OK.

8. Next make the four lines you typed in Step 6 a bulleted list. To do so, select them and click on the Bullets button on the Formatting toolbar. Your document should look like Figure 3.16.

9. In each of these lines, make the word before the colon bold. Select the words (one at a time) and press Ctrl+B to make them bold.

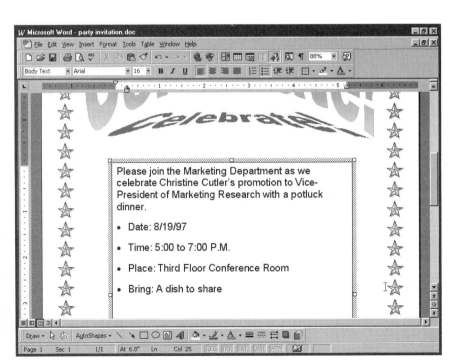

Figure 3.16

The text of the invitation is shaping up with 16-point text and a bulleted list.

10. How about a different bullet character? The little circle is pretty boring. Select the bulleted lines and choose F<u>o</u>rmat, Bullets and <u>N</u>umbering. The Bullets and Numbering dialog box appears.

11. If the <u>B</u>ulleted tab isn't on top, click on it (see Figure 3.17).

12. If you like one of the bullets shown, click on it, click on OK, and then skip to Step 19. Otherwise, click on the Cus<u>t</u>omize button to display the Customize Bulleted List dialog box (see Figure 3.18).

13. Click on the Bullet button to open the Symbol dialog box. (You worked with it this morning, remember?)

CAUTION This Saturday Afternoon session is a bit deceptive, for it might give the impression that text boxes are the normal way of putting text into Word. Actually, they're the exception rather than the rule. Text boxes are useful whenever you place text in an exact spot on a page and you don't want the text's position to change as you manipulate other objects. Desktop publishing requires precise control, which is why we're using text boxes so much in this session. You'll see in upcoming sessions that most other kinds of Word documents don't use them.

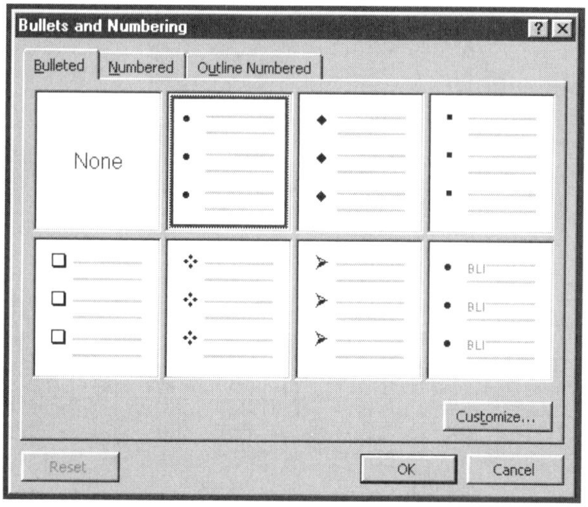

Figure 3.17

You can choose a different bullet character from this dialog box.

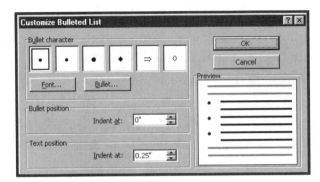

Figure 3.18

This dialog box offers extended options for your bulleted lists.

14. Choose a character you want to use for the bullets (see Figure 3.19). If needed, open the Font drop-down list and choose a different font. Wingdings has some interesting characters you might like.

15. After you select the character you want, click on OK. (I found a star in Wingdings 2 that matches the stars in my page border.)

16. Back in the Customize Bulleted List dialog box, click on the Font button. The Font dialog box opens.

17. If you want your bullet character to appear larger, change the size in the Size list. For example, I set mine to 20 to make them more noticeable next to the 16-point text. Then click on OK.

18. Click on OK to close the Customize Bulleted List dialog box. Your new bullet character appears in your bulleted list, as shown in Figure 3.20.

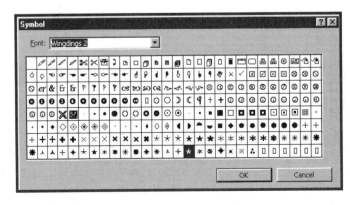

Figure 3.19

Choose your bullet character from the Symbols dialog box.

SATURDAY AFTERNOON Flyers and Newsletters 167

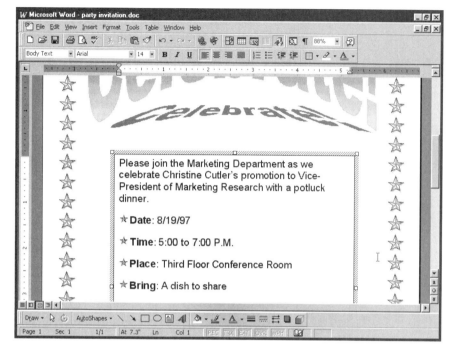

Figure 3.20

Here are my finished bullets, with stars that match my page border.

19. If you want to put more regular text after the bulleted list, position your insertion point at the end of the last bullet point and press Enter. A new line starts with a bullet.

20. To turn off the bullet, click on the Bullets button on the toolbar.

 Another way to turn the bullet off after Step 19 is to press Enter again immediately and then Backspace to get back to the line.

21. Type any additional text that you want. For example, I used the following text:

> If you have time, stop by the receptionist desk in Marketing and sign one of the Good Luck cards for Christine, any time between now and the party.
>
> See you there!

22. Make the closing words ("See you there!" or whatever closing words you put on your flyer) bold by selecting them and pressing Ctrl+B.

23. Now get rid of the border around the text box. Right-click on the border of the text box and choose Format Text Box from the shortcut menu. The Format Text Box dialog box appears.

24. On the Colors and Lines tab, open the Color drop-down list in the Line section and choose No Line. Then click on OK.

25. Zoom out to Whole Page and click away from the text box, so you can see the overall effect (see Figure 3.21).

26. There's one more thing needed to make the flyer perfect. Notice in Figure 3.21 that the text could be moved down a bit. You could resize and move the text box, but here's an easier fix: position the insertion point before the first word of text, and press Enter once. That's it!

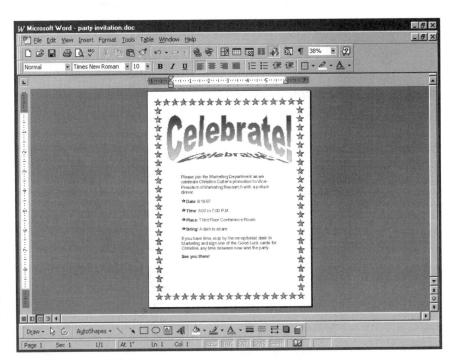

Figure 3.21

The flyer is looking more and more polished.

SATURDAY AFTERNOON Flyers and Newsletters 169

Creating a Map

In the last flyer, the party is being held in a conference room at work; everyone knows how to get there. Now suppose you are creating an invitation to a party that is being held in an unfamiliar location. You need to draw a map, perhaps to print on the back of the flyer.

TIP To print on the reverse side of the flyer, simply feed it back into your printer so it prints on the opposite side. If you are not sure how to feed the paper in correctly, test it as you did in the Saturday Morning session.

If you want a map to your party (or other event), you are unlikely to find a predrawn version, so you probably have to draw it yourself. Luckily, Word comes with some simple but effective drawing tools.

TIP Some computer manufacturers give you a free copy of a mapping program (like AutoMap Streets Plus) when you buy your computer. If you are lucky enough to have such a program, you may be able to cut and paste a map from it into Word, saving yourself the trouble of drawing.

To display the Drawing toolbar, right-click on any toolbar and choose Drawing from the shortcut menu. It appears at the bottom of the screen, as shown in Figure 3.22.

Before you draw your map, you should practice a little with the drawing tools. The following sections explain the various tools and give you some time for practice.

NOTE If you have experience with the drawing tools already, skip to the section "Putting It All Together: Drawing a Map." You don't need to work through the following explanations of the tools.

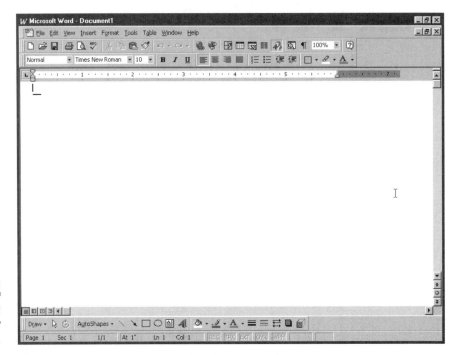

Figure 3.22

The Drawing toolbar, ready for action.

Lines and Shapes

There are two types of tools on the Drawing toolbar: tools that draw shapes and tools that manipulate shapes. Since you can't manipulate a shape before you draw it, look at the drawing tools first:

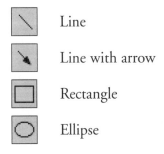

Line

Line with arrow

Rectangle

Ellipse

SATURDAY AFTERNOON Flyers and Newsletters

The procedure is basically the same for all these tools, although it may take you a bit of practice to master them. Start or open a new document on which to practice and follow these steps:

1. Click on the drawing tool you want.
2. Point the mouse pointer where you want the line or shape to begin.
3. Hold down the mouse button and drag to where you want the line or shape to end.
4. Release the mouse button to view the finished line or shape.

TIP If you double-click instead of click in Step 1, you can repeat the procedure from Step 3 to draw more of the same shape. Otherwise you must go back to Step 1 each time.

Practice with the lines and shapes to become comfortable manipulating them.

Drawing AutoShapes

AutoShapes are predrawn shapes that function as the lines and boxes you draw. They're great for people who want shapes like arrows and starbursts but aren't coordinated enough to draw them (or simply don't have the time to do their own drawing).

1. Click on the AutoShapes button on the Drawing toolbar. A menu pops up listing categories of shapes.
2. Point your mouse at the category you want (for example, Block Arrows). A menu of the available shapes in the category appears (see Figure 3.23).
3. Click on the shape you want. Your mouse pointer turns into a crosshair.
4. Drag on the document to draw a box where you want the shape to appear. When you release the mouse button, the shape appears in your document.

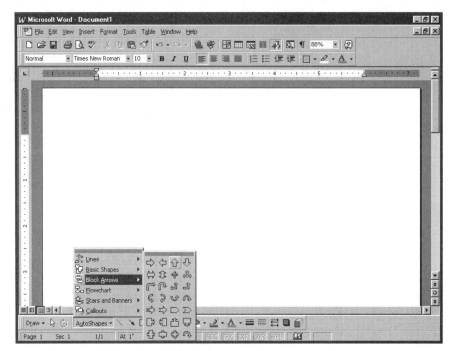

Figure 3.23

Choose a category of AutoShape and then choose the shape.

Manipulating Lines and Shapes

Moving lines and shapes is the same as moving WordArt, which you learned how to use earlier in this session. To move a line or shape, simply click on it to select it, position the mouse pointer over it so that your pointer becomes a four-headed arrow, and then drag the line or shape to its new position. Resizing a line or shape is the same as resizing WordArt, too: just point to one of the line or shape's selection handles and drag it.

Copying and Deleting Lines and Shapes

You can copy lines and shapes the same way you copy anything else in Word:

1. Select the line or shape.

2. Choose Edit, Copy; or click on the Copy button on the toolbar; or press Ctrl+C.

3. Select where you want it to go.

4. Choose Edit, Paste; or click on the Paste button; or press Ctrl+V.

5. If needed, reposition the copy in the exact location where you want it.

Deleting is just what you'd expect: select the object and then press Delete.

Rotating and Flipping Lines and Shapes

Suppose you've drawn an arrow that points up with the AutoShape feature, but you want it to point down. No problem—just flip it.

1. Select the drawing.

2. Click on the Draw button on the Drawing toolbar. A menu appears.

3. Point to Rotate or Flip on the menu. Another submenu appears.

4. Choose Flip Vertical or Flip Horizontal. (To turn the arrow upside down, I chose Flip Vertical.)

As you saw while you had the menu open, the Rotate or Flip submenu also has commands for Rotate Right and Rotate Left. You can use these to rotate your shape 90 degrees. If you want to control the precise amount of rotation, use the Free Rotate feature:

1. Choose Draw, Rotate or Flip, Free Rotate, or click on the Free Rotate button on the Drawing toolbar (see Figure 3.24). The selection handles turn into green circles.

2. Position the mouse pointer over one of the circles so the mouse pointer turns into a circular arrow. Then drag the selection handle to rotate the shape to the exact position you want.

3. Click anywhere away from the shape to finish.

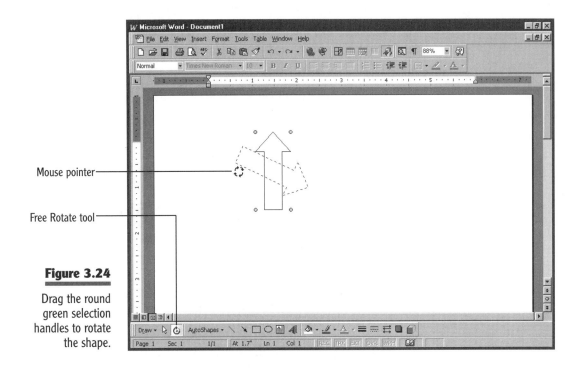

Figure 3.24

Drag the round green selection handles to rotate the shape.

Mouse pointer

Free Rotate tool

Changing a Line or Shape's Appearance

On the Drawing toolbar, there are several tools that control how a drawing appears:

 Fill Color. Open this drop-down list to choose a fill color, and click on the button to apply the color to the selected shape. (This doesn't work with lines.)

 Line Color. Open this drop-down list to choose a line color, and click on the button to apply the color to the line or shape. (If you are working with a shape, it changes the outline color around the shape.)

 Line Thickness. Select the line or shape, and open this drop-down list and select the line thickness to use. If applied to a shape, it changes the border around the shape.

 Line Style. Select the line or shape, open this drop-down list, and select a line style (dotted, dashed, or whatever). If applied to a shape, it changes the border.

 Arrow Style. Select the line, open this drop-down list, and select the type of arrow to use (including None to remove an arrow). (This doesn't work with shapes.)

 Shadow. Select the shape and click on this button to open a list of shadow types. Click on an item to apply it. (This doesn't work with lines.)

 3-D. Select the shape and click on this button to open a list of 3-D types. Click on an item to apply it. (This doesn't work with lines.)

 TIP You can do everything the Drawing toolbar does with more precise control by right-clicking on the shape or line and choosing Format AutoShape from the shortcut menu. (It doesn't matter whether you actually created it with the AutoShape button; Word considers all shapes and lines AutoShapes once they're drawn.)

Putting It All Together: Drawing a Map

Now that you know how to use Word's drawing tools, it's time to get down to business and create your map. You need to make one for your own destination, of course, but here's how I created mine:

1. Switch to Page Layout view, and set the Zoom to Page Width.
2. Near the middle of the page, draw a thick black line. This represents the nearest major road. To do this, draw a line with the Line tool, and while the line is still selected, use the Line Style tool to make it thicker.
3. Place a text box on the road and label the road. Size the text box and text very small, so it isn't obtrusive. Figure 3.25 shows the progress so far.

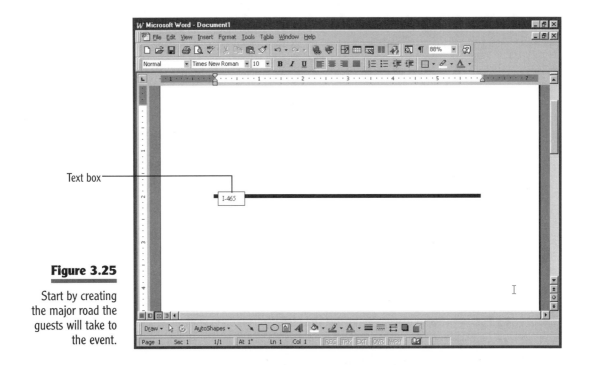

Figure 3.25

Start by creating the major road the guests will take to the event.

4. Next, add a directional arrow to the map so the readers will know which way is north.

   a. Draw an AutoShape arrow.

   b. Right-click on the arrow and choose Add Text from the shortcut menu.

   c. Type **N** and click on the Center button on the formatting toolbar to center it in the arrow.

   d. Format the N with Arial font at a fairly large size (I used 22 points).

   e. Click on the border around the arrow to select it (as opposed to the text inside it).

   f. Open the Fill Color drop-down list on the Drawing toolbar and choose the palest gray for the arrow color. Click away from the arrow to deselect it.

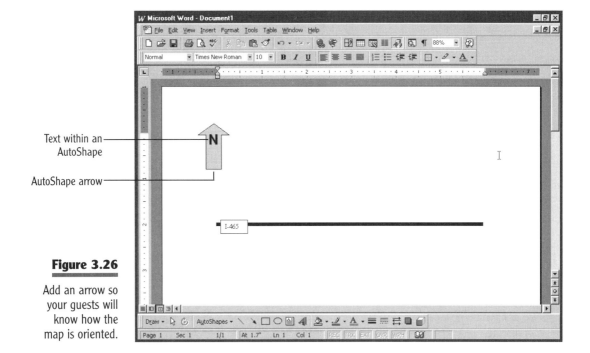

Figure 3.26

Add an arrow so your guests will know how the map is oriented.

When you finish the arrow, it should look like the one in Figure 3.26.

5. Add the secondary roads that the guests will take. Make them slightly thinner than the major road, and label each one with a text box.

6. Now add the building and house number where the event is being held. I made mine a shaded rectangle, as shown in Figure 3.27.

   a. Draw the rectangle with the Rectangle tool.

   b. Use the Fill Color tool to change its color to light blue or some other light color.

   c. Right-click on the rectangle, choose Add Text, and then type the house or building number.

   d. Resize the rectangle as needed to show the number.

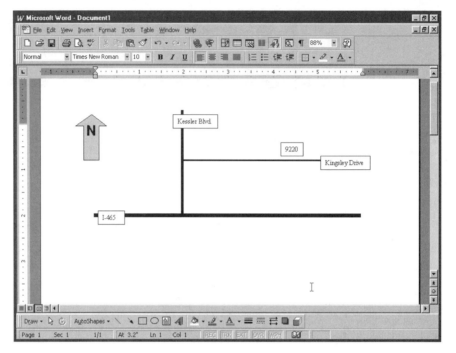

Figure 3.27

Add the secondary roads to the map as thinner lines, and a shaded box for the site.

7. Just to make sure people see the building on the map, I added an arrow pointing to it and a text box for a callout (a comment).

   a. Draw a text box large enough to type about five words near the site.

   b. In the text box, type **This is the place!** and format it as bold and italic.

   c. Right-click on the text box and change the Line Color to No Line, removing the border from it.

   d. Use the Line tool to draw a line from your text to the site.

   e. Click on the Arrow Style button and choose a style that has an arrow at the right end.

   When you finish, the map should look like the one in Figure 3.28.

SATURDAY AFTERNOON Flyers and Newsletters 179

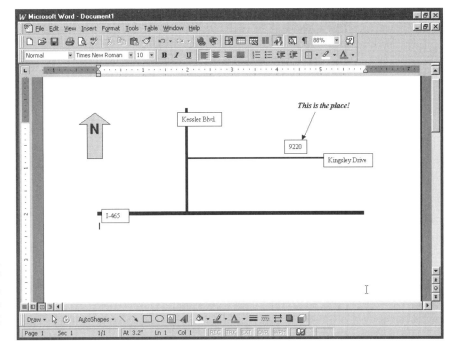

Figure 3.28

Now your guests won't miss the building you want them to notice.

> **TIP** If you aren't sure your map is clear in its directions, you might want to add a text box below the map and supply text-based directions.

Another Way to Highlight a Site

In Step 7 of the preceding procedure, you made the party site stand out by adding a *callout* to it. Callouts are a good way to emphasize something. Another way to call attention to the site is to place a starburst AutoShape around it, as shown in Figure 3.29.

1. Delete the text box and arrow you created earlier. (You can add them back later.)

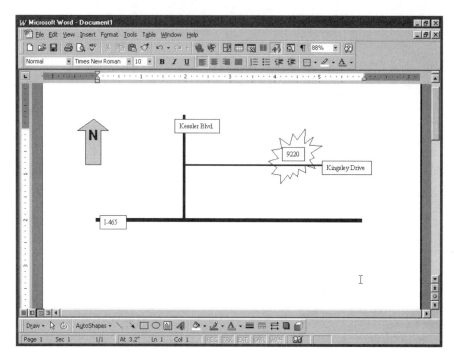

Figure 3.29

Here's another way to make your party site stand out.

2. Open the AutoShapes list on the Drawing toolbar, choose Stars and Banners, and then click on the second shape in the top row.

3. Draw the shape on your map directly over your party site. Don't worry that it covers the site.

4. Use the Fill Color tool to make the starburst a bright yellow.

5. Right-click on the starburst and choose Order, Send to Back.

Creating an Advertising Flyer

The final flyer you'll create is an ad. You can make your ad for anything—a house for sale, a new product your company is making, or a service you plan to offer. For this example, I created a flyer for my brother-in-law's band, Mike's House, advertising an upcoming concert. Then, I made copies on colorful paper and posted them in all the local

nightclubs and coffee shops. Perhaps my herculean efforts will draw a big crowd for the performance, and then he might become rich and famous and buy me a new car! (Charlie, are you listening?)

Importing a Scanned Image

My flyer has a picture of the band. You may want a picture on yours too—perhaps one of the product you're selling, or a photo of your own honest face!

You can scan pictures yourself if you have a scanner attached to your computer. If you don't, you can take your pictures to a copying center. (The local Kinko's in my area has computers with scanners for rent by the hour.)

Scanned images have a variety of file formats, but the most common ones are Tagged Image Format (.tif) and Bitmap Image (.bmp). Other formats you may encounter include .pcx, .gif, .jpg, and .pic. Word accepts pictures in any of these formats, as well as others.

TIP The default setup doesn't install all of Word's graphics import filters. If Word does not offer the format you need to import, rerun the setup program and add the filter you need.

If you have your picture scanned away from your computer, bring it back on a floppy disk. Copy it from your floppy disk to a folder on your hard disk before you import it. (Use Windows Explorer or My Computer in Windows 95; refer to the Windows 95 Help system if you don't know how to copy a file.) When you're ready to import your picture, follow these steps:

1. Start a new document based on the Blank Document template.
2. Choose Insert, Picture, From File. The Insert Picture dialog box appears. It's exactly like the Open dialog box that you use to open documents, except for the name (see Figure 3.30).

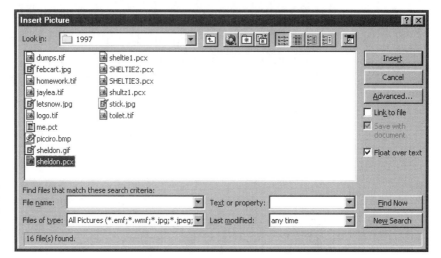

Figure 3.30

Choose your picture from this dialog box.

3. Locate the picture you scanned and double-click on it to import it. (Refer to the Friday Evening session if you need help changing drives or folders.)

NOTE In Figure 3.30, notice the check boxes. You generally won't need to change these, but you might like to know what they are for. Link to file, when selected, maintains a link between the original image and the copy in Word, so if the original changes, Word's copy will change too. If you select the check box, the Save with document check box becomes available. If you turn the check box off, Word will not include the image in the saved file, but will pull it from the original each time the Word file is opened. (I don't recommend this unless you need to make the Word file as small as possible.) The third check box, Float over text, places the image in relation to the page itself, and not the text on the page. The picture stays on this page even if the surrounding text changes—which is useful if you refer to "the picture on page 23" somewhere else in the document.

4. Zoom out to Whole Page view so you can see the scanned image on the page.
5. Drag the image to the correct spot on the page.

SATURDAY AFTERNOON Flyers and Newsletters

6. Add a text box under the picture and add the text for your advertisement.

7. Dress up the ad with different fonts and text sizes, bullets, or any other elements. Use your imagination! My finished product appears in Figure 3.31.

Take a Break

I bet you are tired of sitting. This would be a great time to either lay down and take a quick Saturday afternoon cat nap, or to stand up and do those dishes that are sitting in a pile in the sink. Yuck! I don't know about you but a nice, refreshing siesta sounds the best to me. Regardless, when you return, you'll dive into newsletter land.

Figure 3.31

Here's an advertisement that will really catch people's attention (I hope!).

Creating a Newsletter

Now it's time to move on to "the big project" for the afternoon: a newsletter. You may not believe it, but most of what you need to know to create a great-looking newsletter will be a review—you have already learned a lot so far! In this section, I'll move quickly over the parts you already know, and slowly over the new material, so you finish in time for dinner.

Using the Newsletter Wizard

If you're not the creative type, you may choose to take the easy way out and use Word's Newsletter Wizard to create your newsletter, rather than going through the steps to manually create one. You will end up with a similar product either way, and it will take you only a few minutes. The downside, of course, is you won't be able to create a more detailed and personalized newsletter the next time around because you won't have a grasp of the fundamentals I write about in this section. (And didn't you buy this book to learn Word, rather than to knock out a quick newsletter?)

However, in the interest of fairness to those who really did buy this book for a quick newsletter, here's how to wrangle the Newsletter Wizard:

TIP The Newsletter Wizard is a great help, and you may want to use it even after you have "done it the hard way" in the remainder of this afternoon's session. I'm not trying to steer you away from it; I just don't want you to use it as a substitute for learning Word.

1. Choose File, New and click on the Publications tab. Double-click on Newsletter Wizard.
2. Click on the Next button to begin.
3. Click on the appropriate option button to choose the newsletter layout you want, as shown in Figure 3.32 (Contemporary,

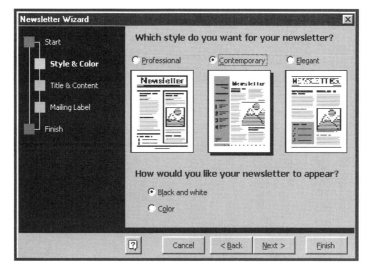

Figure 3.32

Using a Wizard is as simple as clicking on an option button or two.

Professional, or Elegant), and then click on Color or Black and white, depending on whether you have a color printer. Click on Next to continue.

4. In the blanks provided, enter the title for your newsletter, the date, and the volume and issue. Click on Next to continue.

5. When asked whether you want to leave room for a mailing label on the back, choose Yes or No. Then click on Next.

6. Click on Finish. A sample newsletter appears, as shown in Figure 3.33. Make changes to its text as needed to customize it for your own use. The sample text provides instructions for customizing the document.

Okay, now that you've seen the Newsletter Wizard, you'll get down to the business of creating a newsletter from scratch. Think of it as Word boot camp! You may not use all the training you receive in everyday work, but when the time comes to create a humdinger of a newsletter, you'll be glad you bore the brunt of the instruction today.

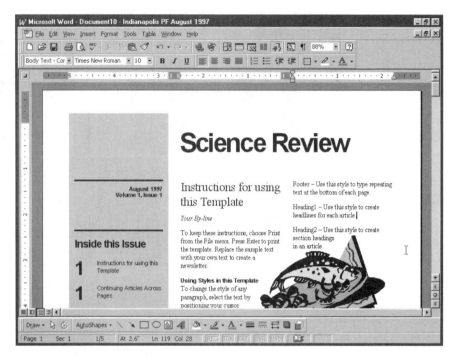

Figure 3.33

The Newsletter Wizard creates a document complete with instructions.

Creating a Masthead

Masthead is publishing jargon for the line that runs across the top of the first page of the newsletter. A masthead normally contains the title of the publication, the sponsoring organization, and the date. Figure 3.34 shows some sample mastheads (1 is a simple masthead with just text in a text box, 2 uses WordArt, and 3 uses an imported image and a text box).

At this point, you can probably create most parts of the first two mastheads in Figure 3.34 on your own. But each one requires at least one skill you haven't learned yet, so work through them now.

Creating Masthead 1

This type of masthead is very easy, because it's just text in a text box. The only difference is you'll need to set a centered tab stop for the third line, which you haven't yet learned to do.

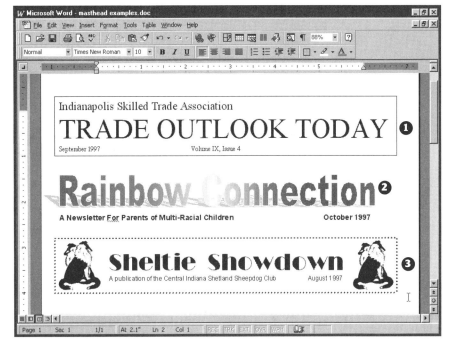

Figure 3.34

Some interesting masthead ideas you may want to copy.

1. Place the text box.
2. Type and format the text. The first line is 18-point Times New Roman; the second line is 44-point Times New Roman. Adjust the point size of the second line as needed so your title exactly fits across the text box. The third line is 10-point Times New Roman.
3. On the third line, press Tab to separate the two phrases.
4. At the left end of the ruler, notice a little black L. This is the default tab stop (left). Click on it once to change to a centered tab stop—a sort of upside-down T.
5. Click on the ruler at the horizontal midpoint of your text box. The second phrase on the third line moves to align with the tab stop you created (see Figure 3.35).

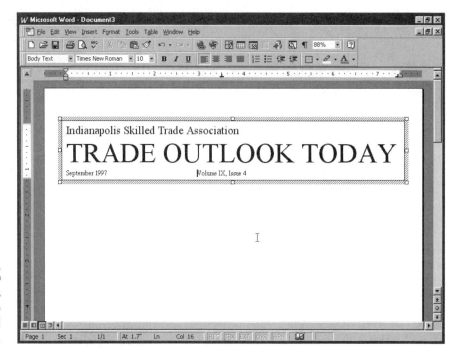

Figure 3.35

The text that aligns with a centered tab stop is centered under the stop.

Creating Masthead 2

Masthead 2 is basically just a line of WordArt with a text box beneath it. Simple, right? You'll group the two pieces together so the masthead becomes a single entity that can be moved and resized as one, rather than two separate pieces.

1. Create WordArt for your title and resize it as needed so it fills the desired space.

2. Place a text box beneath the WordArt and type your text into it. Format it as 12-point Arial bold. Press Tab between the two phrases.

3. Click again on the tab type button at the left end of the ruler to change the tab type to a right tab, which looks like a backward L.

4. Place a right tab stop on the ruler where you want the text in the second line. Depending on your WordArt position, this may be at the right edge of the text box or somewhat indented.

5. Click on the text box border to select it.
6. Press and hold Shift and click on the WordArt. Both objects should be selected (with handles around them).
7. On the Drawing toolbar, open the D<u>r</u>aw menu and choose <u>G</u>roup.
8. To test your masthead as one object, drag it across the screen. When you finish, drag it up to its appropriate spot at the top of the page.

Creating Masthead 3

It may not look it, but Masthead 3 is fairly complicated because there are many steps involved. Luckily, you have already learned almost all the skills you need to complete it. The only new thing here is instead of a border around the masthead, you are going to use a rectangle and format it to resemble a border.

1. Import the picture you want to use (<u>I</u>nsert, <u>P</u>icture, <u>F</u>rom File). Resize it as needed.
2. If you need two copies of the picture (as shown in Figure 3.34), copy it (Ctrl+C) and then paste the new copy into the document (Ctrl+V). Drag the pasted second copy where you want it.
3. Create the text box where you want it, as shown in Figure 3.36.
4. Type some text and format it. Tab between the phrases on the second line. In Masthead 3, the first line is 37-point Barbe Display SSi and the second line is 10-point Arial.

TIP You aren't stuck with just the font sizes on the Font Size drop-down list! For example, in Step 4, 37 point was the perfect size for the text (38 point was too big; 36 too small). It wasn't available on the drop-down list, so I typed the number "37" manually into the Font Size text box on the Formatting toolbar.

NOTE Barbe Display SSi is a font I found on one of those "1001 Fonts" discount disks that you can pick up for bargain prices at your local software store.

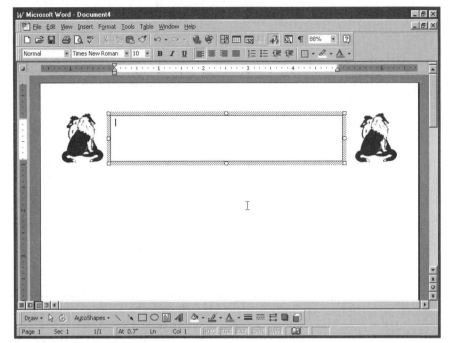

Figure 3.36

Place your graphics and create a text box to fit between them.

5. Set a right tab stop for the second line so it aligns with the end of the first line.

6. Right-click on the text box border and choose Format Text Box. Set the Line Color to None and click on OK.

7. Draw a rectangle where you want a border to appear around the whole grouping. Don't worry, it will cover everything up.

8. Right-click on the rectangle and choose Format AutoShape. Set the Fill Color to No Fill.

9. From the Dashed drop-down list, choose the dots that look like diamonds. From the Style drop-down list, choose 2¼ points and click on OK.

10. Now select all the elements (press and hold Shift while you click on each one) and group them together (Draw, Group).

You did it! Now that you have a good-looking masthead, you can put together the newsletter articles.

Creating Multicolumn Articles

You can create multiple columns in a document in either of two ways: you can use Word's multiple columns feature, or you can create a series of text boxes and link them.

Word's multiple columns feature has received a bad rep in the past for being hard to use. It's improved in the Word 97 release, but it's still not your best choice for newsletters. I'll explain it in the Time-Savers section at the end of this session, but I'll wager you won't find it as useful as the text box method that I show you in the following steps.

NOTE Word's Columns feature works fine if you have a simple article you want to print in multiple columns, but newsletters are typically more complicated. They may have two different stories on the front page, each of which are continued elsewhere. They may also have pictures and other boxes that interrupt the text flow. Word's Columns feature isn't very graceful about handling these complex situations, and if you later need to make changes to the newsletter elements, the multi-columns feature can shift your text in unexpected and unwelcome ways.

TIP A lot of people think of linked text boxes as an "advanced" feature, and most Word books don't cover them. But they're really not that difficult to use, and they give you a much greater degree of control over your newsletter text. In the long run, they're less frustrating than Word's multiple columns feature, too.

Typing Your Article

The first thing you need to do is type your article. It's best to type it in a separate Word document as plain, regular text. Save your work so you won't have to type it again if something goes wrong in the layout phase.

Placing Your Text Boxes

Now jump back to the newsletter document and do the following:

1. View the document in Page Layout view and set the zoom to Whole Page.

2. Click on the Columns button on the Standard toolbar and drag across three columns, as shown in Figure 3.37.

NOTE "Wait a minute," you may think, "I wasn't going to use Word's Columns feature in this task." Well, you're not. You're just pretending to want to use it so you can make column guides appear on the ruler to help you draw the text boxes.

3. Draw a text box from top to bottom on the page and enclosed within the first vertical column marked off on the ruler, as shown in Figure 3.38.

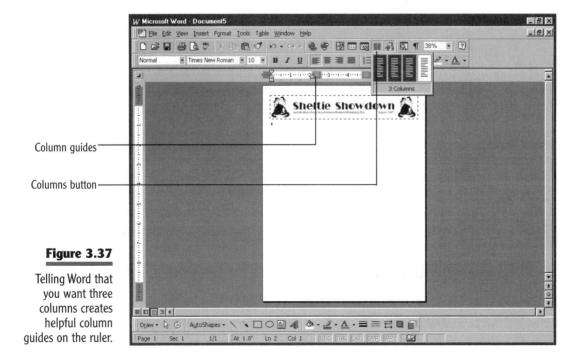

Figure 3.37

Telling Word that you want three columns creates helpful column guides on the ruler.

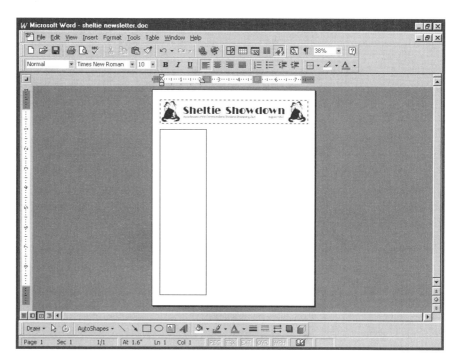

Figure 3.38

This is the first of several text boxes that will hold my article.

4. Click on the text box's border to select it and copy it (Ctrl+C).
5. Click away from the text box to deselect it and paste twice (Ctrl+V).
6. Drag the two copies to the two other columns on the page, as shown in Figure 3.39.
7. Select all three text boxes (Shift+click) and open the Format Text Box dialog box (right-click and choose Format Text Box).
8. On the Colors and Lines tab, set the Line Color to No Line.
9. On the Position tab, deselect the Move object with text check box (see the next section to understand why) and click on OK.

Creating More Pages

If you need additional pages, you have to create them. This is not as easy as it sounds, because Word controls the number of pages according to the amount of text you have in the document. (It doesn't count text box

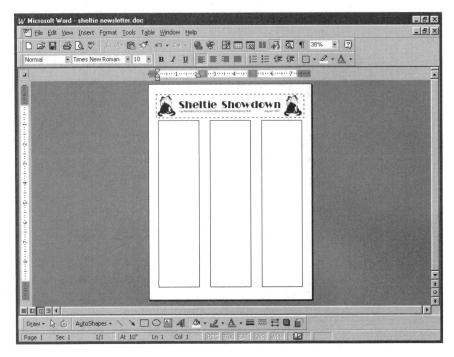

Figure 3.39

Now all three text boxes are in place in their columns.

content as "text in the document.") Unfortunately, you just have to press Enter, adding lines to the regular text of the document (which is actually just an empty shell to hold our text boxes in this newsletter) until another page appears. Then, once it does, place more text boxes on it.

 TIP Step 9 in the preceding section allows you to press Enter to create extra pages without shifting text boxes.

Inserting Your Article

Now you need to copy the article from the regular Word document and paste it into your text frames.

1. Switch to the document containing the article text you typed. Select the whole thing (Ctrl+A) and copy it (Ctrl+C).

2. Switch back to your newsletter document and click in the first text box and paste (Ctrl+V). Don't worry that the text doesn't flow to the other text boxes yet.

3. Right-click on the first text box's frame and choose Create Text Box Link. The mouse pointer turns into a pouring paint can.

4. Click in the second text box (you can't see its border, but you know basically where it is). The text flows into the second text box.

5. If you have more text, right-click on the second text box's frame and choose Create Text Box Link again, and link the third text box to the second.

6. If your article still isn't completely visible, start a new page and place more text frames on it; then link them in.

TIP If an article runs onto another page, you should resize the last text box containing the article on the earlier page and add a small text box at the bottom, into which you should type something like **Continued on page 2**.

7. If you have more articles to place, create more text boxes (on additional pages as needed) to hold them.

The advantage of flowing text from one text box to another becomes apparent when you add or delete text from the article. The text automatically rewraps from one text box to the next as needed.

Cleanup

When you place an article into text boxes, there are always finishing touches and things you want to add later. Here are some ideas:

- Change the Zoom to 100% so you can see the article text clearly.
- Format the article title in a larger, bolder font than the rest of the article.
- Make sure there is vertical space after each paragraph. If not, adjust the paragraph spacing as you learned in this morning's session.

- If you need to fit more text on the page, or if the columns look too narrow, decrease the white space between columns.

When widening text boxes, the danger in dragging them to resize them manually is that they will no longer all be the same size. Here are two methods that will increase the width of each line in the text box without throwing off the column balance:

1. Select all three columns (Shift+click).
2. Right-click on one of their borders and choose Format Text Box.
3. Do either or both of the following:
   - On the Text Box tab, set the Left and Right number to 0.00.
   - On the Size tab, increase the Width setting a couple of clicks (.2 to .3 is good).
4. Click on OK. Figure 3.40 shows my finished first page.

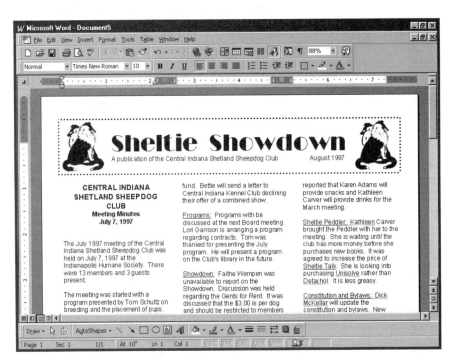

Figure 3.40

The first page of my finished newsletter.

SATURDAY AFTERNOON Flyers and Newsletters 197

Other Text Box Tricks for an Attractive Layout

In the preceding example, there are three simple, equal text boxes on the page. But you can do some fancier things with text boxes to create really interesting layouts. For example, how about making the article title in Figure 3.40 run across the top of the first two columns, as shown in Figure 3.41?

1. Resize the first two text boxes to leave room for a new text box above them.

2. Place the new text box in the empty space.

3. Cut and paste the title text into the new text box and reformat the text as needed to make it look attractive.

4. Delete any extra blank lines at the beginning of the first text box of the article.

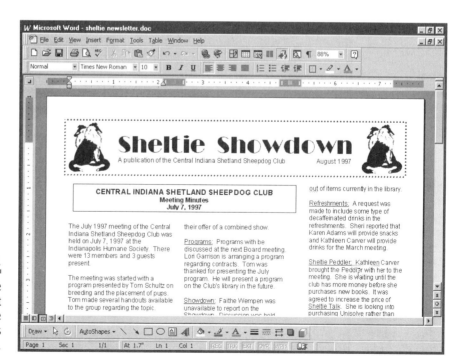

Figure 3.41

You can create an additional text box to make the article title cross multiple columns.

Another scenario: suppose you have a "top story" that you want to highlight. You might make the top story fill two of the three columns, and reserve the last column for, say, a table of contents, as shown in Figure 3.42.

1. Delete the second and third text boxes on the first page, leaving only the first one.
2. Resize the remaining text box to fill two columns.
3. If desired, format the article title to make it larger and more noticeable.
4. Place a third text box in the third column, and put a separate article in it (it's easiest to type directly into the text box if the article is short).
5. If desired, add a shaded background to the third column's text box to differentiate it from the main story.

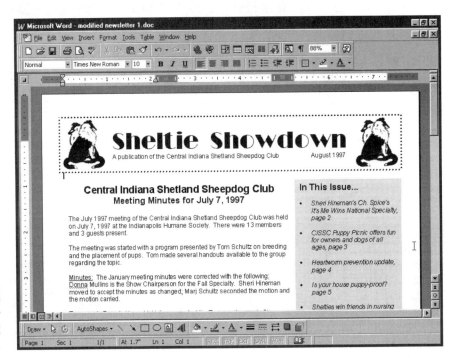

Figure 3.42

Here's another variant you might want to try.

Numbering the Pages

A multipage newsletter should probably have page numbers to keep readers from getting lost. This is especially true if you have articles that run from one page to another. With page numbers in place, you can add references like "Continued on Page 6." The simplest way to add page numbers is to:

1. Choose Insert, Page Numbers. The Page Numbers dialog box appears (see Figure 3.43).

2. Set the position (usually Bottom is best) in the Position drop-down list.

3. Set the horizontal alignment (usually Right) in the Alignment drop-down list.

4. (Optional) If you want a certain font or other formatting, click on the Format button and use the dialog box that appears to specify it. Click on OK when you finish.

5. Click on OK to close the Page Numbers dialog box. The page numbers appear on each page of your newsletter.

You can also create full-fledged headers and footers for each page of your newsletter, but it's not really necessary, and it's a lot of work. If you are interested in learning more about headers and footers, stay tuned for the Sunday Morning session, where you'll look at them in detail.

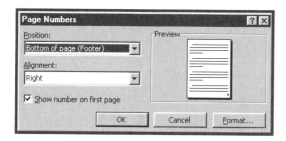

Figure 3.43

Set the positioning for your page numbers here.

Reusing Your Newsletter Setup Next Month

Once you have your newsletter just the way you want it, you should save your work. After all, you don't want to start from scratch every month (or every time the newsletter needs to be published).

There are two ways to reuse your newsletter. One is to base each month's newsletter on the preceding month's. Just save your newsletter as a regular document, and then next month, open it, make changes, and save it under a new name.

Another way is to create a template, as you learned earlier. Before creating the template, you might want to delete all the text that isn't part of the recurring design (for example, all the article text), leaving only the masthead and the frames. Then choose File, Save As, and change the Save as type setting to Document Template (see Figure 3.44). The Templates folder automatically appears when you change the file type to Document Template. Call it something like "Club Newsletter" and click on OK. Then you can start new documents based on the template each month. The advantage to this method is you can't accidentally ruin an important previous issue by using Save instead of Save As, and you won't accidentally include outdated information from the last issue in the new one.

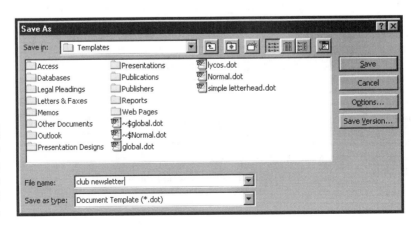

Figure 3.44

Save your newsletter as a template to reuse it in upcoming months.

Using Clip Art in Flyers and Newsletters

Now take some time to look at the clip art Word provides. You can use clip art in flyers, newsletters, or almost any other kind of document. *Clip art* is predrawn artwork that comes with Word. You access it from the Clip Gallery (see Figure 3.45). The Clip Gallery does more than just display clip art; notice in Figure 3.45 four tabs, one for each type of clip that Word helps you organize. You'll focus mainly on the clip art, but keep in mind you can also use it for sounds, videos, and pictures (that is, bitmap images like scans).

To open the Clip Gallery, follow these steps:

1. Display the worksheet where you want the clip inserted (clips float on top of the page, rather than attaching to a particular spot in the text).

2. Choose Insert, Picture, Clip Art.

3. If a dialog box appears telling you there is additional clip art on the

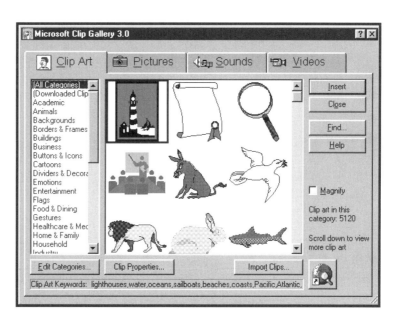

Figure 3.45

In the Clip Gallery, all the various types of multimedia files have their own tabs.

Word 97 (or Office 97) CD, go ahead and put it in your CD-ROM drive (if you don't have it, don't worry about it) and click on OK.

TIP In the dialog box in Step 3, there is a Don't remind me again check box. If you select this check box, you won't see the dialog box in the future—Step 2 will take you directly to the Clip Gallery.

4. Click on the tab for the type of clip you want (Clip Art, for example).
5. Click on the clip category you want from the Categories list. Or, to see all clips, select All Categories from the list, as shown in Figure 3.45.
6. Click on the clip you want.
7. Click on Insert. The Clip Gallery closes and your clip appears in your document.
8. Resize and move the clip as needed.

There's a lot you can do with the Clip Gallery, but it's getting late, so I'll save the information for the Time-Savers section. Have a scrumptious dinner—maybe you should treat yourself to a nice meal out. After all, you have earned it! Then again, with a quick phone call, you could have a delicious pizza delivered to your doorstep in minutes.

Time-Savers

If you've finished this session and still have more time, or if you're curious to learn more, check out the following sections. Since you just covered clip art in the preceding section, I'll expand on this area first.

Importing Clips

If you use your own pictures frequently in Word, you might want to import them into the Clip Gallery so they'll be available for browsing on the Pictures tab (or, if you don't want to bother with that, you can continue to insert pictures with the Insert, Picture, From File command).

Windows 95 comes with several bitmap images (albeit small ones) it uses as wallpaper. While you will probably not use these as pictures in Word very often, they make excellent practice files. Import them into the Clip Gallery now:

1. If the Clip Gallery isn't open, choose Insert, Picture, Clip Art.
2. Click on the Pictures tab.
3. Click on the Import Clips button. The Add pictures to Clip Gallery dialog box appears.
4. Change the drive and folder to display the contents of the Windows folder (see Figure 3.46).
5. Click on the first file and press and hold Shift while you click on the last one. This selects all the files between the two.
6. Click on the Open button. A Clip Properties dialog box appears for Waves, as shown in Figure 3.47.
7. Create a new category to hold these Windows bitmap files by clicking on the New Category button.

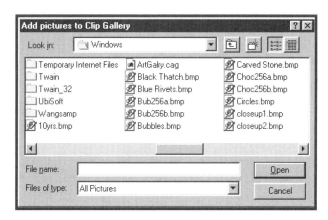

Figure 3.46

You'll find some .bmp (bitmap) images to practice with in the Windows folder.

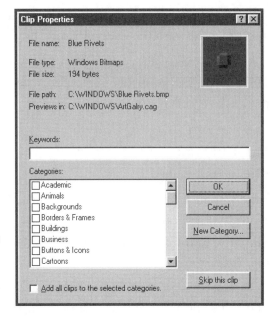

Figure 3.47

For each imported clip, you must give Clip Gallery some information.

8. Type **Windows 95 Bitmaps** in the New Category Name text box and click on OK. Windows 95 Bitmaps now appears on the Categories list, with its check box marked.

9. Type **Wallpaper** in the Keywords text box, since these bitmaps were originally designed as wallpaper in Windows 95.

10. Click on the Add All Clips to the Selected Categories check box.

11. Click on OK. All the bitmap images appear on the Pictures tab of the Clip Gallery, as shown in Figure 3.48.

You can follow the same procedure shown in the preceding steps to import any kind of file as a clip: video, sound, picture, or additional clip art.

Getting More Clips from the Internet

Microsoft has a Web site on the Internet with more clips to download. It includes sounds, videos, pictures, and clip art. To get them, you must

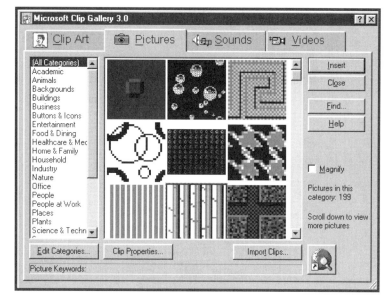

Figure 3.48

Now you can use any of these pictures in Word through the Clip Gallery.

have a way to connect to the Internet (an online service or a dial-up or network Internet connection). To see what's available, follow these steps:

1. Establish your Internet connection. This may involve starting your online service software and connecting, or using Windows 95 Dial-Up Networking to connect to your Internet Service Provider.
2. Minimize the software used to make the Internet connection.
3. Start Word, or switch back to it if it is already open.
4. Choose Insert, Picture, Clip Art. The Clip Gallery appears.
5. Click on the tab representing the type of clip you want to import (Clip Art or Pictures, for example).
6. Click on the globe button in the bottom right corner of the Clip Gallery.
7. If you see a dialog box telling you to click on OK to browse the

Web, do so (you may not see this dialog box at all, depending on your setup). Your browser opens and the Clip Gallery Live page loads.

8. Read the licensing agreement in the upper right pane and click on the Accept button. The upper right pane changes to show the controls in Figure 3.49.

9. Click on the Browse or Search button to choose how you want to use the site. For this example, choose Browse.

10. Click on the button that indicates the kind of clips you are looking for. From left to right, they are Clip Art, Photos, Sounds, and Videos. For this example, choose Clip Art.

11. Open the Select a category drop-down list and choose a category that you're interested in. For this example, choose Animals.

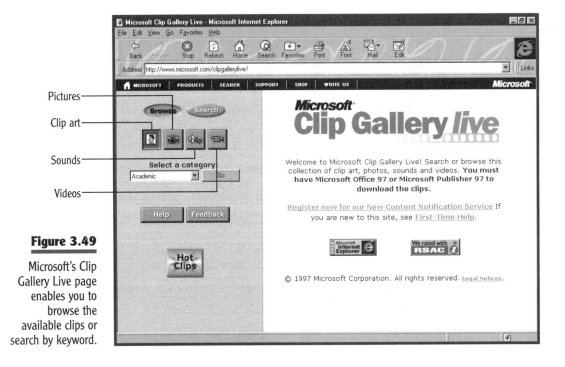

Figure 3.49

Microsoft's Clip Gallery Live page enables you to browse the available clips or search by keyword.

SATURDAY AFTERNOON Flyers and Newsletters

12. Click on Go. The top left pane changes to show the available clips in that category (see Figure 3.50). If there are more clips in the selected category than can be displayed at once, you can see the next group by clicking on the right-arrow button under the clips.

13. Click on the hyperlink (the underlined name) of the clip to start downloading it to your computer. If you are asked to open it or save it to a disk, choose Open.

    It may take a few minutes, depending on the size of the clip and the speed of your connection. When the image transfers, the Clip Gallery reappears on your screen with the new clip added on the appropriate tab in the Downloaded Clips category.

14. Jump back to your browser and get more clips if you want. When you finish, terminate your Internet connection and go back to the Clip Gallery to use your new clips.

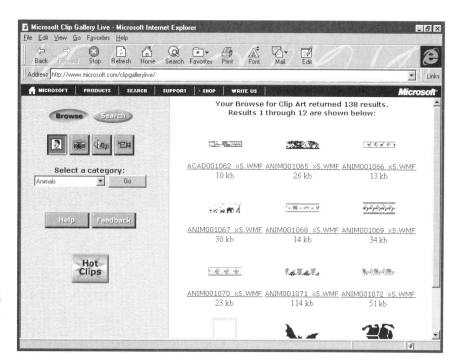

Figure 3.50

The available clips are shown in little preview windows.

Recategorizing Clips

Is it necessary to recategorize clips? Usually not, if you don't have too many of them. You can usually find the clip you want by browsing in the Clip Gallery. But if you want to be really meticulous about your clip filing system, or if you need to manage a large number of clips, you might want to pay attention to the categories and move things around to make the categories more logical.

NOTE You cannot recategorize clips that come with Word—the function only works for ones that you import or download yourself.

Earlier—when you imported the clips from the Windows folder—you saw how to create a new category as you import a clip. But you can also move an existing clip from category to category and make a clip appear in several categories.

1. In the Clip Gallery, click on the clip you want to recategorize.
2. Click on the Clip P__r__operties button. The Clip Properties dialog box appears (see Figure 3.51).
3. Select or deselect check boxes for the various categories to choose which categories the clip will appear in.
4. (Optional) If you need to create a new category, click on the __N__ew Category button, type a name for it, and click on OK.
5. When you finish with the clip, click on OK to close the dialog box.

You can also manage the categories as a group as opposed to an individual clip. This enables you to rename and delete categories.

1. From the Clip Gallery, click on the tab for the clip categories you want to edit (there are separate categories for each clip type).
2. Click on the __E__dit Categories button. The Edit Category List dialog box appears (see Figure 3.52).
3. Select the category you want to act upon.

SATURDAY AFTERNOON Flyers and Newsletters

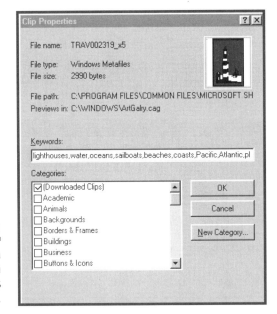

Figure 3.51

You can change a clip's categories in the Clip Properties dialog box.

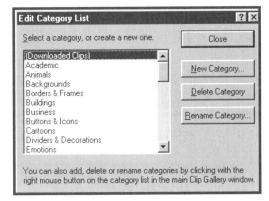

Figure 3.52

You can change and delete categories from the Edit Category List dialog box.

4. To rename the category, click on the Rename Category button. Type a new name in the dialog box that appears, and click on OK.

5. To delete the category, click on the Delete Category button.

6. Select another category and rename or delete it if needed. When you're finished, click on Close.

More Ways to Modify WordArt

WordArt has its own toolbar, made especially to help you make changes to your WordArt objects. It appears automatically when you create a piece of WordArt. Table 3.1 explains these buttons.

Button	Purpose
	Opens the WordArt Gallery dialog box for a new WordArt object
Edit Text...	Reopens the Edit WordArt Text dialog box
	Reopens the WordArt Gallery dialog box for the existing WordArt object
	Opens the Format WordArt dialog box to change lines and colors
Abc	Opens a pop-up array of WordArt shapes
	Enables you to rotate the WordArt (works the same way as the Free Rotate tool on the Drawing toolbar)
Aa	Makes all the letters the same height
Ab	Toggles between vertical and horizontal text orientation
	Opens a pop-up menu of text alignments (centered, left aligned, and so on)
AV	Changes the spacing between letters

Table 3.1 WordArt Toolbar Buttons

To edit a piece of WordArt, double-click on it. This displays the WordArt toolbar (if it isn't visible already) and the Edit WordArt Text dialog box. When you are done making changes to the WordArt, click outside it to deselect it. Like any other drawn object, you can drag it around on the worksheet to reposition it, or you can resize it using the selection handles in the corners.

Multiple Columns without Text Boxes

I promised earlier in this session I would show you the other way to create columns in a document—here you go. I suggest you try out the Columns feature on a regular document with lots of paragraph text rather than on your formatted newsletter file. If you saved your newsletter article as a separate file before you copied it into the text boxes, it would be a good file to use. Otherwise, just find a document you've created that has more than one page and open it up in Word. First, see how the whole thing looks in two columns:

1. Switch to Page Layout view.
2. Click on the Columns button on the Standard toolbar and drag across two columns.
3. Release the mouse button. The entire document is formatted in two columns, as shown in Figure 3.53.
4. Now press Ctrl+Z to undo it or choose Edit, Undo Columns.

Next experiment: what if you don't want the entire document formatted in multiple columns, but only a piece of it? For example, what if you want the article title to run across the entire page width?

1. Select the text you want in multiple columns.
2. Click on the Columns button on the Standard toolbar and drag across two columns.
3. Release the mouse button. The selected text is formatted in two columns, as shown in Figure 3.54.

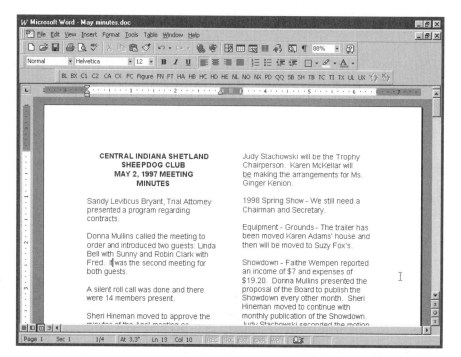

Figure 3.53

Congratulations, you've just created multiple columns without text boxes.

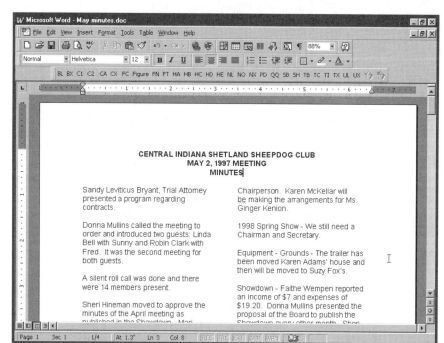

Figure 3.54

By selecting the text before issuing the Columns command, you can control which text appears in multiple columns.

SATURDAY AFTERNOON Flyers and Newsletters 213

Understanding Section Breaks

To understand what's happening with the columns (in the preceding section), you need to absorb a little info about how Word works. Usually, when you apply settings like margins, headers and footers, and number of columns, they apply to the entire document (as shown in Figure 3.53). However, sometimes you may want a single document with different settings for parts of it. Therefore, Word enables you to place *section breaks* to separate parts of the document that should have different settings from the rest. In Figure 3.53, the title is actually in a different section from the rest of the article. To see this, follow these steps:

1. Switch to Normal view.
2. Scroll until you see the article title. Notice the section break line beneath it, as shown in Figure 3.55.

The section break (visible in Figure 3.55) is where the settings are stored for the preceding section. The fact that the title is in a single column is

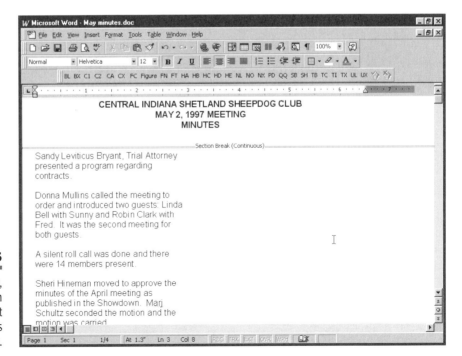

Figure 3.55

In Normal view, you can see section breaks, but not multiple columns side by side.

stored in that section break. If you delete a section break, the text above it takes on the properties of the section beneath it.

1. Position the mouse pointer on the section break line and press Delete. The section break disappears and the title joins the article in its section. (You can tell because the title is scrunched up in the narrow column, like the rest of the article.)
2. Switch to Page Layout view to see the results.

You can insert your own section breaks too—you don't have to rely on the Columns feature to do it. For example, suppose you want a few pages of your newsletter to have different margins from the rest. When you get to the spot where the new margins should begin, do this:

1. Choose Insert, Break. The Break dialog box appears (see Figure 3.56).
2. In the Section Breaks section, choose the type of section break you want:
   - **Next page.** For both a page break and a section break.
   - **Continuous.** Changes settings without starting a new page.
   - **Even page.** For both a page break, a section break, *and* a next section that starts on an even-numbered page.
   - **Odd page.** Same as above except the new section starts on an odd-numbered page.
3. Click on OK.

Figure 3.56

You can insert all types of breaks with this dialog box, but it is most commonly used for section breaks.

Notice you're not limited to section breaks in the Break dialog box. You can also create page breaks (without a section break) and column breaks (a directive to start a new column in a multicolumn section). However, most people don't use the Break dialog box for page or column breaks because their shortcut keys are much easier to use:

Page break: Ctrl+Enter

Column break: Ctrl+Shift+Enter

In Page Layout view, break indicators are not normally visible. You can see them, however, by turning on the display of hidden characters with the Show/Hide ¶ button on the Standard toolbar. Alternatively, you can switch to Normal view, in which all types of breaks appear onscreen.

SATURDAY EVENING

Mail Merge and Tables

- Assembling data in a table
- Creating a merge letter
- Executing a merge
- Using other kinds of data sources
- Creating merged mailing labels

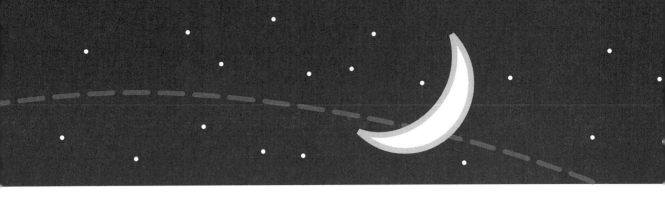

Mass mailings aren't a lot of fun. I've been the newsletter editor for a club of Shetland Sheepdog fanciers for several years now, and every month the worst part is preparing the copies for mailing. But I remember back a few years ago when I had to type each label or envelope on a typewriter. Yeech! That was pretty awful. By comparison, Word's mail merge feature makes the job seem like a sunny day in the park.

Even if you don't have to do mail merges, go ahead and work through this session anyway. You never know when you're going to need to do a mass mailing, whether it's at work or for the church or PTA. Besides, in this session, you'll learn about tables too, which you might find useful for other projects.

The Basic Mail Merge Process

I'm a firm believer in explaining the travel plan to everyone in the vehicle before beginning the journey. That way, nobody needs to ask "Are we there yet?" Mail merging is a multistep process; take a look at the steps first:

1. You'll create a table in Word that contains the names and addresses of where to send the mailing, as shown in Figure 4.1. Each person's name and address information is called a *record*. Column headings are field names.

Figure 4.1

This table holds personalized information (the records) that will appear in the letters.

2. You'll produce a letter with Word commands called *merge codes* in the places to be personalized. For example, there will be a {FIRST} code in the spot where the person's first name should go, as shown in Figure 4.2. Field names appear shaded and in double angle brackets.

3. You'll tell Word to merge the table with the letter, creating individual personalized letters for each person in the table, as shown in Figure 4.3. Notice that the actual info replaces the field names.

4. You'll check your work and then print the letters.

NOTE In the first step, creating the table, I'll pause for a few minutes to tell you about the Table feature in general. This won't help you with your mass mailing, but if you ever want to use the Table feature in other kinds of documents, it'll come in handy.

SATURDAY EVENING Mail Merge and Tables   221

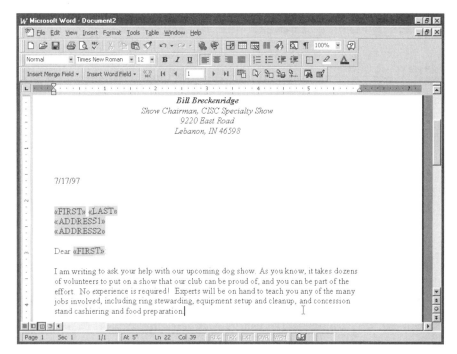

Figure 4.2

This letter contains generic text that will appear in all the letters plus codes for the personalized data.

Figure 4.3

Here's a letter created by merging the table in Figure 4.1 with the letter in Figure 4.2.

Assembling Data in a Table

The first step in a mail merge is to assemble data—in other words, the names and addresses or other information you plan on including.

NOTE For mail merge purposes, there are three ways to assemble the name list. You can create a table and type the data there, import table-like information from another program (such as Excel), or enter names in database fields in Word. I'll show you the way I prefer (using a table) in the following sections, and then I'll explain the other two methods.

Choosing Field Names

Each column in a table represents a field. For example, in Figure 4.1, the fields are FIRST, LAST, ADDRESS1, and ADDRESS2. Before you create the table, decide how many fields (and therefore how many columns) you will need, and what you will call them. For example, each of the following could be a field:

- First name
- Last name
- Street address
- City
- State
- ZIP code

Or you could decide to make each address line a single field:

- First and last name
- Street address
- City, State, and ZIP code

It all depends on what information you plan on using separately. For example, will you ever want to include only the first name, without the last? If so, you will need separate fields for first and last names. Will you ever want to include the city name by itself? If so, you should split the city from the state and ZIP fields.

In Figure 4.1, notice that I took a combination approach. Sometimes I used the first and last names separately, but I didn't need the address broken up except by the lines that it appears on. Therefore, I used the following fields, for a total of four columns.

- First name
- Last name
- Street address
- City, state, and ZIP code

Notice also that I gave each field a more generic name:

- First name = FIRST
- Last name = LAST
- Street address = ADDRESS1
- City, state, and ZIP code = ADDRESS2

I did this because short field names are easier to work with, as you'll see later.

Creating a Table

Now that you know how many columns you need in your table, go ahead and create it by following these steps:

1. Start a new document based on the Blank Document template.
2. Click on the Insert Table button on the Standard toolbar. (It looks like a grid with a blue bar across the top.) A white grid of squares appears beneath it.
3. Drag your mouse across the squares until you darken four squares across and four squares down, as shown in Figure 4.4.
4. Release the mouse button. The empty table appears in your document.

Figure 4.4

The Insert Table button lets you create a table of almost any size by dragging across the squares.

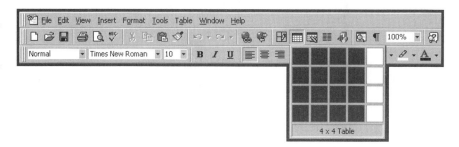

5. Type the field names in the top row, pressing Tab to move from cell to cell. (Each of the boxes in a table is called a *cell*.) When you finish, it should look something like Figure 4.5.

TIP

If you Tab too far, press Shift+Tab to move back one field, or just click on a cell to move the insertion point there.

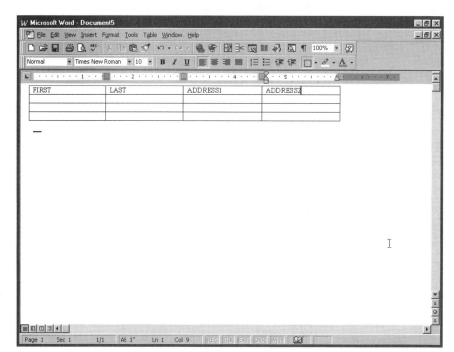

Figure 4.5

My table with the field names in the top row.

Typing Data into a Table

Now you're ready to type your names and addresses into a table. It's fairly straightforward; just move to the cell you want and start typing. When you finish a field, click on a different cell, or press Tab or Shift+Tab to move to the next or preceding cell. Each person's information is contained on one line, and each line forms one *record*.

The tricky part about typing in a table is not the typing, but the moving around from cell to cell; the insertion point doesn't move in a table like it does in a regular document. Table 4.1 provides a quick reference for moving the insertion point around in a table. When you finish, your table will look something like the one in Figure 4.6. Notice that some entries wrap to additional lines; this is okay.

TIP If you've filled up all your rows, no problem. Position the insertion point in the bottom right cell in the table and press Tab. This starts a new row.

TABLE 4.1 MOVING THE INSERTION POINT IN A TABLE

To Move	Press
To the next cell	Tab
To the preceding cell	Shift+Tab
To the next row	Down arrow
To the preceding row	Up arrow
To the first cell in the row	Alt+Home
To the last cell in the row	Alt+End
To the first cell in the column	Alt+Page Up
To the last cell in the column	Alt+Page Down

LAST	FIRST	ADDRESS1	ADDRESS2
Adams	Susan	3621 West 27th Street	Indianapolis, IN 46218
Antle	Gloria	R18, Box 1404	Indianapolis, IN 46241
Bohnke	Lori	482 Capital Hill	Middletown, IN 47356
Burkett	Karen	216 Honey Creek Drive	Arcadia, IN 46030
Carver	Diane	604 Airport Road	Batesville, IN 47006
Creech	Jeannne	343 S. Taft St.	Anderson, In 46013
Fogle	Tamara L.	6009 Debra Ct.	Battle Ground, IN 47920
Garrison	Bud and Carole	25085 Ray Parker Rd.	Dewey AZ 86327
Hartsock	Tom and Jessica	24 Callery Pear Drive	Zionsville, IN 46077
Hineman	Steve and Jenny	4631 S. St. Rd 109	Brownsburg, IN 46112
Junkersfeld	Lyn	8700 SR 43 North	Cambridge City, IN 47327-9471
Karbowski	Ellen	Bedford, IN 47421	Monticello, IN 47960
Kata	Ann	10067 Hereford Lane	Muncie, IN 47302
Kettering	Bettie	8805 E. 200 S	Indianapolis, IN 46241
Lacey	Sheri	8805 E. 200 S	Plainfield, IN 46168
Lasky	Kathy	2828 Manatee Rd.	Grand Rapids, MI 49505
McKellar	Jay and Judy	1725 N. Linwood Ave.	Zionsville, IN 46077
McKellar	Donna Kay	10967 Allisonville Rd.	Tavares, FL 32778
Morphew	Michael	214 Cedar Street	Indianapolis, IN 46218

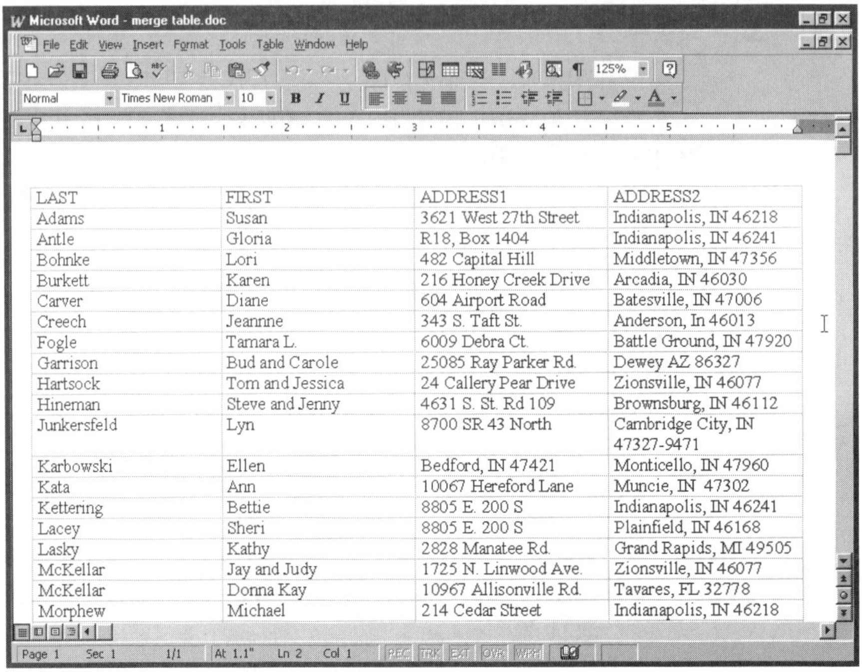

Figure 4.6

Here's my table with all the names and addresses.

NOTE To start a new paragraph in a cell, press Enter. However, for your table of names and addresses, you won't need to do that, because each cell contains only one paragraph.

Inserting and Deleting Rows and Columns

After working with your table for a while, you may decide there are not enough columns. Not a problem; you can add a column.

1. Select the entire column to the left of the new column you want to add. To select a column, move the mouse pointer above the top row until you see a down-pointing black arrow, and then click to select the column (see Figure 4.7).

SATURDAY EVENING Mail Merge and Tables

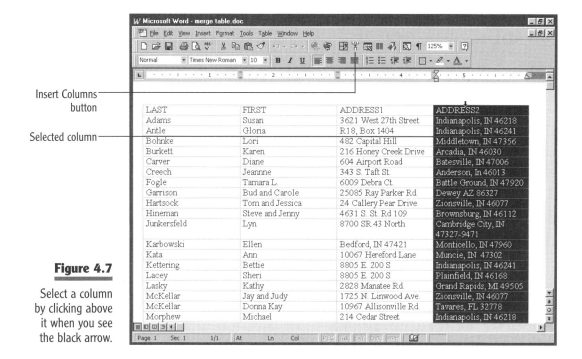

Insert Columns button

Selected column

Figure 4.7

Select a column by clicking above it when you see the black arrow.

2. Click on the Insert Columns button on the Standard toolbar, or choose T<u>a</u>ble, <u>I</u>nsert Columns.

3. Type a new field name at the top of the new column, and type the data in the fields beneath it.

To remove a column, follow these steps:

1. Select the column to be removed.
2. Click on the Cut button on the Standard toolbar or press Ctrl+X.

 NOTE You cannot select a column and press Delete to remove it; this merely clears the column's contents.

As I mentioned earlier, if you want to add a row at the bottom of the table, just position the insertion point in the last cell of the last existing row and press Tab. Easy, eh? To add a row in another spot in the table:

1. Select the row that the new row should appear above. To select a row, move the mouse pointer to the left of the leftmost cell in the row, so the mouse pointer changes to a right-slanted white arrow (different from the default left-slanting one), and click. A selected row appears in Figure 4.8.
2. Click on the Insert Rows button on the Standard toolbar.

NOTE To select more than one row or column at once, hold down the mouse button while you drag straight across (for columns) or straight down (for rows). Then when you insert additional rows or columns, Word will insert the same number of new ones as the number you selected. For example, to insert four rows quickly, select four rows and click on the Insert Rows button.

Insert Rows button

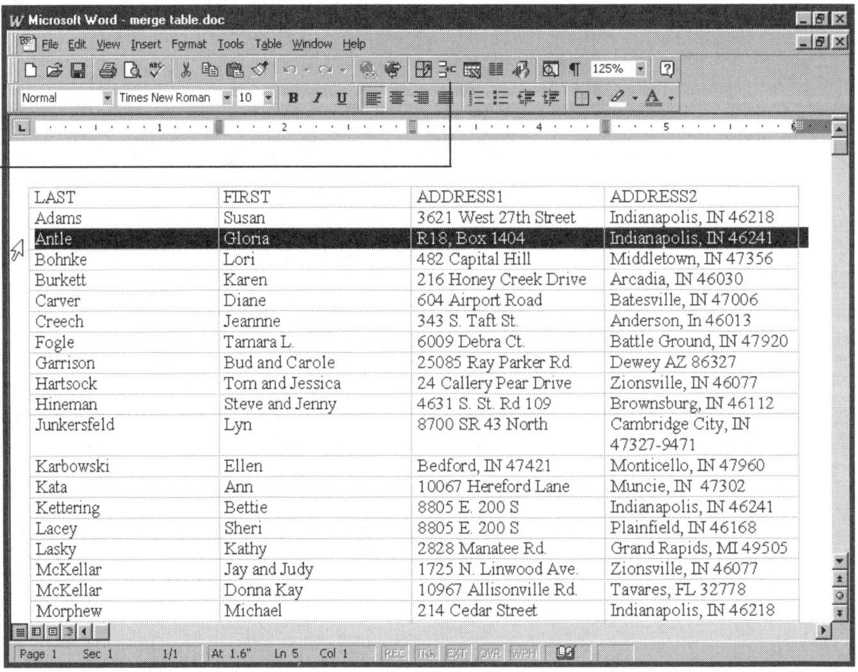

LAST	FIRST	ADDRESS1	ADDRESS2
Adams	Susan	3621 West 27th Street	Indianapolis, IN 46218
Antle	Gloria	R18, Box 1404	Indianapolis, IN 46241
Bohnke	Lori	482 Capital Hill	Middletown, IN 47356
Burkett	Karen	216 Honey Creek Drive	Arcadia, IN 46030
Carver	Diane	604 Airport Road	Batesville, IN 47006
Creech	Jeannne	343 S. Taft St.	Anderson, In 46013
Fogle	Tamara L.	6009 Debra Ct.	Battle Ground, IN 47920
Garrison	Bud and Carole	25085 Ray Parker Rd.	Dewey AZ 86327
Hartsock	Tom and Jessica	24 Callery Pear Drive	Zionsville, IN 46077
Hineman	Steve and Jenny	4631 S. St. Rd 109	Brownsburg, IN 46112
Junkersfeld	Lyn	8700 SR 43 North	Cambridge City, IN 47327-9471
Karbowski	Ellen	Bedford, IN 47421	Monticello, IN 47960
Kata	Ann	10067 Hereford Lane	Muncie, IN 47302
Kettering	Bettie	8805 E. 200 S	Indianapolis, IN 46241
Lacey	Sheri	8805 E. 200 S	Plainfield, IN 46168
Lasky	Kathy	2828 Manatee Rd.	Grand Rapids, MI 49505
McKellar	Jay and Judy	1725 N. Linwood Ave.	Zionsville, IN 46077
McKellar	Donna Kay	10967 Allisonville Rd.	Tavares, FL 32778
Morphew	Michael	214 Cedar Street	Indianapolis, IN 46218

Figure 4.8

To select a row, move the mouse pointer to the left of it and click.

To delete rows, select the rows and click on the Cut button on the Standard toolbar, or choose Table, Delete Rows.

Table Finishing Touches

When your table is the way you want it, save your work. I called mine Merge Table, but you can use any name you want. Then close the file; you won't need to work with it anymore as a separate file (unless, of course, you want to put more names in it later or make corrections).

Creating a Merge Letter

The next step is to create a letter. Armed with the skills you gained in the Saturday Morning session, you should be able to create a letter very easily. The only difference is that instead of including personal information about a recipient, you will insert merge codes.

1. Start a new document, based either on the Blank Document template or your letterhead template you created this morning.
2. If needed, type your return address and the date. (You won't need to do this if you are using your letterhead template.)
3. Press Enter to move the insertion point to the spot where the recipient's name and address should go.
4. Choose Tools, Mail Merge. The Mail Merge Helper dialog box opens.
5. Click on the Create button, and choose Form Letters from the drop-down list (see Figure 4.9).
6. A dialog box appears asking whether you want a new document or the active window. Click on Active Window, because you have already started a document to hold the letter.
7. Back in the Mail Merge Helper dialog box, click on the Get Data button and then on Open Data Source on the drop-down list. The Open Data Source dialog box appears (see Figure 4.10).

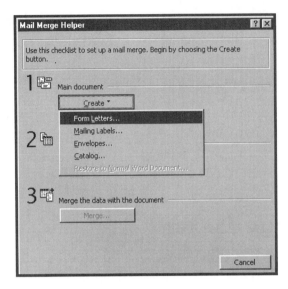

Figure 4.9

First, choose the type of mail merge.

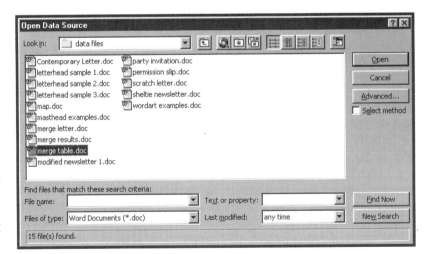

Figure 4.10

Use this dialog box as you do any other that opens files.

 TIP Look back at the Friday Evening session if you can't recall how to navigate dialog boxes that open files.

8. Choose the file containing your table, and click on <u>O</u>pen.

NOTE If, after Step 8, you get a dialog box asking about header record delimiters, it's because you have extra paragraph markers before the table in your data file. Click on Cancel, and then click on Close to get out of the Mail Merge Helper. Reopen your data file and delete any extra blank paragraphs above the table. Save your work, and then try again. You could go ahead with the merge without removing those blanks, but you would have one or more empty letters—letters going to nobody—at the beginning of your stack of personalized letters.

9. Next, you see a message saying that Word found no merge fields in your main document. Don't worry; this is normal. Click on the Edit Main Document button to continue. All the dialog boxes disappear, and your letter reappears with a Mail Merge toolbar across the top.

10. Click on the Insert Merge Field button on the Mail Merge toolbar (see Figure 4.11) and then on the field containing the first names of your recipients. The code is inserted at the insertion point position.

11. If your table separates first and last names (as mine does), press the spacebar and then insert the field containing the last names (LAST, in mine).

12. Press Enter to begin a new line, and insert the field containing the first line of the address.

13. Press Enter to begin a new line, and insert the field or fields containing the second line of the address. On mine, everything is in one field (ADDRESS2), but if the rest of your address is separated, you might need to do the following:

   a. Insert the CITY field.

   b. Type a comma and press the spacebar.

   c. Insert the STATE field.

   d. Press the spacebar twice.

   e. Insert the ZIP field.

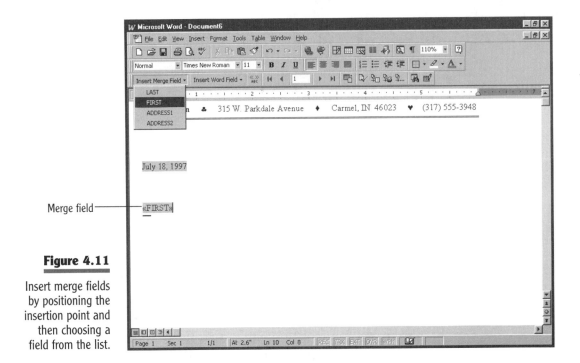

Merge field

Figure 4.11

Insert merge fields by positioning the insertion point and then choosing a field from the list.

14. When you complete the address block, press Enter twice and type your salutation (for example, **Dear**). Do not type any personalization.
15. Now insert the first name field, type a colon, and press Enter twice.
16. Type your letter. If you want to insert any personalization in the letter, insert the appropriate merge fields as needed.
17. Finish your letter normally with a closing and a signature block. My finished letter appears in Figure 4.12.

Executing a Merge

Performing an actual merge is the easiest part of the whole process. It's as simple as clicking on a button. The only complicated part is that there are

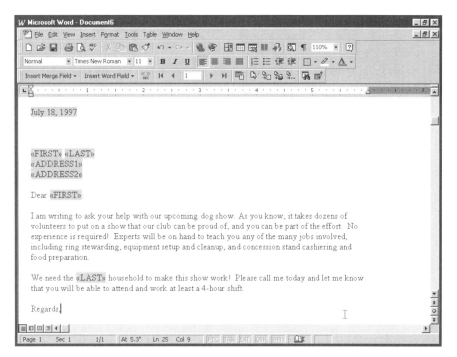

Figure 4.12

A completed letter, ready for merging.

so many choices! Word provides more flexibility than most of us will ever need in the merging department, and a button on the Mail Merge toolbar represents each option.

Table 4.2 explains the Mail Merge toolbar buttons that are used for previewing and printing merges. Just click on the button you want. I'll tell you how to use the various buttons in the sections that follow.

Most of the buttons on the Mail Merge toolbar are designed to help you check your work before you print the merged letters, so you can avoid printing copies you will have to throw away. There are various ways to prevent errors in your mail merge.

Two types of errors occur in a mail merge situation: errors that Word recognizes as errors, such as a missing field column in your data table, and

Table 4.2 Merge Function Buttons on the Mail Merge Toolbar

Button	Name	Purpose
	View Merged Data	Toggles the display between the field names (off) and the actual field data for each record (on).
	First Record	When View Merged Data is on, shows the letter for the first row of the merge table.
	Previous Record	When View Merged Data is on, moves to the letter for the preceding row of the merge table.
	Go To Record	When View Merged Data is on, moves to the letter for the row number that you specify.
	Next Record	When View Merged Data is on, moves to the letter for the next row of the merge table.
	Last Record	When View Merged Data is on, shows the letter for the last row of the merge table.
	Mail Merge Helper	Reopens the Mail Merge Helper dialog box, so you can make changes to its settings if needed.
	Check for Errors	Runs a check to make sure the merge will complete without problems.
	Merge to New Document	Creates a new document that holds the merged letters.
	Merge to Printer	Sends merged letters directly to the printer.
	Mail Merge	Opens the Mail Merge dialog box.

Table 4.2 Merge Function Buttons on the Mail Merge Toolbar (continued)

Button	Name	Purpose
	Find Record	Opens the Find in Field dialog box, with which you can find a particular value in a field. (This is most useful when View Merged Data is on.)
	Edit Data Source	Opens the document containing the merge table, so you can make changes to it.

errors that Word can't help you find, such as Bob's name appearing with Peter's address in your data table. Here are some ways that Word helps you watch for the errors it can detect:

- You can ask Word to check for errors before merging or while merging. Word reports problems such as missing columns in your data table or empty data tables.
- Even if you don't use the Check for Errors feature, if Word runs into a problem that prevents it from completing the merge, it automatically reports the error to you.

For correcting the errors you must identify, Word offers these tools:

- You can preview the merged letters one at a time onscreen by using the View Merged Data button, to make sure that, for example, ADDRESS1 data is placed in the ADDRESS1 field location.
- You can merge to a new document and then view the document onscreen (with each letter on a separate page) before you print.

Asking Word to Check for Errors

Admittedly, I don't use this feature very often, because it very seldom finds an error. If you followed the steps earlier in this session for setting up your data file and letter, you should not have any errors. But if you start branching out on your own, trying more unusual merges, you might find this feature handy. To check your work for errors (without actually performing the merge), follow these steps:

NOTE What do I mean by "more unusual?" Check the Time-Savers section at the end of this session for some ideas. For example, you can create queries that sort or filter the data, or import data from other sources.

1. Click on the Check for Errors button on the Mail Merge toolbar. (It looks like a document with a check mark next to it.) The Checking and Reporting Errors dialog box opens (see Figure 4.13).
2. Click on the top option, Simulate the merge and report errors in a new document, and then on OK.
3. If a dialog box reports no mail merge errors found, click on OK.

It is unlikely that Word will find an error in Step 3, but if it does, take note of the error and Word's suggestion for fixing it, and edit your data file or letter as needed. For some errors, like missing fields, Word will suggest a fix and even fix it for you if you consent.

Later, when you are more experienced, you can save yourself some time when checking for errors by selecting the middle option button in Figure 4.13. This merges the letters to a new document at the same time that it checks for errors. I'll discuss merging to a new document in an upcoming section.

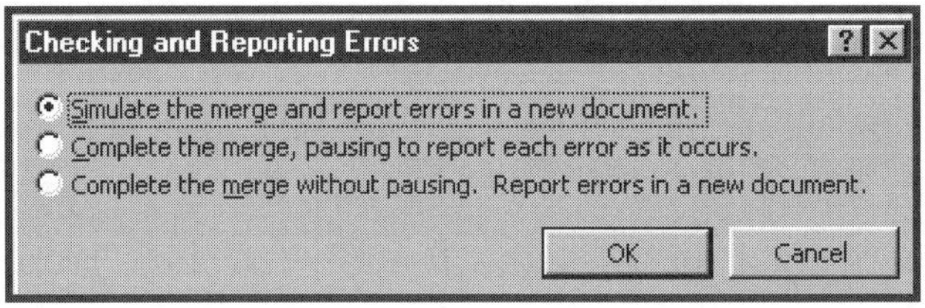

Figure 4.13

For this exercise, choose the top option.

NOTE I ran into an unusual error message while writing this book. Whenever I tried to merge or check for errors, I received this message: "Word could not merge the main document with the data source because the data records were empty or no data records matched your query options." I did not use query options, and my data records certainly were not empty. I was stumped until my mate wandered into the room and said "Have you tried exiting Word and then restarting it?" "No," I said. Sure enough, when I reentered Word and reopened my merge letter, the problem disappeared and everything worked perfectly. The moral: save your work frequently, and if all else fails, reboot.

Previewing Merged Letters One at a Time

To do a quick check before printing, many people find it useful to use Word's View Merged Data feature. This enables you to see one letter at a time onscreen exactly as it will print. You can scroll through the stack of letters with the controls Word provides.

The View Merged Data button on the Mail Merge toolbar toggles between displaying the merge fields (shaded in gray) and the actual names and addresses. Click on the View Merged Data button now. The first name and address appears, as shown in Figure 4.14. From there, you can scroll through the letters with the buttons immediately to the right of the View Merged Data button. You just saw these in Table 4.2. You can return to displaying the field names by clicking on the View Merged Data button again.

Changing Data in a Record

If you find that changes need to be made to one or more data records, you can do either of the following:

- You can reopen the data file and make your changes in the table.
- You can click on the Edit Data Source button on the Mail Merge toolbar (the rightmost button) to open a dialog box showing the

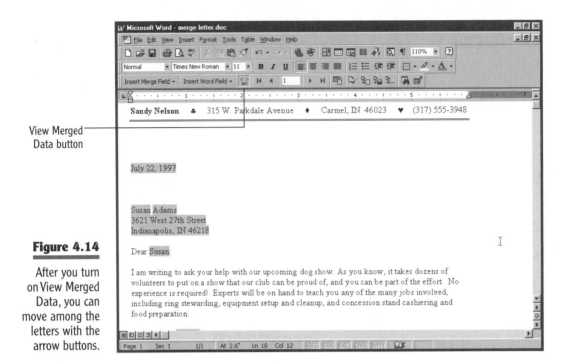

Figure 4.14

After you turn on View Merged Data, you can move among the letters with the arrow buttons.

first record in a data form (see Figure 4.15.) From there you can use the arrow buttons (which work the same as the arrow buttons on the Mail Merge toolbar) to move to the record needing changes, and then type your corrections into the form.

If you do use the Edit Data Source button, any changes you make to the data will also be reflected in the saved version of the data table; you do not have to reopen the data table and make the change there too.

Choosing a Different Data File

Perhaps after looking at the previewed letters, you realize that you have used the wrong data file. No problem. Click on the Mail Merge Helper button on the Mail Merge toolbar to reopen the Mail Merge Helper.

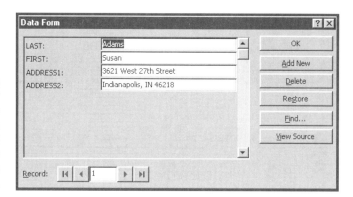

Figure 4.15

This form shows your table data in a slightly different format that you may find easier to work with.

Then click on the <u>G</u>et Data button and select <u>O</u>pen Data Source. Finally, choose a different data source file.

Merging to a New Document

If you checked for all possible errors, and are confident that everything is a "go," you have my permission to skip this section and merge directly to the printer (in the next section). Personally, I'm never that confident. I prefer to merge to a new document first, and then print it.

1. Click on the Merge to New Document button. If there are no errors, the merge completes automatically, and the first letter of the letter set appears onscreen.

2. Scroll down using the scroll bar to view the rest of the letters, checking each one carefully to make sure the merged information is correct, as shown in Figure 4.16.

NOTE If you're viewing the letters in Normal view in Step 2, you'll see section breaks between the letters. You learned about section breaks this afternoon, remember?

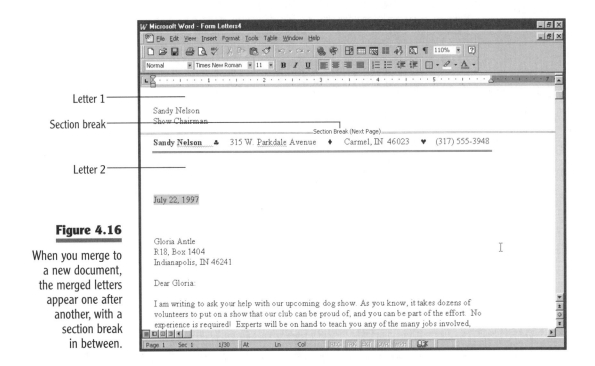

Figure 4.16

When you merge to a new document, the merged letters appear one after another, with a section break in between.

3. When you are confident that all letters are correct, click on the Print button on the Standard toolbar to print the letters.

One advantage of this method is that you can go through the new document containing the letters and delete any letters that you don't want. In the Time-Savers section at the end of this session, you'll learn how to set up filters so you can exclude certain records from the merge, but in my opinion, merging them all and then deleting the unneeded letters is much simpler.

You can also print the letters one at a time. Instead of clicking on the Print button (Step 3) from the document containing the merged letters, choose File, Print, and specify a single page number in the Pages text box.

NOTE What happened to your generic letter with the fields in it? It's still open. Open the Window menu and choose to redisplay it.

Merging to a Printer

Merging directly to a printer takes guts, because if there are errors that Word can't detect, and you don't notice them until after you merge, you will waste paper and printing toner or ribbon. Still, many busy people swear by it.

1. Click on the Merge to Printer button on the Mail Merge toolbar. The Print dialog box opens.
2. Click on OK. The merged letters print.
3. Check your letters as they come off of the printer to make sure everything merged correctly.

 TIP If some letters do not merge correctly, there is no need to reprint the whole stack. Just merge to a new document and then delete all the letters that printed correctly before you reprint. Also, you can use the Query feature (described in the Time-Savers section) to choose which records to print.

Save Your Work!

If you plan to do the same merge again, you should save your letter. When you reopen it, it will be ready to merge again; the data table will still be attached. If you make changes in your data table, the changes will show up. The data table is not really part of the letter file; it's simply linked to it.

If you merge to a new document, you will also have an open document containing all the letters. You will probably *not* want to save it, because you will most likely never need to resend this particular letter to the same people. If you ever need to recreate the letters (for example, to reprint a specific one that didn't get mailed), you can easily run the merge again on your saved letter.

Using Other Kinds of Data Sources

So far in this session, you've used my favorite data source—a Word table. I do a mail merge every month for a newsletter, and I keep the mailing list in a Word table. This way, I can make changes to the addresses throughout the month as needed, without opening the merge document.

However, there are two other ways to create or retrieve data, and in the interest of fairness to people who prefer them, I'll explain each one briefly. If you're not interested in using other data sources, skip this section.

Using Data Sources from Other Programs

If you are a Microsoft Office user, you probably have Microsoft Excel installed on your computer, and possibly Microsoft Access too. You can use data from either of these programs in your Word mail merge. You can also use data from almost any other popular spreadsheet or database program, although it might require a little bit more setup than Excel or Access.

Using Data from Excel

If you already have data in Excel that you want to use in your mail merge, follow these steps.

1. In Excel, open the workbook containing the data, and check the following:
   - If you don't want to use the entire worksheet in the merge, create a named range in Excel for the range to use. (See Excel's Help system if needed.)
   - Make sure there are no blank rows at the top of the worksheet, if you are not using a named range.

 Make sure that the first row in the worksheet or range contains column headings to use as field names.

2. When you are satisfied with the set up of your data in Excel, save your work and close Excel.

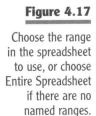
CAUTION Excel allows you to split and merge cells so that not every row has the same number of columns in it. This is very helpful for creating printed forms in Excel, but it can really mess things up in a mail merge. Don't use worksheets with split or merged cells for Word mail merge data—or if you must, un-split or un-join the offending cells first.

3. In Word, start a new document, based either on your letterhead template or on the Blank Document template.

4. Start a mail merge as you did before (<u>T</u>ools, Mail Me<u>r</u>ge), but when you get to the Open Data Source dialog box, open the Files of <u>T</u>ype drop-down list and choose MS Excel Worksheets (.xls).

5. Locate and select the Excel workbook containing the data and click on Open. A Microsoft Excel dialog box appears, as shown in Figure 4.17.

6. Choose the named range if you created one, or choose Entire Spreadsheet to use the whole sheet, and then click on OK.

7. Complete the merge normally.

Figure 4.17

Choose the range in the spreadsheet to use, or choose Entire Spreadsheet if there are no named ranges.

Microsoft has carefully designed all the Office programs to work seamlessly together; this is why it's almost as easy to use Excel data as it is to work with data in Word itself. It's easy with Access data too, as you'll see in the following section.

Using Data from Access

Access is a database program ideally designed for keeping track of things like address books. Therefore, it's a good bet that if you use Access, you've got some names and addresses in it. Here's how to use them in a Word mail merge:

1. If needed, open Access and refresh your memory with the name of the database file and the table or query within the database file that holds the data. Then exit Access.

NOTE   A *query* in Access is a set of criteria that plucks certain records from one or more tables and assembles them in a particular order. For example, you might have a query that picks out only people with ZIP codes greater than 55555. You can create simple queries as you merge in Word, as you'll see in the Time-Savers section at the end of this session.

2. In Word, start a new document, based either on your letterhead template or on the Blank Document template.
3. Start a mail merge as you did before (Tools, Mail Merge), but when you get to the Open Data Source dialog box, open the Files of Type drop-down list and choose MS Access Databases (.mdb).
4. Locate and select your Access database and click on Open. A Microsoft Access dialog box appears, as shown in Figure 4.18.
5. Click on the Table or Query tab to choose which you want to work with, and then click on the name of the table or query to use. Finally, click on OK.
6. Complete the merge normally.

Figure 4.18

You can use either tables or queries from Access in your mail merge.

Using Data from a Text File

Text files can be the trickiest of data sources, not because they're inherently difficult, but because they have errors in them more often than other types of sources. For example, notice the data in Figure 4.19. It is an ordinary text file (.txt) opened in Word. As you can see, the fields are separated into columns by tabs, but on some lines there is more than one tab between certain columns. Whoever created this table added the extra tabs to make the data line up neatly on the page, but this messes up a mail merge.

Why? Because when importing data from text files, Word relies on separator characters to tell it when one column ends and the next one begins on each line. Tab is the separator character used in Figure 4.19. When Word encounters two tabs in a row, it thinks that the second tab represents another field, and there is simply no data in the space between them. Rows with extra tab stops end up with more columns than the other rows, and Word becomes very confused.

To clean up a text file before using it as a data file, you must remove the extra tabs. There's no good way to do this; just do it manually, moving the insertion point to each extra one and deleting it.

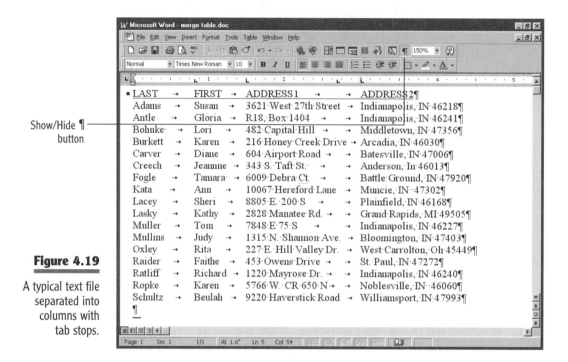

Figure 4.19

A typical text file separated into columns with tab stops.

Show/Hide ¶ button

> **NOTE** Word can search for and replace two tab stops in a row with a single tab stop. Use Edit, Replace and search for ^t^t. Replace it with ^t. Re-run the Replace until it finds no more. This will not take care of extra single tabs and the ends of lines, but it will save you some work searching for double tabs within the lines.

> **TIP** Converting text to a table is a useful general-purpose skill to have, so you may want to learn this even if you do not have data in a text file right now.

After you remove all the extra tabs, check your work by converting the text to a table.

1. Select all the data. (Just drag across it.)

2. Choose Table, Convert Text to Table. The Convert Text to Table dialog box appears (see Figure 4.20).

3. If the correct number of columns does not appear in the Number of Columns text box, you can either type the correct number or leave it as-is. Either way, you will be able to spot errors in the table later.

CAUTION The number that appears in the Number of Columns text box is the number of columns in the row with the most tab stops. If you have four columns but the text box shows a 5, you know that you missed an extra tab stop in at least one row. You can Cancel at this point and go looking for it, or you can continue and fix the error after you create the table.

4. In the Column Width box, enter a number that will make the table come out at approximately six inches. For example, if you have four columns, use 1.5". (Actually, you can leave this set to Auto if you prefer, but the table you get will not be very readable.)

5. In the Separate text at box, make sure that Tabs is selected.

6. Click on OK. Your text becomes a table.

7. Look for errors caused by extra tabs and make corrections. For

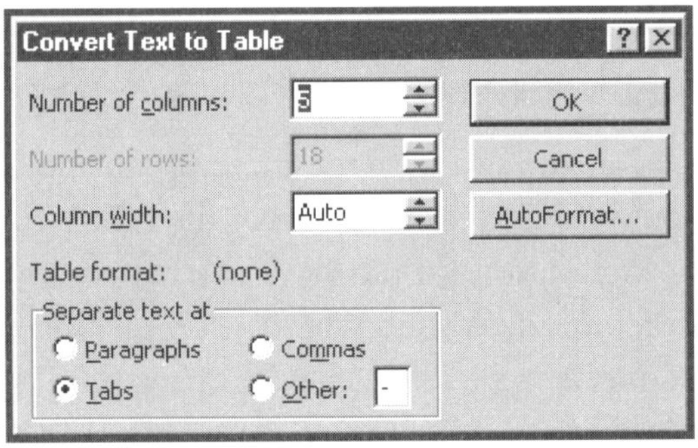

Figure 4.20

Although you can use a text file as-is in your merge, it is best to check for stray tab stops by converting the text to a table.

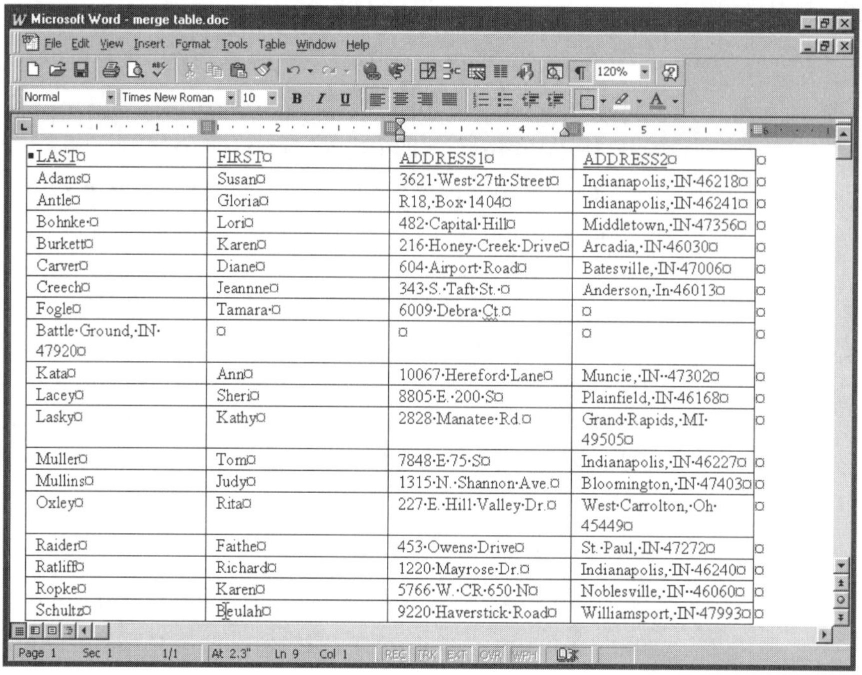

LAST	FIRST	ADDRESS1	ADDRESS2
Adams	Susan	3621 West 27th Street	Indianapolis, IN 46218
Antle	Gloria	R18, Box 1404	Indianapolis, IN 46241
Bohnke	Lori	482 Capital Hill	Middletown, IN 47356
Burkett	Karen	216 Honey Creek Drive	Arcadia, IN 46030
Carver	Diane	604 Airport Road	Batesville, IN 47006
Creech	Jeannne	343 S. Taft St.	Anderson, In 46013
Fogle	Tamara	6009 Debra Ct.	
Battle Ground, IN 47920			
Kata	Ann	10067 Hereford Lane	Muncie, IN 47302
Lacey	Sheri	8805 E. 200 S	Plainfield, IN 46168
Lasky	Kathy	2828 Manatee Rd.	Grand Rapids, MI 49505
Muller	Tom	7848 E 75 S	Indianapolis, IN 46227
Mullins	Judy	1315 N. Shannon Ave.	Bloomington, IN 47403
Oxley	Rita	227 E. Hill Valley Dr.	West Carrolton, Oh 45449
Raider	Faithe	453 Owens Drive	St. Paul, IN 47272
Ratliff	Richard	1220 Mayrose Dr.	Indianapolis, IN 46240
Ropke	Karen	5766 W. CR 650 N	Noblesville, IN 46060
Schultz	Beulah	9220 Haverstick Road	Williamsport, IN 47993

Figure 4.21

Extra tab stops are easy to notice once you convert the text to a table.

example, in Figure 4.21, an extra tab forced the last part of a person's address into a new row. I moved that data up into the correct row and deleted the blank row.

8. Save the data in its table form as a Word file, and use it to perform a mail merge.

Creating a New Data Source with a Word Form

As you were using the Mail Merge Helper you may have noticed that you could choose to create a data source file rather than open one. This method works well if you do not have the names and addresses already typed into a file ahead of time. Word prompts you to save your work when you're done, so you end up with a separate data file much like the Word table that you created earlier in this session. This is simply a different way of getting to the same result. To create a new data source, follow these steps:

1. In Word, start a new document, based either on your letterhead template or on the Blank Document template.

2. Start a mail merge as you did before (<u>T</u>ools, Mail Me<u>r</u>ge), but when you click on the <u>G</u>et Data button, choose Create Data Source. The Create Data Source dialog box appears, as shown in Figure 4.22. Word creates the fields in the Field names in header row scroll box by default if you don't specify otherwise.

3. The list on the right (see Figure 4.22) contains a ready-made list of fields. Do any of the following as needed:

   - To remove a field you don't want to use from the list, click on it and then click on the <u>R</u>emove Field Name button.
   - To add a new field to the list, type its name in the <u>F</u>ield name text box and then click on the <u>A</u>dd Field Name button.
   - To rearrange fields, click on a field you want to reposition and then click on the up or down arrow button in the dialog box to move it up or down in the list.

4. When you are satisfied with the fields and their order, click on OK. The Save As dialog box opens.

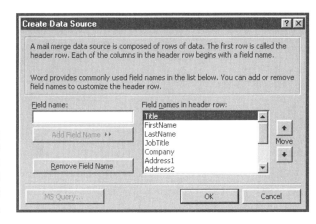

Figure 4.22

Here's where you set up the fields you'll use in the data source.

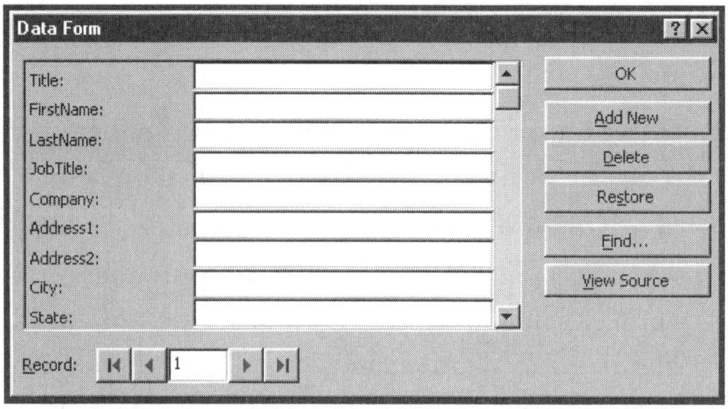

Figure 4.23

Word creates a data entry form with the fields you choose.

5. Enter a name to save your data file, and click on Save.

6. Next, you see a message that your data source contains no records. Click on the Edit Data Source button, and a data entry form appears, like the one shown in Figure 4.23.

7. Enter information into the fields for the first record.

8. If you need to enter another record, click on Add Record, and then enter another. When you finish entering records, click on OK.

9. Create your form letter by inserting merge fields, as you learned earlier, and complete the mail merge normally.

If you need to add, edit, or delete records, just click on the Edit Data Source button on the Mail Merge toolbar to reopen the form. From there you can move from record to record using the arrow buttons at the bottom of the form, or delete a record by displaying it and then clicking on the Delete button.

Take a Break

Have you reached information overload yet? Don't worry—the day is almost over. Look at what you've accomplished so far this weekend; just with most of this session under your belt, you're now adept at merging tables and other items with form letters. You definitely deserve a few minutes to collect your thoughts. Next, you'll tackle other merges, such as creating mailing labels, envelopes, and catalog listings from existing data.

Creating Merged Mailing Labels

Form letters are certainly not the only thing you can create with a mail merge. In fact, the most common thing I use mail merge for is mailing labels that I print out and stick on the newsletters that I mail to club members. Creating a sheet of mailing labels is really no harder than creating a form letter.

1. Start a new document based on the Blank Document template.
2. Choose Tools, Mail Merge to open the Mail Merge Helper dialog box.
3. Click on the Create button and choose Mailing Labels.
4. A box appears asking whether you want to use the active window (your blank document) or start a new document. Click on the Active Window button.
5. Click on the Get Data button, and either open or create a data source.
6. Next you see a message that Word needs to set up your main document. Click on Set Up Main Document to continue.
7. A Label Options dialog box appears, as shown in Figure 4.24. At the top of the dialog box, choose the type of printer you are using: Dot matrix or Laser and ink jet.
8. In the Tray drop-down list, choose how you will feed the labels into the printer. Choose Manual if you will feed each sheet of labels in by hand, or choose a paper tray (such as Upper, Lower, or AutoSelect Tray) if you are going to put the labels in the regular paper tray.

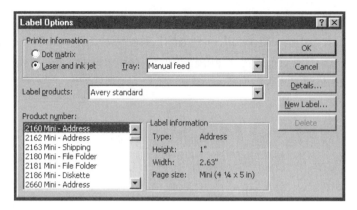

Figure 4.24

Because you told Word you wanted labels, it gives you the chance to set the label size and specifications.

 TIP Even though sheets of labels fit into my laser printer's paper tray, I feed label sheets in manually so they don't crumple and wrinkle as much.

9. Look on the box that your labels came in and find the Avery number. Even if the labels were not made by Avery, they should still have an Avery equivalent number on them.
10. Select the Avery number from the Product number list.

 NOTE If you don't have an Avery number, measure a single label on the sheet, and choose an Avery number that has the same measurements and number of labels per sheet as the labels that you have. To find out how many labels there are per sheet, choose a label and then click on the Details button. However, because all label sheets are normal paper size, if you match up with the right size label, the number of labels per sheet should automatically be correct too.

11. Click on OK. The Create Labels dialog box appears.
12. Click on the Insert Merge Field button and choose the first field that you want on the label.

13. Add the rest of the fields you want, separating them with spaces and line breaks as needed. You may also want to add a blank line at the top of the label, and add some spaces (for example, five) at the beginning of each line, as I did in Figure 4.25.
14. Click on OK. Word creates a sheet of label placeholders, which you can see on your screen behind the Mail Merge Helper dialog box.
15. In the Mail Merge Helper dialog box, click on the Merge button. Then in the Merge dialog box that appears, click on the Merge button again. Word creates a sheet of labels, ready for you to print, as shown in Figure 4.26.

◆◆◆

Choose your label sheets carefully. There are label sheets designed for each type of printer: dot matrix, ink jet, and laser. If you use the wrong type in your printer, it can damage the printer. For example, labels designed for dot matrix or ink jet use are apt to melt inside a laser printer, jamming up the printer mechanism and requiring costly repair.

◆◆◆

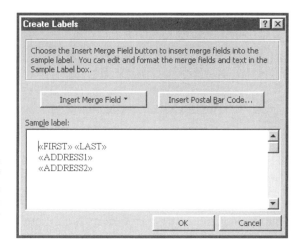

Figure 4.25

Insert merge fields to form a normal-looking address for a single label.

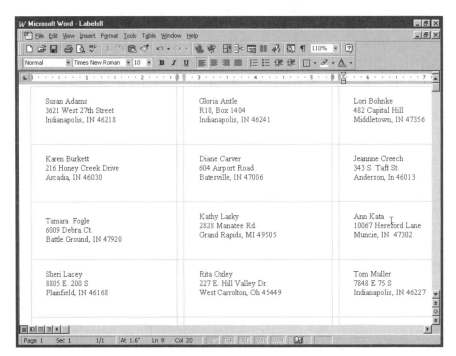

Figure 4.26

You can print this document on a sheet of labels.

Creating Merged Envelopes

Creating envelopes is much the same as creating labels, except for a dialog box or two.

1. Start a new document based on the Blank Document template.
2. Choose Tools, Mail Merge to open the Mail Merge Helper dialog box.
3. Click on the Create button and choose Envelopes.
4. A box appears asking whether you want to use the active window (your blank document) or start a new document. Click on the Active Window button.
5. Click on the Get Data button, and either open or create a data source.

6. Next you see a message that Word needs to set up your main document. Click on Set Up Main Document to continue.

7. An Envelope Options dialog box appears, as shown in Figure 4.27. Choose the envelope size you want from the Envelope size drop-down list. (The default is 10, which is a standard business-size envelope.)

8. If you want to reposition the return address or the mailing address on the envelope, use the controls in the Delivery address and Return address sections of the dialog box. (I never change these—the defaults work just fine.)

9. Click on the Printing Options tab and choose the correct orientation for your envelopes. (You already determined this in this morning's session; turn back and refresh your memory if needed.)

10. Click on OK. An Envelope Address dialog box appears. It's exactly the same as the box you saw in Figure 4.25, except for its title.

11. Insert merge fields into the dialog box just as you did with mailing labels, and then click on OK.

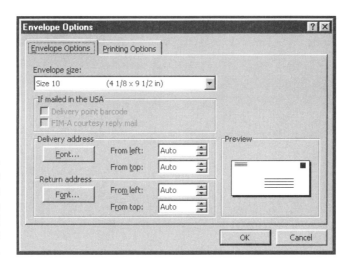

Figure 4.27

Set the envelope size and the position of the addresses printed on it.

12. Back in the Mail Merge Helper, click on the Merge button, and then click on the Merge button in the Merge dialog box that appears. Word creates the envelopes, ready to print, as shown in Figure 4.28. Notice Word remembered your return address from when you entered it in this morning's session.

13. Load your printer with envelopes, or feed them in manually, and print.

TIP If you want to change the return address, choose Tools, Envelopes and Labels, and type your change in the Return Address box.

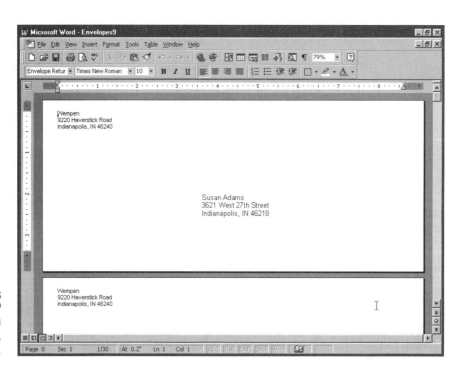

Figure 4.28

Each envelope is a separate section, ready to print.

Merging a Data Table into a Catalog Listing

A catalog listing is just like any of the other merged documents except that more than one record appears per page. It's called a catalog because it creates a listing of the chosen fields from each record, one after the other, as shown in Figure 4.29. By now, the merge process should seem pretty familiar to you.

1. Start a new document based on the Blank Document template.
2. Choose Tools, Mail Merge. The Mail Merge Helper dialog box opens.
3. Click on the Create button and choose Catalog.
4. A box appears asking whether you want to use the active window (your blank document) or start a new document. Click on the Active Window button.

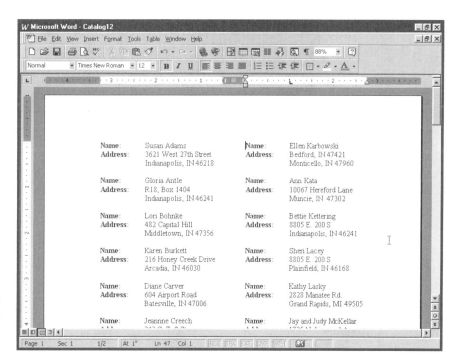

Figure 4.29

Here is a catalog of names and addresses I created.

5. Click on the <u>G</u>et Data button, and either open or create a data source.

6. Next you see a message that Word needs to set up your main document. Click on <u>S</u>et Up Main Document to continue, and you're faced with a blank document, just like when you created a form letter.

7. Insert the fields for one record. Word will duplicate them for you to make the catalog.

8. Format any text around the fields, and the fields themselves, as desired. For example, in Figure 4.30, I created an address book list with one blank line between records, and the words "Name" and "Address" in boldface to introduce the fields.

9. Click on the Merge to New Document button on the Mail Merge toolbar to perform the merge, as shown in Figure 4.31.

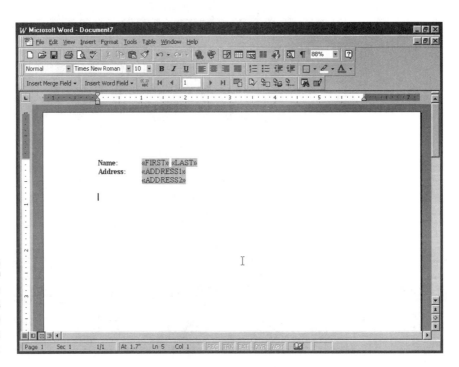

Figure 4.30

Set up a single record, just as you would set up the fields in a form letter.

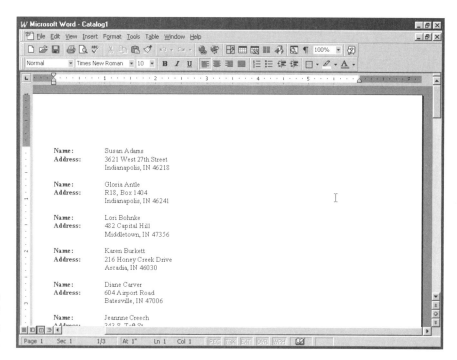

Figure 4.31

The result of merging the fields in Figure 4.30.

Depending on the length of the data in each field, you might want to divide the list into two or more columns using the Columns feature you learned about this afternoon, so that your catalog listing looks like the one in Figure 4.29.

Time-Savers

This has been a short but fairly intense session. You'd be surprised how many Word users are intimidated by mail merging, and now you're one of the elite few who can handle it! If you're not too tired, check out the following extra bits of information that will help you in the long run.

More about Tables

In this section, I'll show you how to format a Word table. Table formatting doesn't matter for the purposes of your mail merge, because you don't print the table. The table is merely a storage tank for the names and addresses. However, tables are good for much more than just holding data for a mail merge; you can insert them into reports (like the ones you'll create tomorrow morning), use them to create multicolumn lists, and place them on Web pages. Therefore, it's useful to know a little bit about table formatting. So take a few minutes now to work through the following exercises that teach you how to make your table more presentable.

Adjusting the Column Widths

As you entered names and addresses into your table, you may have noticed that some of the longer entries wrapped to additional lines in the cell, making some rows taller than others.

Just for the sake of neatness, you may want to resize your columns to take into account that some columns hold more information than others. For example, you might want to make the FIRST and LAST columns narrower, and add some space to the ADDRESS1 and ADDRESS2 columns. As I've said, there's no reason to do this if you are using the table only for mail merge, except to practice for the time when you use a table in a document where appearance counts.

To resize a table column, drag the column's right border. For example, if you have two columns and you want to make the left one smaller, drag its right side (in other words, the line separating the two columns) to the left.

1. Make sure that nothing is selected in the table. (More on this shortly.)
2. Position the mouse pointer over the right edge of any cell in the leftmost column that needs resizing, so the mouse pointer turns into a vertical double line with arrows to the right and left of it.

3. Drag the line to make the column to its left larger or smaller (see Figure 4.32). A dotted line shows where the new right border of the column will be located.

4. Repeat for each column, working from left to right, until all columns in the table are the width you want.

The reason you should start with the leftmost column is that the column to the right of the one being resized also changes size, so that the overall table width remains the same. By working from left to right, you make each column the size you want and it stays that way.

TIP If you want to resize a single column and you don't want the columns to its right to change size, just press and hold Shift as you drag. The column size change will make the table as a whole larger or smaller, but no other columns will change width.

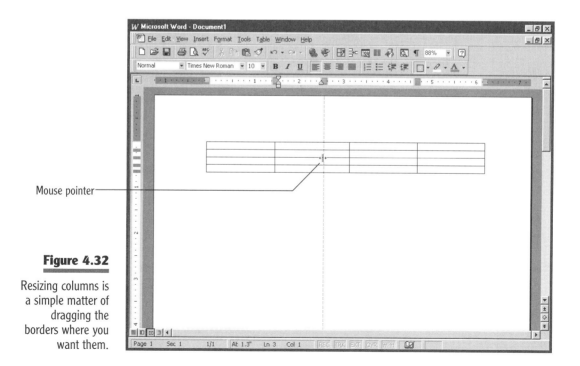

Mouse pointer

Figure 4.32

Resizing columns is a simple matter of dragging the borders where you want them.

In the preceding steps, I told you to make sure nothing was selected in the table before you began. If you drag a cell's right border when the cell (or any text in it) is selected, it changes only that cell. To change only one cell's width, follow these steps:

1. Point the mouse pointer at the bottom left corner of the cell, so that the pointer changes to an arrow pointing up and to the right, and then click to select the cell.
2. Drag either the right or left border of the cell to change its width.
3. Click away from the table to see the result.

Figure 4.33 shows a table with a wide variety of individual cell widths. As you can see, it's somewhat messy, and you will probably not use this feature very often.

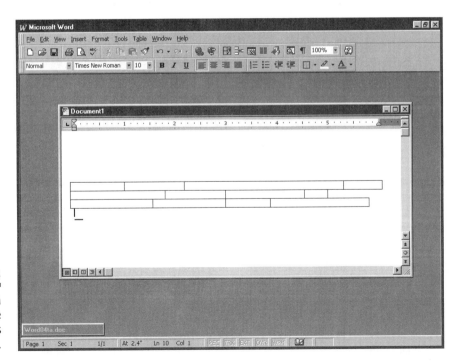

Figure 4.33

If you drag when a cell is selected, the dragging affects only that cell.

You can also resize a table cell (or row) vertically, the same way you changed the column widths:

1. Position the mouse pointer over the horizontal divider at the bottom of a row, so the mouse pointer changes to a double horizontal line with two arrows.
2. Drag the line up or down to resize the row above the line.

To change the height of a specific cell, select the cell first before dragging.

CAUTION When you resize the height of a cell or row, you set a fixed height for it, which means that the cell (or row) is no longer free to become larger or smaller as the text in it changes. This can cause major problems if you have more text in a cell than will display in the cell's fixed height; one or more lines of text may disappear entirely. (The text is still there, and will reappear when you increase the height of the cell, but it doesn't display or print until you do so.) For this reason, I almost never resize heights in a table.

Splitting and Merging Table Cells

This skill is not one you may use very often, but it certainly comes in handy when you need it! Word enables you to merge two or more cells into one, or split a cell into two separate cells. (Of course, this makes the table useless for mail merge, so you would never do this to a table you were using for that purpose.)

The most common reason to merge cells is to create a centered title over a group of cells. For example, in Figure 4.34, the top row has been merged into a single cell that titles the cells beneath it.

1. Select the cells that you want to merge.
2. Choose T<u>a</u>ble, <u>M</u>erge Cells.
3. Type the text you want in the new cell, and click on the Center button on the Formatting toolbar, if it needs to be centered.

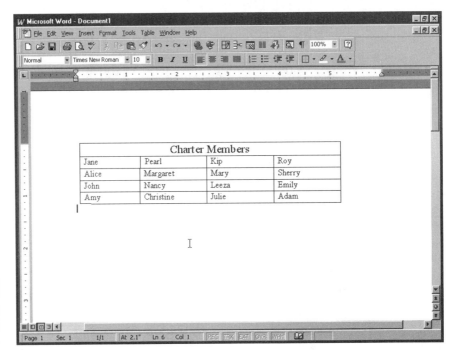

Figure 4.34

Merging cells can create a single cell for a title.

NOTE If you merge cells that already contain text, the contents of each of the merged cells will appear as a separate line in the new cell.

Splitting cells comes in handy primarily when you are using a table as a layout tool for creating a form. I won't get into this explicitly in this book, but I started an example in Figure 4.35, and it doesn't require any skills besides the ones you're learning in this book. In Figure 4.35, the cell containing the company name is a merged cell that merges two rows, and the Price and Qty cells are split from a single cell.

To split a cell:

1. Select the cell to split.
2. Choose Table, Split Cells. A Split Cells dialog box appears.

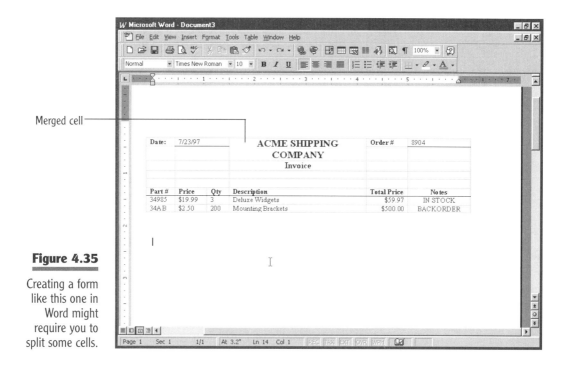

Figure 4.35

Creating a form like this one in Word might require you to split some cells.

3. In the Number of columns text box, enter the number of pieces into which you want the cell split horizontally.
4. In the Number of rows text box, enter the number of pieces into which you want the cell split vertically. (This is less common.)
5. Click on OK.

Formatting a Table

Formatting a table is basically the same as formatting regular text in a document. You can:

- Select text in a cell, or an entire cell, and change the font, font size, and font attributes (like bold, italic, and underline).
- Remove the border from a cell, just as you remove borders from paragraphs. By default, tables start out with borders on all sides of

each cell. If I need borders around certain cells, or only on certain sides, I usually remove all the borders from the entire table and then add them back selectively with the Border control on the Formatting toolbar.

- Change the text and background color for each cell in the table individually (by selecting a cell before you make the changes) or for the whole table (by selecting the whole table first).

You can also use Word's Table AutoFormat tool to apply any of several predesigned formats to your table.

1. Click anywhere in the table.
2. Choose Table, Table AutoFormat. The Table AutoFormat dialog box opens (see Figure 4.36).
3. Choose a format from the Formats list. You can preview each one in the pane to the right of the list.
4. In the Formats to apply area, deselect or select check boxes for various items until the sample looks the way you want it.
5. In the Apply special formats to area, do the same thing: select or deselect check boxes until the sample looks good.
6. Click on OK.

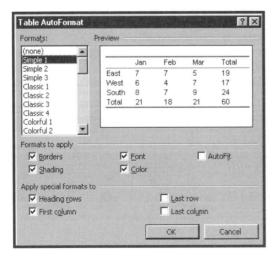

Figure 4.36

Table AutoFormat provides a shortcut to dressing up a table.

Sorting and Filtering Merge Data

Ready to get really techie? When doing a mail merge, you can sort the output by a certain field, and you can narrow down the records you want included. Why might you want to do this? Here are some ideas:

- Sort labels and envelopes by ZIP code to take advantage of the Postal Service's cut rates.
- Mail merge in batches—first just print letters for the people whose last names begin with A through M, and print the others later.
- Add a field for LAST CONTACT to your data, and keep track of the last time you wrote to each person. Then you can send a letter only to people you have not contacted in the last six months, for example.

Sorting Your Data

There are two ways to sort data. One is to sort the Word table that contains it beforehand.

1. Open the document containing the Word table that you're using as your data source.
2. Select the column by what you want to sort. For example, if you want the data sorted by last name, select the column containing last names.
3. Choose T<u>a</u>ble, <u>S</u>ort. The Sort dialog box opens, as shown in Figure 4.37, with the column you chose in the first Sort by box.

TIP You can use the T<u>a</u>ble, <u>S</u>ort command to sort regular paragraphs in a document by the first letter; the paragraphs don't have to be in a table.

4. Choose <u>A</u>scending or <u>D</u>escending. Ascending is A to Z; descending is Z to A.
5. Make sure the Header row option button is selected, because your column has a field name at the top that you do not want sorted.

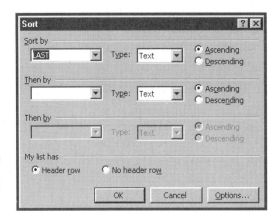

Figure 4.37

You can sort data in a table with the Sort dialog box.

6. If you want to sort by any other columns (for example, to sort by first name if the last names are the same), enter information for the secondary sort in the Then by section.

7. Click on OK. Word sorts the table for you.

In Excel, when you select a single column to sort, only that column gets sorted; surrounding columns do not move. Names and addresses can be scrambled. This is not a problem in Word, however; even though you selected only one column in Step 2, Word keeps all rows together as it sorts.

The other way to sort data is to do it while merging.

1. Start a normal merge with Tools, Mail Merge, and choose your merge type and data source.

2. If it's not still open, reopen the Mail Merge Helper dialog box by clicking on the Mail Merge Helper button on the Mail Merge toolbar.

3. Click on the Query Options button. The Query Options dialog box opens.

4. Click on the Sort Records tab.

5. Open the Sort by drop-down list and choose the field that you want to sort by (see Figure 4.38).
6. Choose Ascending or Descending.
7. If you want to sort by additional fields, select them in the Then by section.
8. Click on OK.
9. Continue the merge normally.

Filtering Records with a Query

A query is like a filter into which you pour your records. The ones you want are trapped by the filter and retained; the others fall through and are discarded. (No, they aren't permanently discarded; they're just not used in the particular mail merge you're doing.) To try a simple query that chooses only records that have a last name that begins with A through L, perform the following steps:

1. Start a normal merge with Tools, Mail Merge, and choose your merge type and data source.
2. If it's not still open, reopen the Mail Merge Helper dialog box by clicking on the Mail Merge Helper button on the Mail Merge toolbar.

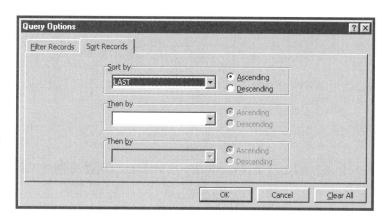

Figure 4.38

You can choose to sort as a query option during the merge.

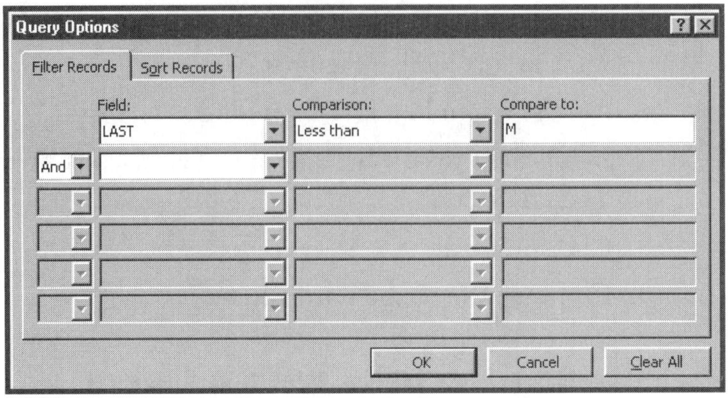

Figure 4.39

This query will find all records where the last name begins with A through L.

3. Click on the Query Options button. The Query Options dialog box opens.
4. Click on the Filter Records tab, if it is not already on top.
5. Open the first Field drop-down list and choose the field containing the criterion by which to filter (for example, LAST).
6. Open the first Comparison drop-down list and choose the comparison operator you want. For example, I chose Less than because I wanted last names with first letters from A to L—that is, less than M.
7. In the first Compare to box, type the value to compare to. For example, I typed M. Figure 4.39 shows my settings for this filter.
8. If you want to set up additional criteria, enter them on subsequent lines. If only one criterion needs to be met, change the And drop-down value to Or.
9. Click on OK.
10. Continue the merge normally.

Filtering Records by Record Number

Another way to filter records is by their place in the data source list. Word considers the first record in the table (or other data source) to be record 1, the next one record 2, and so on. To use only the first ten records, for example, you would do this:

1. Set up the merge normally, up to the point where you are ready to merge.
2. If the Mail Merge Helper dialog box is open, click on the Merge button to open the Merge dialog box. If it isn't, open the Merge dialog box directly from the Mail Merge toolbar by clicking on the Mail Merge button (the one with an ellipsis).
3. In the Merge dialog box (see Figure 4.40), in the Records to be merged section, click on the option button next to From and enter the starting record number in the text box (for example, 1).
4. In the To text box, enter the ending record number (for example, 10).
5. Click on Merge to finish the merge.

Well, if you made it this far this evening, it is probably late at night! So get some well-deserved sleep, and I'll see you tomorrow morning, when you'll plunge into long documents and reports.

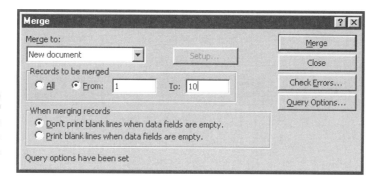

Figure 4.40

Choose a range of records (rows) in the Merge dialog box.

SUNDAY MORNING
Reports and Long Documents

- Creating an outline
- Using styles
- Creating running headers and footers
- Making a table of contents
- Generating an index

It always feels a bit intimidating to sit down and start writing a long document like a book or a major report for a client. Knowing that the final product will be dozens, even hundreds of pages changes the way you approach a writing project. And rightly so—long documents have their own special challenges. Luckily, Word provides all the right tools to handle them.

What Makes Longer Documents Different?

All documents are basically the same, despite their length. There is no magic formula that says a document with a certain number of words is considered a "long document" and subject to special rules. You don't have to do anything special to create a long document if you don't want to.

You've heard the old saying, "A long journey begins with a single step." Well, taking a single step is one way to start a long document, whether it's the next great American novel or the technical specifications for a new invention. Just type. If it turns out to be longer than you expected, that's fine.

That's one philosophy—here's another: If a document is longer than a few pages (ten, for example) in its final form, you may encounter additional problems, such as:

- The organizational structure may not make sense.
- You may forget to write about some topics you intended to cover.

- Readers may not have a way to find specific topics easily.
- The pages of hard-copy printouts may get out of order, confusing the reader.
- The formatting of headings and other elements may be inconsistent.

Word provides tools that guard against each of these dangers. You can use these tools with a document of any length, but most people don't bother with them unless the document is long enough to make the danger likely. For example, most people don't put page numbers on a two-page document because it's unlikely anyone will be confused as to their order. Similarly, most people don't put a table of contents (TOC) in a report shorter than 10 pages because readers could flip through the report almost as quickly as they could read a page number on a TOC and turn to that page.

In this session, you'll find out about Word's "long document anti-confusion safeguarding tools" (no, that's not Microsoft's term for them, it's mine) and learn when to use them.

NOTE If you're lucky, you already need a long document, and you can begin to create it as you work through this session. If not, you may want to insert dummy text under various headings, creating a long document for the purpose of practice only. You can then save your work and replace the dummy text with real text when you need to create a real report.

Creating an Outline

How many times have you started writing something with one idea in mind, only to finish with a product completely different from your expectations? This happens to me frequently. If you're writing a creative piece about your favorite cheese, and you end up with an ode to garlic chicken pizza, your essay has evolved and perhaps improved. But if you're presenting a report on cheese sales in Wisconsin over the past year, your

ideas should flow in an organized manner, with little deviation from the main theme.

In a long document, the danger of "theme shift" becomes greater as the document grows longer. In your zeal to write the information on page 1, you probably aren't thinking about page 100. You just write, and one idea leads to another. By the time you reach page 100, your idea may have morphed into something you didn't intend.

An outline can help keep you on track. Most professional writers start every long document with an outline. I began this book with an outline, as I have with almost all my other publications. An outline lists the topics you want to cover, in the order you want to address them. When the outline is complete, you can go back through and fill in the expository text under each heading, and presto, you have a final product. For example, Figure 5.1 shows part of the outline for this book.

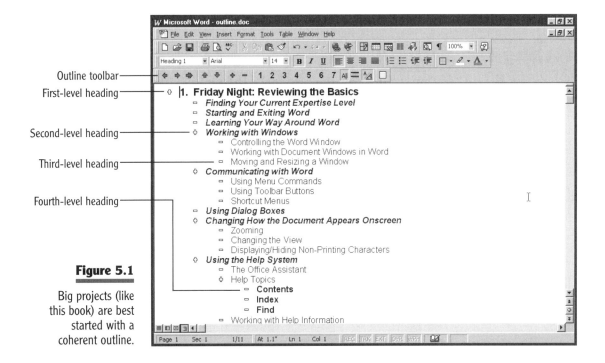

Figure 5.1

Big projects (like this book) are best started with a coherent outline.

Compare the outline in Figure 5.1 with the table of contents at the beginning of this book. Similar, eh? An outline shows the headings you plan to use in the document. Or, if your document won't have headings, the outline shows the major topics you plan to cover.

TIP If your document is more than a few pages, I strongly encourage you to break it up with headings. They make the document much easier to follow.

In a Word outline, you can tell the level of each heading by the amount of indentation and the size and font of the typeface. For example, in Figure 5.1, first-level headings (chapter titles) are aligned with the left margin and are formatted in 14-point Arial bold. Second-level headings (major headings within a chapter) are indented slightly and formatted in Arial 12-point bold italic. Third and fourth level headings are indented even more and formatted with different attributes. Figure 5.1 shows the screen in Outline view; you'll do all your outlining work in this view.

Starting the Outline

To start an outline, follow these steps. If you don't have a document you need to create, use the table of contents from this book to create your outline.

1. Start a new document based on the Blank Document template.
2. Switch to Outline view (<u>V</u>iew, <u>O</u>utline). The Outline toolbar appears.
3. Type the first-level heading. For example, if your document is organized by chapters, type the first chapter title. Notice that in the Style box, the words "Heading 1" appear.
4. Press Enter, and type another heading for the unit of equal value to the one you just typed. If you're following along with this example, type the other chapter titles. Go ahead and enter all the first-level headings, as shown in Figure 5.2.

SUNDAY MORNING Reports and Long Documents

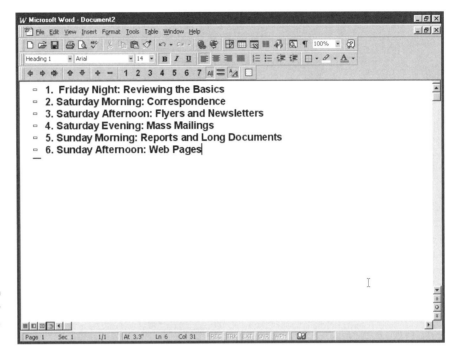

Figure 5.2

Start the outline by typing the first-level headings.

5. Position the insertion point at the end of a first-level heading line, and press Enter, starting a new line.

6. Press Tab. Notice the words "Heading 2" in the Style box.

TIP In Outline view, Tab does not function as it normally does in other views. Instead, it changes the outline level of the line that contains the insertion point. The insertion point can be anywhere in the line; it doesn't have to be at the beginning. To subordinate a line (to "demote" it), press Tab. To elevate the line to a higher level (to "promote" it), press Shift+Tab.

7. Type the headings that belong under the first-level heading, pressing Enter to separate them.

8. When you finish, go back to Step 5 and reposition the insertion

point for another of the first-level headings and repeat Steps 6 and 7 until all the first-level headings have second-level headings beneath them, as shown in Figure 5.3.

9. Next, add the third-level headings by adding lines under second-level ones. Don't forget to press Tab to indent the new lines and change the style box entry to "Heading 3."

10. Add more levels as needed, until your outline is complete. Word can handle up to seven levels. When you finish, you should have a multilevel outline you can be proud of, like the one in Figure 5.4.

NOTE A plus sign next to a heading on an outline means there are subordinate headings ("subheads") beneath it. A minus sign means there are none. This is not so important when all levels are visible (like now), but it is handy when you collapse the outline to show only certain heading levels, as you'll learn to do later in this session.

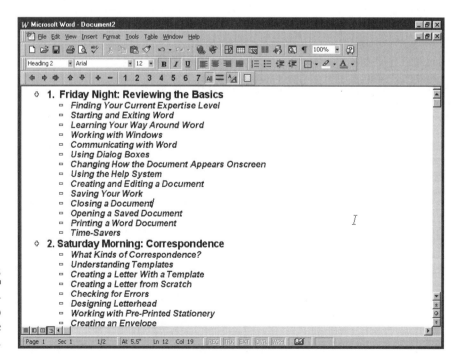

Figure 5.3

Add the second-level headings to the outline (Heading 2).

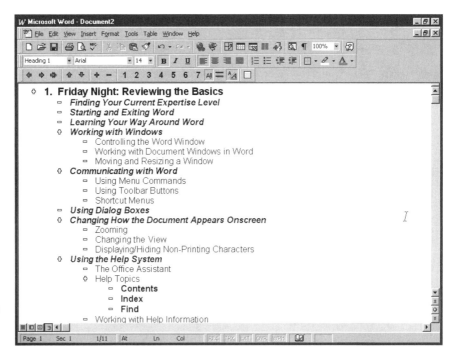

Figure 5.4

The finished outline with four levels.

A Look at the Outlining Toolbar

The Outlining toolbar appears when you enter Outline view; it disappears when you leave Outline view. Its buttons provide shortcuts to change the outline level, location, and appearance of a line. In the following sections, you'll learn how to do each of these things using the buttons available (see Table 5.1).

Promoting and Demoting Lines

Now that you have a rough outline, you may decide some of the lines are improperly indented (the wrong outline level). There are several ways to correct them.

Table 5.1 The Outlining Toolbar

Button	Name	Purpose
⇦	Promote	Promotes the current line one outline level.
⇨	Demote	Demotes the current line one outline level.
⇒	Demote to Body Text	Demotes the current line from a heading to body text. This will be useful later, when you begin typing body text under the headings.
⇧	Move Up	Moves the current line up one line.
⇩	Move Down	Moves the current line down one line.
✚	Expand	Displays invisible subheads if the insertion point is on a heading line that contains them.
▬	Collapse	Hides visible subheads if the insertion point is on a heading line that contains them.
1	Show Heading 1	Hides all outline levels lower than Heading 1.
2	Show Heading 2	Hides all outline levels lower than Heading 2. (The 3 through 7 buttons function equally on their respective outline levels.)
All	Show All Headings	Shows all outline levels, including body text.

Table 5.1 The Outlining Toolbar (continued)

Button	Name	Purpose
	Show First Line Only	Hides all but the first line of multiline paragraphs. Does not affect which outline levels appear.
	Show Formatting	Toggles the display of different fonts and sizes for different outline levels on or off.
	Master Document View	Toggles the display between Master Document view and Outline view (you'll learn about master documents in the Time-Savers section at the end of this session).

To outdent a line so it is a higher outline level (promoted), place the insertion point anywhere in the line and then do one of the following:

- Click on the Promote button on the Outline toolbar.
- Press Shift+Tab.
- Open the Style drop-down list on the Formatting toolbar and choose a higher heading level. For example, if the line is currently Heading 2, choose Heading 1.

To indent a line so it is a lower outline level (demoted), place the insertion point anywhere in the line and then do one of the following:

- Click on the Demote button on the Outline toolbar.
- Press Tab.
- Open the Style drop-down list on the Formatting toolbar and choose a lower heading level. For example, if the line is currently Heading 2, choose Heading 3.

Moving Outline Lines

You saw in Table 5.1 that the Outlining toolbar provides buttons (Move Up and Move Down) for moving, and you are free to use them if you like:

1. To move a single line, click anywhere in the line, or click on the plus sign next to the line to select all the subordinate lines as well.
2. To move the line (and any subordinate lines), click as needed on the Move Up or Move Down button on the Outlining toolbar.

However, I seldom use these buttons because there is an easier moving method: drag-and-drop. In this example, I moved the heading "Using the Help System," and everything under it, to a new spot following the subheads beneath "Working with Windows." Follow these steps to move part of the outline:

1. Position the mouse pointer over the plus sign (or minus sign) next to the line you want to move, so the mouse pointer turns into a four-headed arrow.
2. Drag the selection to the new location. A horizontal line shows where it will go, as shown in Figure 5.5.
3. Release the mouse button to drop the selection into its new location. All subordinate lines move with it.

TIP Although you will rarely need to do so, you can also move an individual line with drag-and-drop. Just select the line, and only that line, first. Then drag the selection rather than the plus sign to the new location.

To avoid selecting the subordinate lines, position the mouse pointer to the left of the plus sign, so the pointer turns into a right-pointing arrow. Then click. This selects the individual line only.

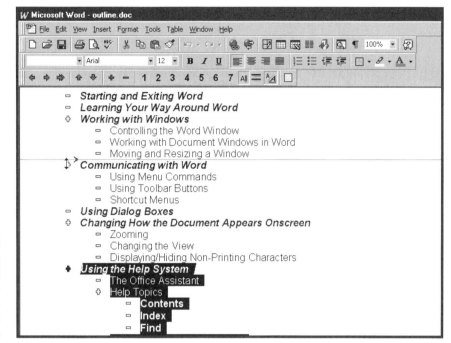

Figure 5.5

Drag the plus sign to move all subordinate entries under the line as well as the line itself.

Changing the Visibility of Outline Levels

When you're looking at the innards of a chapter three outline levels deep, it's easy to lose track of the big picture, like not seeing the forest for the trees. Word enables you to "collapse" the more minor outline levels so you can view the chapter titles and/or the major headings in a list.

Work through the following steps to see how to expand and collapse your outline.

1. Click on the 1 button on the Outlining toolbar. The outline collapses so only the first-level headings (Heading 1 style) are visible, as shown in Figure 5.6.
2. Click on the 2 button. The outline expands so you can see the second-level headings (Heading 2 style), as shown in Figure 5.7.

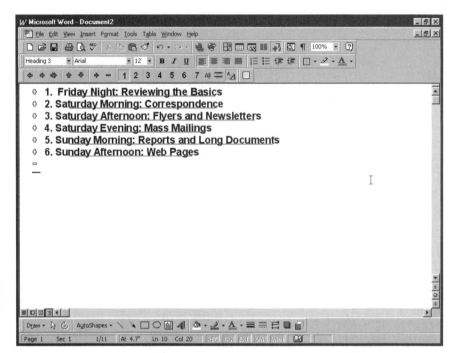

Figure 5.6

Here is the outline after clicking on the 1 button.

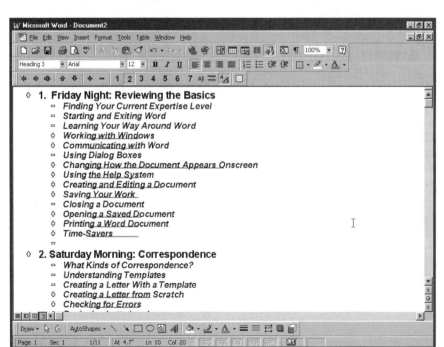

Figure 5.7

Here's the outline after clicking on the 2 button.

NOTE The plus sign means there are levels beneath a heading, while the minus sign indicates no subordinate headings.

3. Click on the 3, 4, and 5 buttons, respectively, and notice how the display changes. When you come to the number beyond which you have no outline levels, the display no longer changes. For example, if you have only three outline levels, buttons 4 and 5 won't respond.
4. Click on the 1 button to change back to first-level headings only.
5. Click anywhere in one of the heading lines to select the line.
6. Click on the Expand button on the Outlining toolbar. The outline expands one level, but only under the selected heading, as shown in Figure 5.8.
7. Click anywhere in one of the subordinate heading lines that just appeared, and click on the Expand button again.

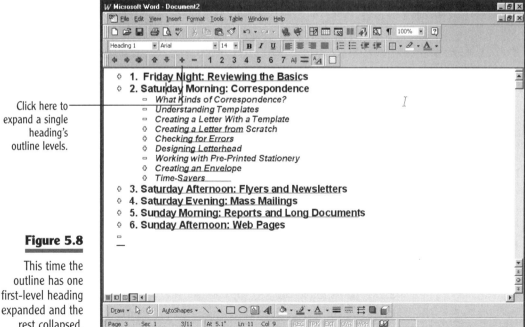

Click here to expand a single heading's outline levels.

Figure 5.8

This time the outline has one first-level heading expanded and the rest collapsed.

8. Now click on the Collapse button twice to collapse the outline two levels, back to first-level only.
9. Click on the All button on the Outlining toolbar to redisplay all levels.

Think you've got it now? If not, go through the steps again just to make sure.

Writing the Actual Document

Now that you have your headings, it's time to write the text. You may want to write only the first few pages right now (or type nonsense text) and save the serious writing for another time, after this weekend. Here's how to begin:

1. Switch back to Normal view.
2. Scroll up to the top of the document.
3. Position your insertion point at the end of a heading under which you need to type body text, and press Enter.
4. Type the text.
5. Repeat Steps 3 and 4 as needed.

Even though you have outlined the entire work in a single Word file, you may decide to split it into several files. For example, in writing this book, I split each chapter into a separate file. To do this, copy into a blank document the portion of the outline corresponding to each chapter, and save each file. For example, to create a separate file for Chapter 1:

1. On the outline, select all the lines that pertain to Chapter 1.
2. Click on the Copy button on the Standard toolbar.
3. Click on the New button on the Standard toolbar to start a new document.
4. Click on the Paste button on the Standard toolbar.
5. Click on the Save button on the Standard toolbar, and save the file under the name "Chapter 1."

6. Do the same thing for each of the other chapters, until you have separate chapter files.

7. Save your outline and close it. You may need to refer to an outline of the entire book or report later.

Styles Offer Consistency

Ever wonder how Word identifies headings in Outline view? It's all due to *styles*. Recall that you change the outline level of a line by opening the Style drop-down list on the Formatting toolbar and choose a different style. But what is a style, anyway?

A style is a predefined set of formatting you can apply in a single step to a paragraph or individual characters. For example, suppose you want to use 12-point Arial type for each paragraph and indent the first line half an inch. Set up a style with these attributes and call it "Body Text," and apply the style to all your paragraphs. This becomes more and more useful the longer the document gets. Styles played an essential part in producing this book, ensuring that the headings and body text look exactly the same on every page.

Styles are particularly helpful when making changes. For example, suppose you find that your report is too long. You could change every paragraph to 10-point type individually, but a much easier way would be to change the definition of Body Text to 10-point type. All the paragraphs formatted with the Body Text style would change automatically.

Where Do Styles Come From?

Styles are stored with a template. To see which styles are available, open the Style drop-down list on the Formatting toolbar. For example, the Blank Document template gives you the following styles:

Normal   Heading 2
Default Paragraph Font   Heading 3
Heading 1

If you start a document based on one of the other templates, you will have different styles at your disposal. For example, the Contemporary Letter template has dozens of styles, including Slogan, Attention, Return Address, and Company Name.

Assigning a Style to a Paragraph

To assign a style, follow these steps:

1. Position the insertion point anywhere in the paragraph, or select multiple paragraphs to apply it to many.
2. Open the Style drop-down list on the Formatting toolbar and choose the style you want to assign.

If your style contains character formatting as well as paragraph formatting (for example, font attributes as well as paragraph spacing or indents), you must either select the entire paragraph or place the insertion point in the paragraph in Step 1. If you select some (but not all) of the paragraph, the character attributes of the style will apply only to the selected text.

In the Time-Savers at the end of this session, you will learn how to assign shortcut keys to styles. If a style has a shortcut key assigned, you can press the key combination instead of performing Step 2 in the preceding steps.

Setting Up the Styles You Want

If you don't like the styles available in your document's template, you have a variety of options:

- Modify an existing style. This is easy, but the original style will no longer be available.
- Create a new style based on an existing one. This is slightly harder, but it preserves the original style.
- Borrow styles from other templates for use in your document.

Modifying a Style

For this exercise, you can use the outline file you've worked with in this chapter, or if you split your project into multiple files, you can use any of them (I worked with my Chapter 1 file).

There are two ways to modify a style: the easy way and the more complicated, yet powerful way. First, the easy way:

1. Select a Heading 2 line (to select the line, move the mouse pointer to the left of the line so the pointer turns into a right-pointing arrow, and then click), as shown in Figure 5.9.

2. Open the Font drop-down list on the Formatting toolbar and choose Times New Roman.

3. Open the Size drop-down list on the Formatting toolbar and choose 14.

4. Click once in the Style box on the Formatting toolbar so the words "Heading 2" are highlighted.

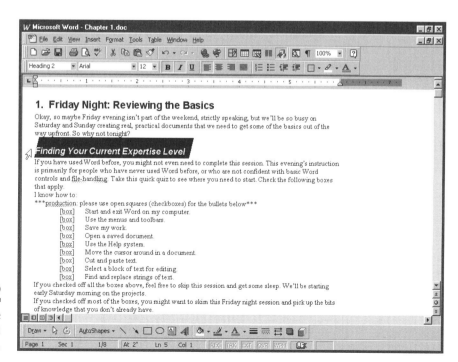

Figure 5.9

Select an example of the style you want to modify.

CAUTION In Step 4, if you click twice, an insertion point will appear in the box. If this happens, simply drag across the words Heading 2 to select (highlight) them.

5. Press Enter. The Modify Style dialog box appears (see Figure 5.10).
6. Click on OK. The style's definition changes to reflect your modifications. You can scroll through the document and verify that every instance of the style has changed.

You can make many formatting changes to a style this way. For example, you can add a border to the paragraph, set the line spacing, the tabs, and the indents—any formatting you can do to a single paragraph can be attached to a style.

There is another way to modify a style, but it's more complicated, albeit advantageous, because you can set up styles before applying them in your document.

1. (Optional) Select a line that uses the font you want to change.
2. Choose F*o*rmat, *S*tyle. The Style dialog box appears (see Figure 5.11). If you chose a style in Step 1, it appears on the list.
3. If the style you want to change is not selected, click on it. If the style you want to change does not appear at all, open the *L*ist drop-down list and choose All Styles to make it visible.
4. Read the description of the current style in the Description area and decide what you want to change.

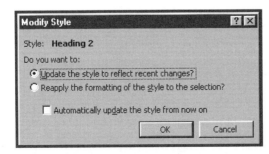

Figure 5.10

Word verifies that you really want to change the style.

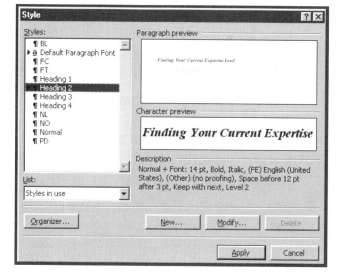

Figure 5.11

You can make changes to any style from the Style dialog box.

5. Click on the Modify button. The Modify Style dialog box appears, as shown in Figure 5.12.

6. Change any of the style's settings shown in Figure 5.12:

    ○ **Name.** Change the style name if needed. For example, you might change Heading 1 to Chapter Title.

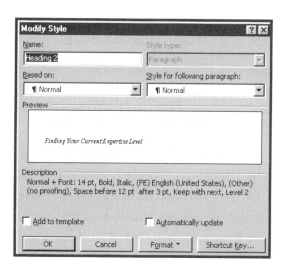

Figure 5.12

Specify the changes to make to the style here.

- **Based on.** Notice in the description that each style starts out based on another style and is modified. In Figure 5.12, you see that Heading 2 is based on the Normal style. To change the basis style, choose a different one.
- **Style for following paragraph.** When you press Enter at the end of a paragraph, the style of the following paragraph is determined by the setting. For example, after a heading, you probably want a body paragraph, so you would choose the style you're using for body paragraphs (like Normal).
- **Add to template.** If the style is not currently part of the template attached to the document, you can add it by clicking on this check box so all future documents based on the template will have access to it.
- **Automatically update.** In the preceding steps, when you changed a style by example, Word showed you a confirmation box asking whether you wanted to modify the style. If you mark this check box, Word will bypass that question in the future (I don't recommend that you do this, however; see the following Caution).

The automatic update feature may seem like a good idea because it saves time. But sometimes you may need to reapply the original style to a paragraph.

For example, suppose you have a paragraph formatted with Heading 2 style, and as you edit, you change it to use the Courier font, just to see what it looks like. But then you decide it's wrong, and you want to go back to the original style definition.

If you do not have Automatically update checked, you can simply click in the Style box and press Enter, and when asked whether you want to update or revert, choose Revert. But if Automatically update is on, you won't be asked what you want to do, and the style's definition will change to the Courier font. Then you'll have to go into the Modify Style dialog box and change the font back the more time-consuming way.

7. Click on the Format button and choose the formatting type you want to change from the pop-up list. A dialog box for that formatting type appears.

8. Make your changes and click on OK to return to the Modify Style dialog box. You have already seen these dialog boxes in earlier sessions this weekend, so you should have no trouble working with them.

9. Click on OK to close the Modify Style dialog box.

10. Click on Apply to apply the style change and close the Style dialog box.

One of my favorite changes is altering the Normal style so there is an extra line of space after each paragraph (you did this yesterday morning to your letter text). In Step 7, choose Paragraph, and set the After setting to 12 point (or the number of points to which your font size is currently set). Because most other styles are based on Normal, this change sets blank space after them.

If you change the Normal style, you may get more changes than you bargained for, because almost all the other styles are based on Normal. For example, suppose Normal uses the Arial font, and Heading 4's definition is Normal+16 point+bold. Heading 4 therefore uses the Arial font because a font change was not specified in the definition. If you change the Normal font to Courier, Heading 4's font will change too. For this reason, some people don't like to use Normal for their body text. Instead, they create a new font called BodyText (or some other similar name) and use it for their paragraphs. You'll learn to create a new style in the following section.

Creating a New Style

When you create a new style, you leave the existing styles intact. You can create a new style if all the existing styles in the document are used or there is no existing style similar to what you want. For example, you might create a Body Text style for the body text or a new style for bulleted list items.

NOTE To delete any styles you aren't going to use, see "Deleting Unneeded Styles from the Document" later in this session. However, deleting unused styles serves no practical purpose because their presence doesn't alter the document in any way.

There are also two methods for creating new styles: an easy one and a more difficult, yet powerful one. First, try out a new style for bulleted list items using the easy method.

1. In your document, type the first paragraph you want to make a bulleted list. Or, if the paragraph is already typed, select it.
2. Apply the closest style you have in your style list. Your new style will be based on it. For most text excluding headings, Normal will probably be the closest.
3. Click on the Bullets button on the Formatting toolbar.
4. Make any additional changes to the paragraph text. For example, you could assign a different bullet character with Format, Bullets and Numbering, or you could change the text's indentation by dragging the tabs and indent markers on the Ruler.
5. Click in the Style box on the Formatting toolbar and select the current style name.
6. Type the new style name—for example, Bullet List (see Figure 5.13).
7. Press Enter. The new style is created.

You can also use the same Style dialog box you saw back in Figure 5.11 to create new styles. The advantage of this method is that you can see at a glance what styles already exist and create several without closing the dialog box.

1. Choose Format, Style. The Style dialog box opens (see Figure 5.11).
2. Click on the New button. The New Style dialog box appears (see Figure 5.14).
3. Type a name in the Name field. Try to be as descriptive, yet brief, as possible.

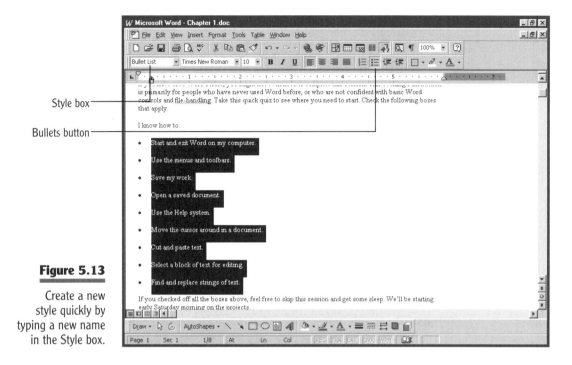

Figure 5.13

Create a new style quickly by typing a new name in the Style box.

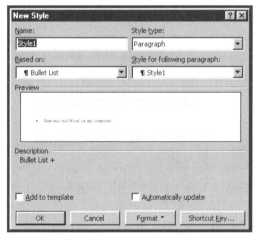

Figure 5.14

Create a new style here.

4. Open the Based on drop-down list and choose an existing style upon which to base the new one (Normal is good if you don't have another in mind).

5. In the Style type drop-down list, choose Paragraph.
6. In the Style for following paragraph drop-down list, choose the style that will usually follow this style. For example, if the new style is a heading, a body paragraph will usually follow it. If the new style is for body text, more body text will usually follow it.
7. (Optional) If you want the style added to the template (and not just to this document), click on the Add to template check box.
8. Click on the Format button and choose a type of formatting for the style.

Character and Paragraph Styles

In Step 5 of the style-creation process, you chose between character and paragraph style types. What's the difference? Paragraph styles affect entire paragraphs. In other words, if you position your insertion point anywhere in a paragraph and apply a style, the entire paragraph will receive it. In contrast, character styles affect only selected text. You must select text first and then apply a character style to it. If you apply a character style when the insertion point is resting in a paragraph, the style will not be applied to the surrounding text. Paragraph styles are the more commonly used type.

This may confuse you because paragraph styles can apply character formatting. In addition to the paragraph formatting, such as line spacing, a paragraph style can apply a certain font and font size to the paragraph, too. But don't let this mislead you—the style is still a paragraph style, and it still applies to the entire paragraph.

The only exception is if you select some (but not all) of the text in a paragraph before you apply a paragraph style. In this case, the paragraph receives all the paragraph attributes in the style, but only the selected text receives the character formatting in the style.

9. Use the dialog box that appears to set the style's formatting, and click on OK to return to the New Style dialog box.
10. Repeat Steps 8 and 9 as needed until the style is completely set up.
11. Click on OK to return to the Styles dialog box.
12. Click on Apply to apply the style to the currently selected paragraph in your document, or click on Close to close the dialog box without immediately applying the new style.

Borrowing Styles from Other Templates

Suppose you start a document based on the Blank Document (Normal) template, but later you think to yourself "golly, there were some fabulous styles in the Elegant Letter template that I could sure use in this report." Easy enough—just attach the Elegant Letter template to your document. When you do so, all its styles become available to you.

To attach a different template to use its styles, follow these steps:

1. Choose Tools, Templates and Add-Ins. The Templates and Add-Ins dialog box appears (see Figure 5.15).
2. Click on the Attach button. The Attach Template dialog box opens.
3. Choose the template to attach, and click on Open. The new template's name appears in the Document template box.

Figure 5.15

Use this dialog box to attach a different template.

NOTE Select the Automatically update document styles check box if you want any paragraphs in the document to appear with the new template's definition of a style formatted with the same name. For example, if the document currently has a Bullet List style and the template you are attaching also has one by the same name, marking this check box will cause everything already in your document with the Bullet List style to change its formatting to match that of the Bullet List style in the incoming template.

4. Click on OK.
5. Now open the Styles drop-down list on the Formatting toolbar. Notice that all the new template's styles are available to you.

Deleting Unneeded Styles from the Document

You do not need to delete styles to have a good-looking document; unused styles sit harmlessly out of the way. However, you may want to trim your style list to only the styles you actually use to save yourself scrolling through a long list of styles each time to find the one you want to apply.

When you delete styles from your document, you are merely making them unavailable in this particular document. You are not deleting them from the template. To delete styles from the template, see the section that follows this one.

To delete styles from the document, follow these steps:

1. Choose Format, Style. The Style dialog box appears (see Figure 5.16).
2. Click on the style you want to delete from the Styles list.
3. Click on the Delete button. A dialog box appears asking if you want to delete the style.
4. Click on Yes. The style disappears from the list.
5. Delete more styles if you want, or click on Close to return to your document.

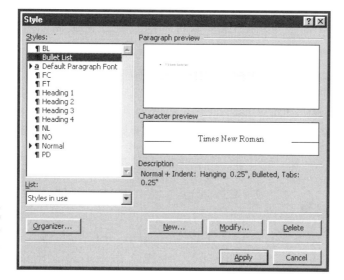

Figure 5.16

You can not only add but also delete styles from here.

Changing Which Styles Are Stored with a Template

When you were creating and modifying styles, there was an Add to template check box, remember? If you mark that check box for any new or modified style, Word will add that style to whatever template is in use on the document. Deleting styles from the template is just a bit more involved.

1. Close the document you're working on (saving if necessary), and any other document that uses the template. You won't be able to modify the template if an open document is using it.
2. Open the template, as you learned to do Saturday Morning.
3. Choose Format, Style and delete the unneeded styles just as you learned in the preceding steps. (You can also add or modify styles if you want.)
4. Close the Style dialog box and save your work.
5. Close the template and reopen your document.

NOTE If you modify a style directly in the template and then reopen the document that uses it, the style changes should be reflected in any paragraphs that use that style. If they are not, you can use a work-around to force it. Just attach a different style sheet to the document (for example, Normal) and make sure the Update styles in document check box is marked. Then reattach the style sheet you want, and make sure the check box is once again marked. This should force all styles in the document to update.

Take a Break

Are your pets telling you it's time to go for a walk? Is your mate giving you dirty "take out the trash" looks? Take a moment and go tend to your daily reality, and then stop back here when all your normal plates are spinning again.

Creating Running Headers and Footers

Look up at the top of the page you're reading right now. Notice the page number? Notice the text that identifies what book you're reading and what session you're in? This is a running header. If this information was at the bottom of the pages, you would see a running footer instead. They're standard practice in almost all books because readers want and need them. Could you imagine reading a book with no page numbers and if you had no clue about the chapter or book name? It would be easy to forget what you were reading, and nearly impossible to refer a friend to a certain passage on a certain page.

You can use running headers and footers in your own documents for a more professional and polished look; they are definitely a nice touch for business reports and presentations. They're not difficult to set up, and your readers will appreciate them.

TIP There is a separate page number feature (Insert, Page Numbers) in Word that inserts a page number in the header or footer. If page numbers are all you need, you can use this as a shortcut instead of diving into the header or footer itself. However, since you're here to learn today, and not to cut corners, continue reading to learn how headers and footers work.

Headers and footers don't show up in Normal view. You can see them in Page Layout view, but they appear gray and you can't edit them; they're there for informational purposes only, so you can gauge how close to them your regular text is running.

Opening the Header and Footer for Editing

To start using the header and footer area, select View, Header and Footer. When you do so, the view automatically changes to Page Layout, and the header and footer areas become editable. The header appears first, as shown in Figure 5.17, but you can switch to the footer by clicking on the Switch Between Header and Footer button on the Header and Footer toolbar.

Table 5.2 shows all the buttons on the Header and Footer toolbar. I'll explain most of them in more detail as you go along.

Creating a Simple Header or Footer

To create a header or footer, just type in the Header or Footer box! It's very simple. Each header and footer box has three predefined positions:

- **Left.** Left-aligned at the left margin.
- **Center.** Centered on a tab stop in the middle of the line.
- **Right.** Right-aligned at a tab stop the right margin.

When you start typing in a header or footer, you start out at the left position. Press Tab to move to the center or right position.

Table 5.2 Header and Footer Toolbar Buttons

Button	Name	Purpose
Insert AutoText ▼	Insert AutoText	Opens a drop-down list of AutoText phrases to insert.
	Insert Page Number	Inserts a page numbering code.
	Insert Number of Pages	Inserts a code for the number of pages in the document.
	Format Page Number	Opens the Format Page Number dialog box.
	Insert Date	Inserts a date code.
	Insert Time	Inserts a time code.
	Page Setup	Opens the Page Setup dialog box.
	Show/Hide Document Text	Toggles the document text display on or off.
	Same as Previous	Makes one section's header and footer the same as the preceding section's. (Available only in multi-section documents.)
	Switch Between Header and Footer	Toggles the display between the header and footer on the page.

SUNDAY MORNING Reports and Long Documents 305

TABLE 5.2 HEADER AND FOOTER TOOLBAR BUTTONS (CONTINUED)

Button	Name	Purpose
	Show Previous	In a document with more than one header or footer, shows the previous header or footer.
	Show Next	In a document with more than one header or footer, shows the next header or footer.
Close	Close Header and Footer	Returns you to regular document viewing and editing.

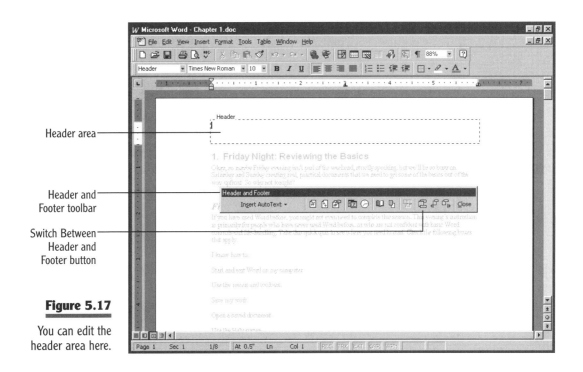

Figure 5.17

You can edit the header area here.

Header area

Header and Footer toolbar

Switch Between Header and Footer button

Ready to try it out? Follow these steps to create a simple header and footer in your document:

1. If you have not done it already, choose View, Header and Footer to make the header and footer areas accessible.
2. Type your company's name (or make one up, like Acme Corporation, if you don't have one).
3. Press Tab to move to the center position, and then press Tab again to move to the right position.
4. Type **Prepared by** and then **your own name** (see Figure 5.18).
5. On the Header and Footer toolbar, click on the Switch Between Header and Footer button. The footer appears.
6. Press Tab to move to the center position.
7. Click on the Insert Page Number button on the Header and Footer toolbar. This inserts a code that automatically prints the correct page number on every page.

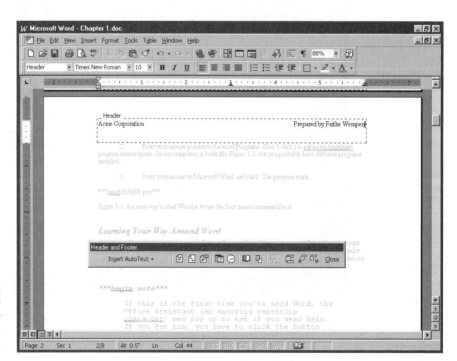

Figure 5.18

This simple header uses plain text with no special codes.

8. Click on Close to exit from header and footer editing.
9. Click on the Print Preview button on the Standard toolbar and examine the header and footer on each page. Looks pretty good, eh?

Inserting Codes in a Header or Footer

In the preceding steps, you used a Page Number code to place the correct page number on each page. But there are lots more codes you can use; you saw some of them in Table 5.2, when I introduced you to the Header and Footer toolbar buttons. You can insert any of these by clicking on the appropriate button when editing the header or footer:

 Page number. Places a different, appropriate page number on each page.

 Number of pages. Places the same total number of document pages on each page.

 Date. Places the date when the document is being printed on each page. If you print it again tomorrow, for example, tomorrow's date will show.

 Time. Places the time when the document is being printed on each page.

For example, Figure 5.19 shows a header that prints the date, time, page number, and number of pages. Notice that I added the words "page" and "of" to help the page numbers make more sense.

You can also insert other information into the header or footer. Notice the Insert AutoText drop-down list on the toolbar; you can choose from a variety of information bits from there. For example, if you want to insert the date on which the document was created (rather than printed), you could choose Created on from the drop-down list. When you use these AutoText codes, it not only inserts the appropriate codes but also supporting text to help you understand it. For example, in Figure 5.20, notice that Word inserted the words "Created on" as well as the created-on date.

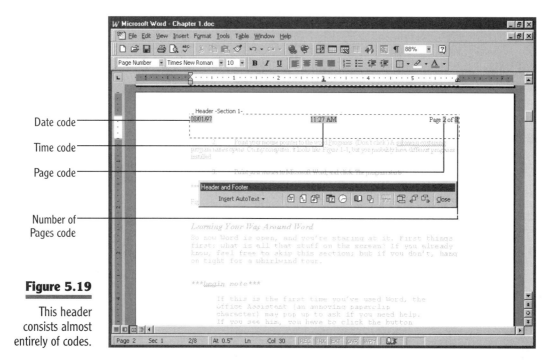

Figure 5.19

This header consists almost entirely of codes.

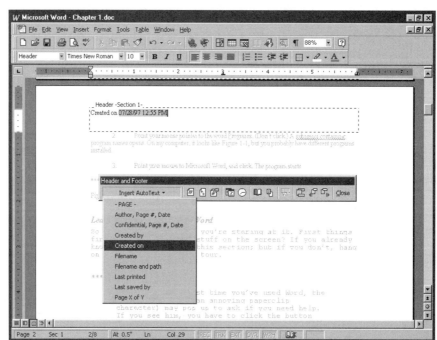

Figure 5.20

When you insert AutoText codes, you often get both text and codes.

Where does AutoText find the information to retrieve? Simple. Close the header and footer area and choose File, Properties to display the Properties dialog box for the document. On the Summary tab you'll find a variety of fields into which you can enter information. AutoText pulls this information into your header or footer when you request it (see Figure 5.21).

In that same dialog box, there is also a Custom tab. Click on it to access extra fields that AutoText can also pull into your header or footer, as shown in Figure 5.22. To set a value for one of these custom fields, follow these steps:

1. In the Properties dialog box (File, Properties), click on the Custom tab.
2. In the Name list, choose the field you want to use.

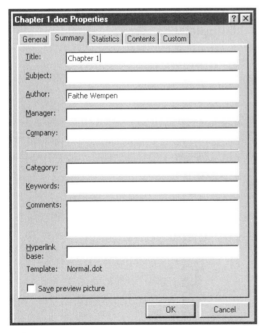

Figure 5.21

Choose File, Properties to access the dialog box from which AutoText pulls its data.

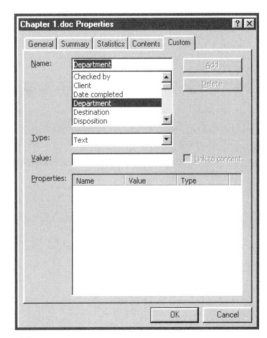

Figure 5.22

You can also set up any of dozens of custom fields if you plan to use that information in the header or footer.

3. In the Type list, choose the type of data the field should hold (for example, Text, Number, Date).

4. In the Value field, type the value that you want associated with that field. For example, in Figure 5.23, I associated my editor's name with the Editor field.

5. Click on the Add button. (If the Add button is unavailable, click again on the field name to make the button available.)

6. Assign values to more fields, and click on OK when you finish.

Now you can go back to your header and footer and insert AutoText for that field, and the value you specified will be inserted.

Why go to all this trouble, when you could just type the editor's name directly into the header or footer? It's a matter of organization. If you work on lots of documents, you may forget who the editor is on a specific project. If the editor's name is entered into the Properties dialog box, you won't have to try to remember it later.

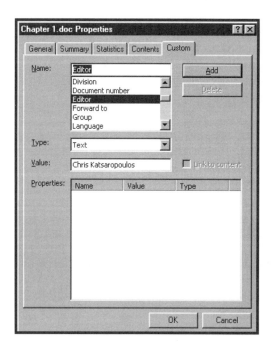

Figure 5.23

Choose the field and enter the value that should be inserted when you use that field as AutoText.

Formatting Your Header or Footer

Formatting header and footer text is easy. While you're viewing the header or footer, drag across the text to select it. Include any codes—they can be formatted too. Then apply any formatting you want. You can change the font, the size, the tab stops, add a border around one or more sides—anything you can do to normal text.

TIP I think it looks especially nice to add a bottom border under the header and a top border above the footer. This sets off the header and footer text smartly from the rest of the document.

Varying What Appears in the Header and Footer

There are times when you don't want the same header and footer on every page. For example:

- You might want a different header or footer on the first page. For a blank first page, you simply tell Word that you want a different header or footer on the first page and then you leave it empty.

- If you are printing the final copy double-sided, you may want different headers and footers for the even and odd pages.

- If you have different chapters or sections in the same document, you may want different headers and footers for each section.

The first two are easy to accomplish; the third is a little trickier. To use a different first page header or footer, or to set up odd and even ones, here's what to do:

1. Select <u>V</u>iew, <u>H</u>eader and Footer to redisplay the header or footer areas if needed.

2. Click on the Page Setup button on the Header and Footer toolbar. The Page Setup dialog box appears (see Figure 5.24).

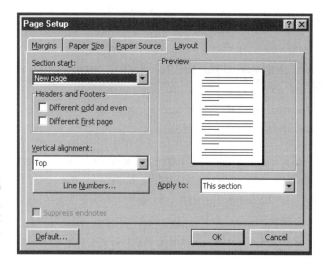

Figure 5.24

Use this dialog box to specify different headers and footers as needed.

3. In the Headers and Footers section of the dialog box, click on one or both check boxes:

    ○ Different odd and even
    ○ Different first page

4. Click on OK to close the dialog box.

5. Type the text for your various headers and footers in the appropriate header and footer boxes. Use the Page Up and Page Down keys to move between pages until you have done all the headers; then click on the Switch Between Header and Footer button and do all the footers.

    ○ If you marked both check boxes, you will have three sets to do: First Page, Odd Page, and Even Page. Figure 5.25 shows how the header box looks different when you're viewing the first page of the document.

    ○ If you marked only the Different odd and even check box, you will have two sets: Odd Page and Even Page.

    ○ If you marked only the Different first page check box, you will

SUNDAY MORNING Reports and Long Documents **313**

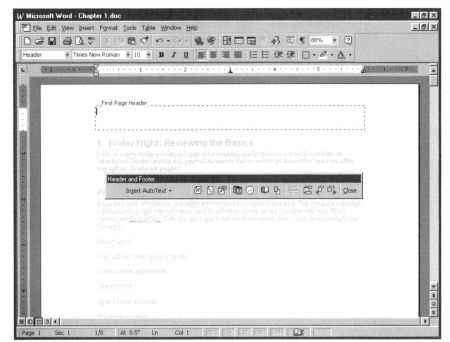

Figure 5.25

When you specify a different first-page header and you're on the first page of the document, you can enter the different header.

have two sets: First Page and regular. (For example, the headers will be First Page Header and Header.)

Changing How Page Numbers Look

You aren't stuck with the generic Arabic numbering that appears when you insert page number codes; you can use a variety of number formats. The key is the Format Page Number button on the Header and Footer toolbar.

1. Click on the Format Page Number button on the Header and Footer toolbar. The Format Page Number dialog box appears (see Figure 5.26).
2. Open the Number Format drop-down list and choose the number format you want.
3. Click on OK.

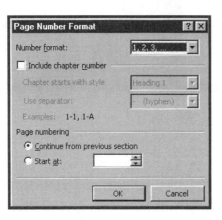

Figure 5.26

You can set up page number formatting for the codes that you insert into your headers and footers here.

You can also start the numbering at a number other than 1. Just reopen that Format Page Number dialog box (see Figure 5.26) and click on the Start at option button. Then enter the number at which you want to start in the text box. The default is 1.

Headers and Footers for Multiple Sections

The easiest way to work your headers and footers for multiple sections is to make them the same across all sections in the document. To do this, just make sure that when you are viewing that section's header or footer, the Same as Previous button is pressed on the Header and Footer toolbar. If it isn't, click on it to select it. This transfers the previous headers and footers to the new section, including both the text and the page numbering formats.

Sometimes, however, you may want different headers and footers for each section. To do this, make sure that the Same as Previous button is *not* pressed. This opens up header and footer boxes for each section, into which you can type the new header and footer text.

You may also want different page numbering for each section. The default is for page numbering to continue uninterrupted from section to section, and that's fine in most cases. For example, the page numbering in this book does not start anew with every chapter; it continues sequentially throughout the whole book. However, sometimes a section may need its own numbering. For example, the table of contents in this book is numbered separately, with Roman numerals. To set up separate page numbering for a section, do the following:

1. Display a header or footer for that section.
2. Make sure the Same as Previous button is not pressed on the Header and Footer toolbar.
3. Click on the Format Page Number button to open the Format Page Number dialog box.
4. Click on the Start a̲t option button and type the page number that the section should begin with.
5. Choose the appropriate number format from the Number format drop-down list.
6. Click on OK.

Creating a Table of Contents

A lot of people think that creating a table of contents is a big deal, but it's not really hard or time-consuming. A table of contents is basically just a list of the headings in your document along with corresponding page numbers. Take a look in the front of this book for an example.

If you already have your headings coded with consistent styles, you're ready to go. For example, all your first-level headings must have the same style, all your second-level headings must have the same style (different from the first-level headings), and so on.

1. Position the insertion point where you want the table of contents to appear. It must appear in the same document as the text it refers to, but it can be in its own section.

TIP To put the table of contents in its own section at the beginning of the document, move the insertion point to the beginning of the document and press Enter. Then insert a section break (Insert, Break). Press the Up arrow key a couple of times to move the insertion point above the section break, and then continue with these steps.

2. Select Insert, Index and Tables. The Index and Tables dialog box opens.
3. Click on the Table of Contents tab (see Figure 5.27).
4. Click on each of the formats in the Formats list, and select one that you like. The From template one takes its styles from the current template; the other formats are fixed.
5. If you used only Word's default heading styles (Heading 1, Heading 2, Heading 3, and so on), skip to Step 7. Otherwise, click on the Options button. The Table of Contents Options dialog box opens (see Figure 5.28).
6. Find each of the styles used for headings on the list of styles, and type a number next to each one that corresponds to its proper outline level. For example, my publisher uses HC for major headings in a chapter, so I typed 1 next to HC. Then click on OK.

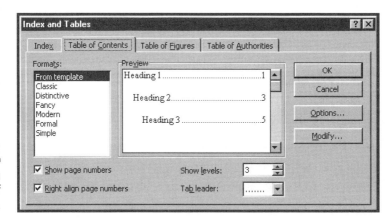

Figure 5.27

Here's where you set up your table of contents definition.

SUNDAY MORNING Reports and Long Documents

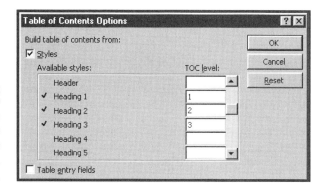

Figure 5.28

Choose which styles should be included in the table of contents, and at what level.

> **TIP** In the Table of Contents Options dialog box, you'll notice that Heading 1, Heading 2, and so on have numbers next to them. Don't worry about removing these numbers for the styles you aren't using; if the style is not in use, Word will ignore the number next to it when it compiles the table of contents.

7. Click on OK. Word generates the table of contents. Figure 5.29 shows one created using the Distinctive format.

> **NOTE** Notice that the table of contents entries in Figure 5.29 appear in gray, indicating that they are fields. They will print in regular black-and-white, however, without the gray.

Experimenting with TOC Formats

Now that you have created a table of contents, take some time and experiment with the various formats.

1. Click anywhere in the existing TOC.
2. Reopen the Index and Tables dialog box (Insert, Index and Tables).
3. Pick a different format from the Formats list.

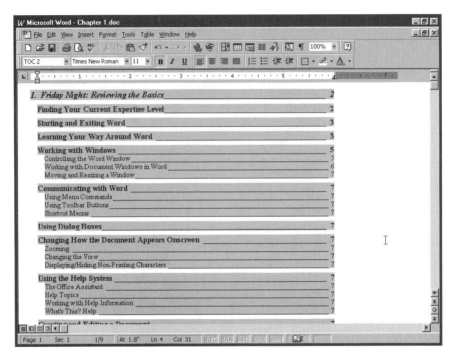

Figure 5.29

Here is the table of contents for my document.

4. If you want to suppress the page numbers, deselect the Show page numbers check box. (This is useful for creating an outline of the chapter under the guise of a TOC.)

5. If you want the page numbers to be a few spaces away from the end of each heading, turn off the Right align page numbers check box. (Warning: this makes the page numbers harder to read.)

6. Pick a different leader character from the Tab leader drop-down list.

7. Click on OK. A message appears asking if you want to replace the selected table of contents.

8. Click on OK. If you don't like the new results, try again, or press Ctrl+Z (Undo) to reverse the TOC replacement that you just performed.

Changing the Formatting of the TOC Styles

When Word generates the TOC, it assigns specific styles to each level of entry. The headings that came from style Heading 1 (plus whatever styles you typed a 1 next to) appear in a style called TOC 1. The headings that came from Heading 2 (plus the styles you typed a 2 next to) appear in TOC 2 style, and so on.

You already know how to modify styles, and TOC styles are even easier to change than regular ones because they automatically update all other lines that use that same style. You'll see what I mean as we modify the TOC 2 style in the following steps:

1. Select a TOC 2 line in the table of contents.
2. Format it the way you want it, using any of the formatting commands. You can change the font, the font size, the indentation, or any other attributes.

Notice that all other instances of TOC 2 style have already changed to match the modifications you made to that one line. You don't have to save the style change.

Creating an Index

Tables of contents are easy, as you just saw. An index is a bit more complicated. For an example of an index, look in the back of this book. An index lists all the important words alphabetically and tells what page number they appear on. Here's how to create an index in Word:

1. First, do one of the following:
   - Mark each instance of each term to be indexed (very time-consuming, but creates the best index).
   - Create a concordance file consisting of one instance of each word to be indexed (a great time-saver but sometimes produces an inferior-quality index).

2. Next, run Word's Index command, which builds the index automatically. (This is the easy part.)

NOTE Actually you can do both the tasks in Step 1 if you want to; there's nothing to prevent it. However, each is rather involved, so most people stick with one method or the other.

I'll explain each of the procedures in the following sections.

Marking Terms to be Indexed

Let's assume for a moment that you want to make the best index possible, and you don't care how much time it takes. If that's the case, manually marking each index term is the way to go. Because you control the wording, you can make an index that makes the most sense. For example, suppose you have a heading "Starting and Exiting Word" in your document. You could mark that heading to be indexed in two places—under S for starting word and under E for exiting Word. You can also create multiple levels in the index. For example, you could have a major entry in the index called Word and underneath it, Starting and Exiting as subentries.

TIP Marking terms is not difficult, but—as I said before—it is time-consuming. For the purpose of this exercise, you may want to mark only a few pages in your document, and come back to fully index it after the weekend is over.

1. Choose Insert, Index and Tables. The Index and Tables dialog box opens.
2. Click on the Index tab.
3. Click on the Mark Entry button. A Mark Index Entry dialog box appears, as shown in Figure 5.30.
4. Position your insertion point in the document immediately before the term to be indexed.

SUNDAY MORNING Reports and Long Documents

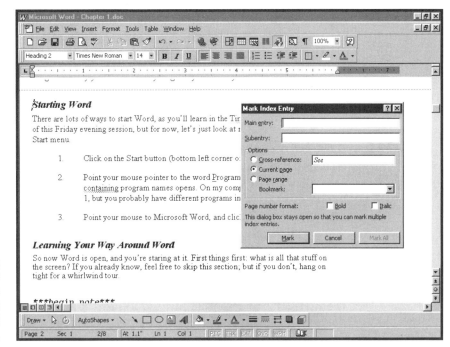

Figure 5.30

Here's where you set up the entries you want in your index.

5. In the Mark Index Entry dialog box, click in the Main entry text box and type the major entry you want for the term. For example, for Starting Word, my main entry might be **Word**.

6. If there is a subentry for the term, enter it in the Subentry text box. For example, if Word was my main entry, my subentry might be **Starting**.

7. Click on the Current page button to indicate that the page number referenced should be the current page.

8. Click on Mark.

TIP If you want certain entries to appear in bold or italic, click on the Bold or Italic check boxes for them before you click on Mark in Step 8. However, if you use this feature, make sure you do so using some sort of consistent rule. Otherwise it will simply look sloppy.

9. If you want to index the same term another way (for example, you might also list it under S for Starting Word), replace the text in the Main entry and Subentry text boxes with different text and click on Mark again. Figure 5.31 shows text marked with two different index entries. A colon separates the main entry from the subentry.

NOTE If you cannot see your index entries onscreen as in Figure 5.31, click on the Show/Hide ¶ button on the Standard toolbar.

10. Move the insertion point to the next term and repeat the procedure until all terms are marked.

You may have noticed two other options in the Mark Index Term dialog box: one for cross-references and one for bookmarks. These are less commonly used, but still valuable.

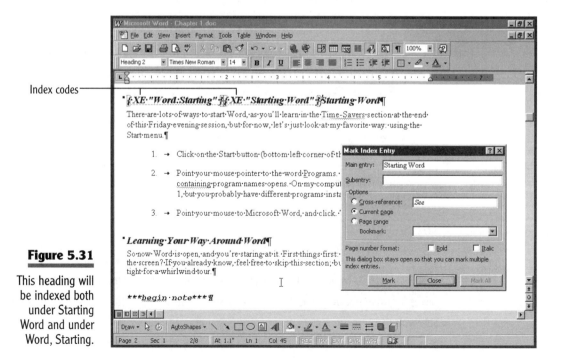

Figure 5.31

This heading will be indexed both under Starting Word and under Word, Starting.

The cross-reference option is for those times when one term is a synonym for another and you think the reader might try to look up the subject by the alternate term. For example, suppose I consistently referred to quitting the Word program in this book as "Exiting Word," but my readers don't know that. I anticipate that they might look it up in the index under "Closing Word" or "Shutting Down Word," so I need cross-references for those that point to Exiting Word. Figure 5.32 shows how the Index Mark Term dialog box should be set up to alleviate this problem.

The Bookmark option is for times when you want to reference a range of pages in your index. For example, suppose you have a three-page section that explains the parts of the Word screen. To reference that entire section in the index under "Parts of the Screen," you first need to create a bookmark for that section.

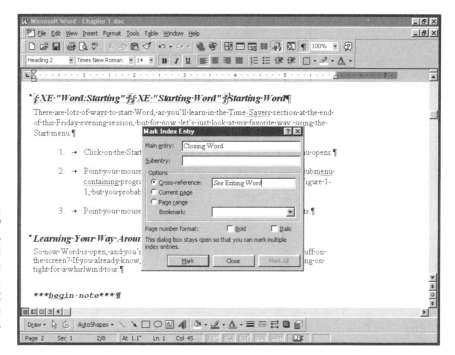

Figure 5.32

Cross-references help the reader find the terms you have chosen to use in your document when there are alternative terms that you didn't use.

Then you can reference the bookmark in the index.

1. Select the entire range that you want to include in the index entry. For me this means selecting a heading in my document and all the text under that heading.
2. Choose Insert, Bookmark. The Bookmark dialog box appears (see Figure 5.33).
3. Type a bookmark name in the Bookmark name text box. You cannot use any spaces, but you can run several words together, like "ScreenParts" or "Partsofthescreen."
4. Click on the Add button. Now you have a bookmark by that name.
5. Click to place the insertion point at the beginning of the bookmarked range.
6. Reopen the Index and Tables dialog box (Insert, Index and Tables) and click on the Mark Entry button again to return to the Mark Index Entry dialog box.
7. In the Main entry text box, enter the wording you want to appear in the index. For example, I entered "Parts of the Word Screen."
8. Click on the Page range option button.
9. Open the Bookmark drop-down list and choose the bookmark you just created.

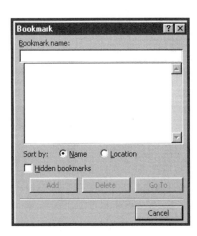

Figure 5.33

Set up a bookmark for the range of text that you want to index as a group.

SUNDAY MORNING Reports and Long Documents

10. Click on the Mark button.
11. Continue marking entries as needed.

You can stop here if you want and skip to the "Generating the Index" section later in this session or next, you can create a concordance file to mark additional entries.

Creating a Concordance File

The following is an alternative method to marking index entries manually; you don't have to do it if you went the manual route and you're satisfied with your work. It can save you lots and lots of time, but the index you get may be short of perfect. It works by identifying words that you always want indexed when they appear in your document. For example, you can tell Word to always index the phrase "Starting Word" under "Word, Starting." But you may get false matches, and your index may contain entries that you did not intend. For example, if you had a sentence in the "Opening a Document" section that said:

You already learned about starting Word in a previous section, so I won't go into that now.

Word would identify this as a place to list with "starting Word" in the index. Then your reader would turn to that page expecting to learn about starting Word but there would be no information about it there. Even with its limitations, this method has legitimate uses, so here it is, in case you want to try it.

1. Start a new document based on the Blank Document template.
2. Create an empty two-column table. Start with about 20 rows; you can add more later as needed.
3. In the first column, enter the text you want Word to search for and mark as an index entry. Make sure to enter the text exactly as it appears in the document. For example, you might enter **Starting Word**.
4. Press Tab to move to the second column.

5. In the second column, type the index entry for the text in the first column. For example, you might type **Starting Word**. Or, if you wanted a main entry and subentry, you might enter **Word:Starting**.

6. Press Tab to go to the next line, and enter another word to be indexed. Repeat until you have a complete list of words to be indexed. Figure 5.34 shows one that I started for my document.

7. Save and close the concordance file.

8. Choose Insert, Index and Tables, and click on the Index tab if it is not already on top.

9. Click on the AutoMark button. An Open Index AutoMark dialog box appears (much like the regular Open dialog box) where you can choose the concordance file.

10. Locate and select the concordance file and click on Open. Word marks all the words in your document automatically, as shown in Figure 5.35. Index entries appear in parentheses.

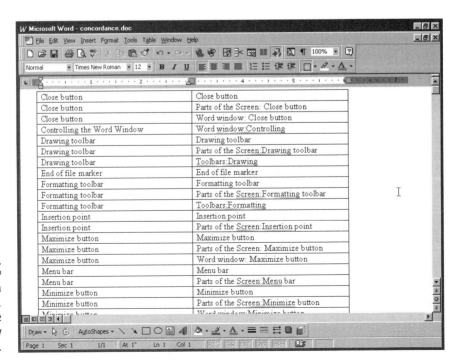

Figure 5.34

Here's a start on a concordance file. In reality there would be many more entries.

SUNDAY MORNING Reports and Long Documents

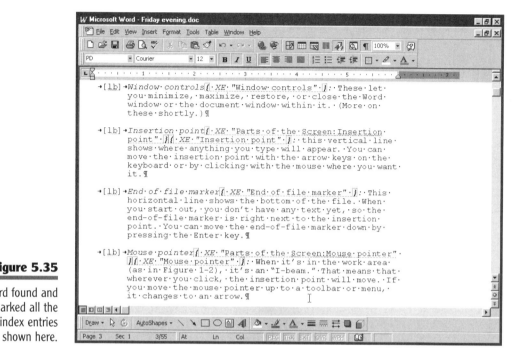

Figure 5.35

Word found and marked all the index entries shown here.

TIP

Here's a way to check your work, to see if you've included all the important words. First, make a list of every word in your document. To do this, select the entire document (Ctrl+A), copy it (Edit, Copy), and then start a new document (click on the New button) and paste the text into it (Edit, Paste). Then replace every space with a paragraph mark. (Edit, Replace, then press the spacebar in the Find what field. Click in the Replace with field, and then click on the Special button and choose Paragraph Mark. Then click on Replace All.) Sort the list alphabetically (Table, Sort). Then delete all the blank paragraph marks at the beginning of the document, all duplicate words, and any words that you don't want indexed. You'll be left with a list of words to be indexed. Now go through this list and compare it to your concordance file, and add any missing significant words to the concordance file's table.

Generating the Index

Now comes the easy part—generating the index. It's easy because Word does practically all the work for you.

1. Position your insertion point where you want the index to appear. You may want to start a new section and page (<u>I</u>nsert, <u>B</u>reak), and type the word **Index** at the top of the page.

2. Choose <u>I</u>nsert, In<u>d</u>ex and Tables, and click on the Index tab if it is not already on top.

3. Click on either the In<u>d</u>ented or the Ru<u>n</u>-In button in the Type area, depending on the style you want. Indented puts each subentry on a separate line; Run-In puts them all together. See the Pre<u>v</u>iew area in the dialog box for examples. I used Indented.

4. From the Forma<u>t</u>s list, choose a format. Check out the Pre<u>v</u>iew area to see what each will look like. I went with Fancy.

TIP If you want to specify your own formatting for the index, for example, use a different font or font size, choose From Template from the Formats list and then click on the Modify button to open the Style dialog box to modify the formatting of the index styles.

5. Choose a number of columns and put the number in the C<u>o</u>lumns text box. The default is 2.

CAUTION Don't use more than two columns for the index unless you plan on making the font size in the index rather small. Otherwise each line will be too short to hold enough text for most entries and will wrap unattractively.

6. (Optional) If you want to right-align the page numbers, click on the <u>R</u>ight align page numbers check box and then choose a leader character from the Ta<u>b</u> leader drop-down list. I left my page numbers unaligned.

SUNDAY MORNING Reports and Long Documents

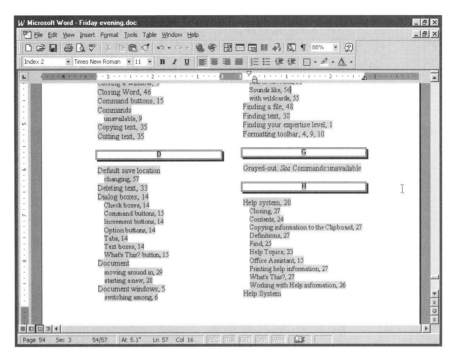

Figure 5.36

Here's a completed index.

7. Click on OK. Word generates the index. A very simple and short example appears in Figure 5.36. Gray background will print as normal white.

Time-Savers

Whew! This has been another intense session, and I don't blame you if you're tired out and ready for lunch. But just in case you finished early, here are some more nifty techniques that can save you time and energy.

Using the Report Templates

Word comes with three report templates: Contemporary, Professional, and Elegant. You can use these the same as you use other templates to start a report and cut down on the upfront work you have to do. I didn't cover these in the main part of this chapter because, frankly, you've learned so much already in this book that these templates are beneath you now. They're good if you're in a hurry, but you no longer need to rely on them because you are now good enough with Word to create your own professional-looking results.

Organizing Files with a Master Document

Back on Friday night, I told you that there was a Master Document view in Word, and I promised that I would explain it. So here we go. With a master document, you can combine two or more document files into a document window, and create indexes and tables of contents as if they were a single document. What's more, the files remain separately saved, so you can still edit them separately whenever you need to.

This book is a good example of a project that can benefit from the Master Document feature. Each session is a separate file in Word, but when I printed it, I wanted a single TOC and index, and the page numbers ordered sequentially. By combining all the sessions in a master document, I achieved all these things easily.

Creating a Master Document

To create a master document, follow these steps:

1. Start a new document based on the template that contains the styles you are using in your documents. This may be Blank Document or it may be something else.
2. Switch to Master Document view (View, Master Document). The Outlining toolbar appears (just like in Outline view), along with a new toolbar, the Master Document toolbar (see Figure 5.37).
3. Click on the Insert Subdocument button. The Insert Subdocument dialog box appears. (It's a normal Open-type dialog box.)
4. Choose the first file to insert into the master document (I used Friday Evening, the first chapter in this book) and click on Open.
5. Repeat Steps 3 and 4 until all the subdocuments you want are inserted (see Figure 5.38).

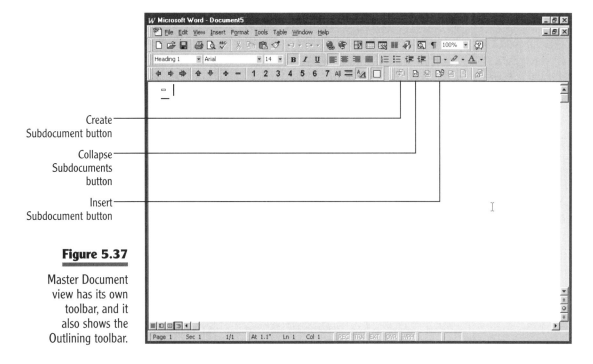

Figure 5.37

Master Document view has its own toolbar, and it also shows the Outlining toolbar.

Create Subdocument button
Collapse Subdocuments button
Insert Subdocument button

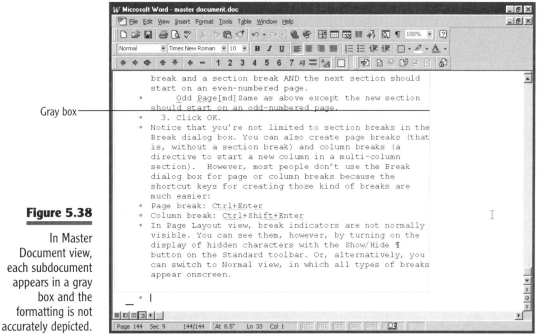

Figure 5.38

In Master Document view, each subdocument appears in a gray box and the formatting is not accurately depicted.

Gray box

Figure 5.39

If there are different definitions for the same style, Word asks whether you want to differentiate (Yes) or standardize (No).

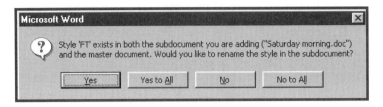

Things that could go wrong, and what to do:

- You may see a warning box like the one in Figure 5.39, telling you that both documents use the same style. It wants to know whether it should create an additional style to differentiate them. If you really want the documents to have different style formatting, click on Yes to All. If you want all the formatting to match (recommended), click on No to All. Or you can click on Yes or No to make judgment calls on each style individually.

- You may see a warning box that the incoming subdocument uses a different template from the one in the master document, and that the master document's template will be used. All you can do is click on OK—but don't worry about it.

Collapsing and Expanding Subdocuments

To get an overall picture of the master document, you may want to collapse the subdocuments so that you just see their names. You can collapse them by clicking on the Collapse Subdocuments button on the Master Document toolbar (pointed out in Figure 5.37). When you do so, you're asked whether you want to save your master document. Click on OK and a Save As dialog box appears. Name your master document and click on OK. When your subdocuments are collapsed, the Collapse Subdocuments button turns into an Expand Subdocuments button; use that to reopen them.

Working with a Master Document

You may have noticed that the formatting appears somewhat messed up in Master Document view (see Figure 5.38). You can view the document normally (including accurate formatting) by simply switching to Normal or Page Layout view.

TIP I like working in Normal rather than Page Layout view when working with a master document because I can see the section breaks more easily.

From there, you can do anything to the master document that you can do to a regular document. Each subdocument is in its own section, so you can apply the same or different formatting to sections. Here are some recommendations:

- Number pages sequentially through the whole document, but set up separate header/footer text for each subdocument. To do this, first create the first section's header and footer and include a page number code. Then move to the second section and display the header and footer. Click to deselect the Same as Previous button on the Header and Footer toolbar, and replace the old text with new text. However, leave the page number code alone. Do the same for each subdocument.

- To create a table of contents, first number all the pages sequentially as described above. Then create a new subdocument to hold the table of contents. Switch back to Master Document view to do this. Position the mouse pointer at the beginning of the master document and click on the Create Subdocument button on the Master Document toolbar. (It's pointed out in Figure 5.37.) Have Word generate the TOC in the empty subdocument.

- Use the same procedure as with the TOC for the index, except create the new subdocument at the end of the master document.

Assigning Shortcut Keys to Styles

If you apply styles to every paragraph in your document, you will get tired of using the Styles drop-down list very quickly. One way to avoid using it is to assign shortcut key combinations to the styles that you apply most often.

1. Open the template containing the styles, or open a document that uses the template.
2. Choose Format, Style. The Style dialog box appears.
3. Choose the style you want from the Styles list, and click on the Modify button. The Modify Style dialog box appears.
4. Click on the Shortcut Key button. The Customize Keyboard dialog box appears.
5. Press the key combination that you want to assign to the style. If that key combination is already in use, its current assignment appears, as shown in Figure 5.40. You can override the current assignment if you want, but you will no longer be able to use the key combination for its original purpose.
6. Experiment until you find a key combination that is not taken or that you don't mind overriding, and then click on Assign.

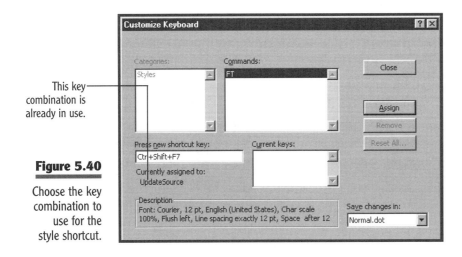

Figure 5.40

Choose the key combination to use for the style shortcut.

This key combination is already in use.

7. Click on Close to return to the Modify Style dialog box.
8. If you did not open the template itself (but rather a document that used it), click on the Add to Template check box.
9. Click on OK to return to the Style dialog box.
10. Click on Close to close the Style dialog box.

 TIP Here are some key combinations that are unassigned by default, to save you the trouble of trial-and-error in finding them:

    Ctrl+F1
    Ctrl+Shift+F1
    Alt+F2
    Ctrl+Shift+F2
    Ctrl+Alt+(F3-F12)
    Ctrl+Alt+Shift+(F3-F12)
    Alt+Shift+F3
    Alt+Shift+F4
    Ctrl+Shift+F4
    Alt+Shift+F5
    Alt+Shift+F7
    Alt+Shift+F8
    Alt+Shift+F10
    Alt+Shift+F11
    Alt+F12
    Alt+Shift+F12
    Alt+Shift+Delete
    Ctrl+Shift+Delete
    Alt+Shift+Insert
    Ctrl+Alt+Insert
    Ctrl+Shift+Insert
    Ctrl+Alt+End
    Ctrl+Shift+Page Down
    Ctrl+Shift+Page Up

Creating a Toolbar of Style Buttons

I saved the best trick for last in this chapter. This is one that I use myself every single day, and it's a real godsend if you have to work with styles a lot.

I work for several customers, and each one has their own template containing the styles they want me to use. I can attach the template to the document (Tools, Templates and Add-Ins) and apply the styles with the Style drop-down list, but scrolling through the list of styles each time is very time-consuming. I could assign shortcut keys to the styles, but since each customer has different styles, I couldn't possibly remember the shortcuts for each style.

My solution has been to create a toolbar with buttons that apply each style in a template (or at least the most commonly used styles in that template). I have different toolbars for different customers, so when I start a new document, I display the correct toolbar and hide the others (View, Toolbars) as needed.

Figure 5.41 shows my Prima toolbar, which I used to write this book for Prima Publishing. Each style name in this template is a two-character abbreviation.

Ready to create your own toolbar? Rather than have you make a big complicated one like mine, I'll walk you through something easier—you'll make a toolbar for the Elegant Report template, so you can use its styles in the report that you are writing.

1. Attach the Elegant Report template to the report that you've been working on in this chapter (Tools, Templates and Add-Ins).
2. Right-click on any toolbar and choose Customize from the menu that appears. The Customize dialog box opens.
3. Click on the New button. The New dialog box appears.
4. Type **Elegant Report** in the Toolbar name box.
5. Open the Make toolbar available to drop-down list and choose Elegant Report.

SUNDAY MORNING Reports and Long Documents

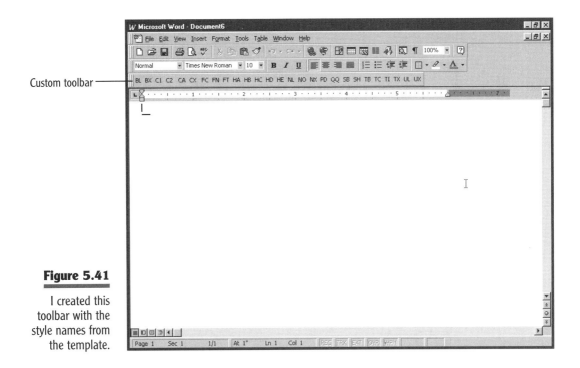

Figure 5.41

I created this toolbar with the style names from the template.

6. Click on OK. A little floating toolbar appears next to the Customize dialog box, as shown in Figure 5.42.

7. Drag the toolbar by its title bar and drop it directly under the existing toolbars at the top of the screen, as shown in Figure 5.43.

8. Click on the Commands tab in the Customize dialog box.

9. Choose Styles from the Categories list. You'll see a list of the styles in the Commands list.

10. Drag the first style that you want to have toolbar access to up to the blank toolbar and drop it there. A button for it appears, as shown in Figure 5.44.

11. Since you will want to include many buttons on the toolbar, get rid of the word "Style" on the button (you know it's a style). Right-click on the new button.

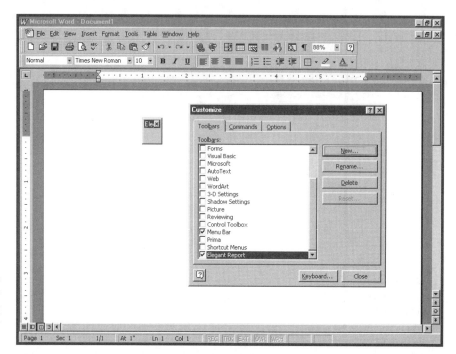

Figure 5.42

Your new toolbar does not yet contain any buttons.

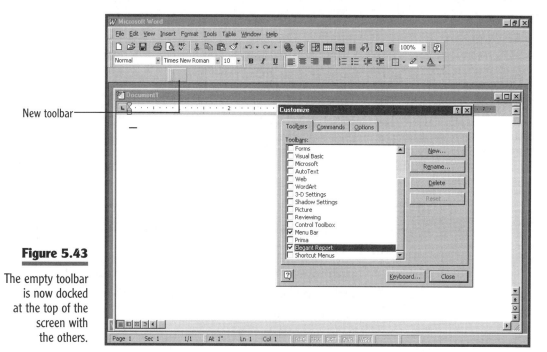

New toolbar

Figure 5.43

The empty toolbar is now docked at the top of the screen with the others.

SUNDAY MORNING Reports and Long Documents

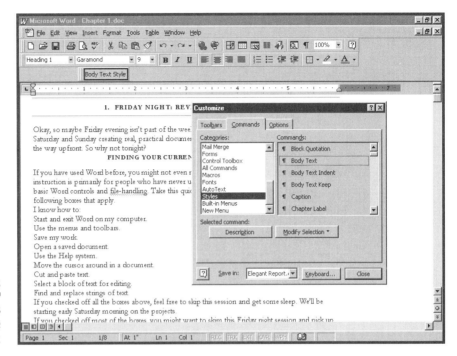

Figure 5.44

The style now has a button on the toolbar.

12. In the shortcut menu that appears, click in the Name text box and delete the word "Style," and then press Enter. The button's name changes.

13. Add more buttons to the toolbar using Steps 10 through 12 until all the styles that you will use most often appear there. Here's a suggested list:

- Block Quotation
- Body Text
- Indent
- Caption
- Chapter Subtitle
- Chapter Title
- Heading 1
- Heading 2

- Heading 3
- List
- List Bullet
- List Number

14. Click on Close to close the Customize dialog box.

There you have it! Now you can access this toolbar whenever you work with a document based on the Elegant Report template. If you open a document and the toolbar is not displayed, just right-click on any toolbar and choose it from the list.

This concludes the Sunday Morning session. Go have some lunch, take a little nap, and I'll see you back here shortly for the grand finale—creating Web pages.

SUNDAY AFTERNOON
Web Pages

- Creating a simple Web site
- Adding hyperlinks
- Using graphical hyperlinks
- Inserting images on a page
- Publishing the pages

I hope you're not too worn out from your weekend studies to appreciate this chapter, because I've saved one of the most fun topics for last. If you've been surfing the Internet (and who hasn't these days), you've doubtless seen lots of pretty impressive Web pages. With Word, you can create your own pages for the world to see. They may not have all the flash and animation that you find at professional sites, but they'll certainly hold their own against most other people's personal pages.

A Crash Course in Internet Jargon

To make sense out of this chapter, you should have some basic knowledge of the Internet. If you do—great. See you in the next section. But if not, hold on tight and I'll take you through it very quickly.

The *Internet* is a vast interconnected network of computers all over the world. Most of the connected computers make information available to the public, and many of them provide Internet access to individuals and businesses as well.

Most ordinary people don't have computers that are directly a part of this big network (the Internet) because it's expensive to maintain the connection 24 hours a day, even when you aren't using it. So instead, they get an account with a *service provider*, who has a big, powerful computer that's hard-wired into the Internet full time. They pay their monthly fees, and the service provider gives them an ID and a password that let them connect to the big computer with their modems. The big computer provides them with an on-ramp to the Internet (also called the "Information Superhighway") for as long as they stay connected by modem.

There are many different kinds of files available on the Internet, and several ways of accessing them. You can look up text-only information through a series of menus on a *Gopher* system, and you can download all types of files to your own computer with *FTP*. However, the most popular Internet feature is the *World Wide Web*, or *Web* for short.

While you are connected to the Internet, you can use a *Web browser* program that runs on your PC to request various *Web pages* from all over the world and display them on your computer screen. The most popular Web browsers are Netscape Communicator (which you can download for free from **http://www.netscape.com**) and Microsoft Internet Explorer (which comes free with Microsoft Office products, including Word).

These Web pages are nothing more than simple text files with some HTML coding that tells the Web browser how to format the text and from what location to pull in pictures. HTML stands for Hypertext Markup Language. Here is an example of some HTML coding:

```
<p>Elvis <i>lives!</i></p>
```

When your Web browser receives the HTML text, it reads it like this:

```
<p>     Begin a new paragraph.
```
Elvis Print the word "Elvis."
```
<i>     Make the text that follows italic.
```
lives! Print the word "lives!" in italic.
```
</i>    Stop making text italic now.
</p>    End the paragraph.
```

The end result shown by your Web browser looks something like this:

Elvis *lives!*

NOTE Don't worry—you won't have to learn HTML coding with all its brackets and obscure abbreviations. You can apply special styles in Word that will handle the conversion to HTML codes automatically when you save your work.

To request a Web page from the computer that it resides on, you have to know its complete name and address; it's just like mailing a letter. This name and address is called a Uniform Resource Locator, or URL. (It's pronounced *You Are Ell*, not *Earl*.) A page's URL consists of http:// plus the address of the computer, a slash (/), and the name of the page itself. For example, here is a (fictitious) URL:

> http://acmecorp.com/~wempen/index.html

Some HTML documents end in .htm rather than .html. Sometimes you may see a Web page address that does not have a document name, but only a site address, like this:

> http://acmecorp.com/~wempen

When there is no filename, as above, most browsers look for a file with the name index.htm or index.html. In other words, if I call my welcome page "index.htm," I don't have to include its name in the address I give people when I invite them to look at my page.

TIP One way to keep both public and restricted-access Web pages at the same address is to link all the public ones through the index.htm page, but not the restricted ones. Then give your restricted pages unusual names that nobody would guess. Give their names out only to the people you want to be able to access them.

You can jump from page to page with *hyperlinks*, which are *hot* links to other URLs. They're called "hot" because you can click on one to make your Web browser open that URL. Hyperlinks can point to other Web pages at your own address, or to pages at any site anywhere in the world.

For example, suppose you have a small appliance repair business. You might want to have three Web pages:

- A welcome page that introduces your business
- A page that lists the brands you are factory-authorized to repair
- A page showing a map to your workshop, for customers who want to drop off appliances to be fixed

Each of your three pages can contain hyperlinks to the other two pages, so your readers can jump freely among them. In addition, your brands page might contain hyperlinks to the Web sites of the appliance manufacturers.

NOTE If you were writing a sales letter, you would probably include all three of these elements on one page together. So why break them up into separate pages on the Web? Well, strictly speaking, you don't have to. But having separate pages for different types of information has several advantages. Your readers don't have to scroll through information that doesn't interest them, and if you need to make a change to one of the pages, the other pages stay available while one is down for repairs. It also makes your Web site (your collection of pages) look bigger and more impressive.

How Web Pages Differ from Other Documents

Web pages are different from regular documents in several ways. One is that they're designed to be viewed onscreen rather than printed. As you know from your work so far this weekend, not everything that looks good onscreen looks equally good on a printout, and vice versa. Just something to be aware of.

Another difference with Web pages is the way you start a new document. To create Web pages in Word, you use one of the special HTML-based templates that contains styles designed to translate smoothly into HTML.

You then create your document normally in Word, using the special HTML styles. When you save, Word translates it into HTML format.

 TIP If you start a normal document and then later decide you want to save it as an HTML document, you can—use the File, Save As HTML command rather than the normal Save or Save As.

Creating a Simple Web Page

First, you'll start out with a very simple exercise. You'll create a Web page and save it in HTML format, and then open a Web browser and look at it.

 NOTE The default installation routine doesn't install all of Word's Web tools. If you start to follow these steps and your system doesn't seem to have the right components installed, you need to rerun the setup program. First, close Word. Then open the Windows 95 control panel (Start/Settings/Control Panel) and double-click on Add/Remove Programs. Insert your Word or Office CD into the CD drive and double-click on Microsoft Word or Microsoft Office on the Install/Uninstall tab. This reruns the setup program and enables you to add components. You'll need to add Web Page Authoring (HTML) if it doesn't already have a check mark.

1. Choose File, New. In the New dialog box that appears, click on the Web Pages tab.
2. Double-click on the Blank Web Page icon. This starts a new document based on that template. It looks just like any other document, except there are some different toolbar buttons.

 NOTE Notice that you are now in Online Layout view. (Open the View menu and see for yourself.) Word switches you to this view whenever you're working with a Web page.

3. Choose File, Properties. A different Properties dialog box appears—not the one you have worked with before (see Figure 6.1).

 NOTE The regular Properties for the document haven't vanished completely; you can access the regular Properties dialog box by clicking the More button shown in Figure 6.1.

4. In the Title box, type the title for the page. This title will appear in the title bar of the Web browser window. For example, type **Bad Poetry**. (Might as well make this example a fun one!)
5. Click on OK to close the dialog box.
6. Open the Style drop-down list and choose Heading 1.
7. Type the major heading for the page. This is like a title except it appears in the document itself instead of in the title bar. For example, type **The Bad Poetry Page**, and then press Enter.

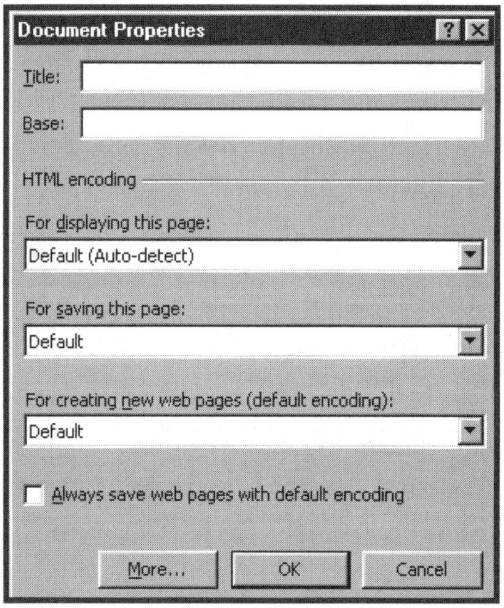

Figure 6.1

Web page documents have a different set of properties from normal documents.

8. Now type an introductory paragraph to explain the page to the reader. Notice that the style is already set to Normal, so you don't have to change it. For example, type the following text:

   The following is the worst poem I have ever read. I hope that it will be as horrific and memorable to you as it has been to me for many years.

   Press Enter when you finish.

9. Now it's time to write the poem. Format the poem's title as Heading 2 (open the Style drop-down list and choose Heading 2).

10. Type **Cruel Fence** and press Enter.

11. Change the style to Block Quote.

12. Type the poem shown here. (I know; it's awful.) When lines should appear together, press Shift+Enter at the end of a line; when there should be a line between them, press Enter by itself.

    The garbage sits, pristine, at the curb.
    The thin plastic bags strain at their seams.

    Do I smell a dead squirrel carcass?
    Sour milk?
    Mold-infested gouda?
    Mayhap an over-ripe cantaloupe?

    The cruel fence mocks me,
    Alas I will never roll there.

    Woof.

    When you're finished, it should look like Figure 6.2.

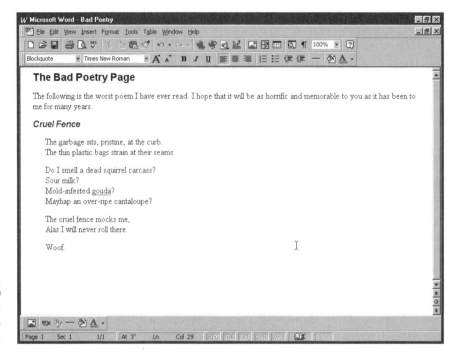

Figure 6.2

The finished Bad Poetry Web page in Word.

NOTE Shift+Enter creates a line break without starting a new paragraph. (This works in regular documents, too—not just Web pages!) When Word converts it to HTML, it will insert the code <BR> for a line break rather than <P> for a new paragraph in these places.

13. Choose File, Save or click on the Save button. The Save dialog box opens. Notice that the file type is already set to HTML.
14. Enter the name under which you want to save the document (for example, BadPoet) and click on Save.

CAUTION Even though Bad Poetry appeared in the title bar after you entered the title in the Properties dialog box, the document was not yet saved. This may be confusing, because normally Word puts the document's filename in the title bar. Keep in mind that the Web page title and the filename are two different things.

15. Choose File, Web Page Preview. The page opens in your default Web browser (probably Internet Explorer), as shown in Figure 6.3.

16. When you finish looking at it, close your Web browser and return to Word.

Just for fun, take a look at the HTML source code. Source code is the actual HTML coding, with all those brackets and whatnot, that I told you Word created behind the scenes. To check it out, choose View, HTML Source. Word shows you the entire mess, as shown in Figure 6.4. When you finish looking, click on the Exit HTML Source button on the Standard toolbar.

There now, that wasn't too difficult, was it? Of course, it gets a little trickier if you want a fancier page with more than just text on it. Fortunately, Word provides a wizard that helps you build fancy pages fairly painlessly, and you'll see it in action later in this session.

Figure 6.3

Web Page Preview gives you a look at how your readers will see the page.

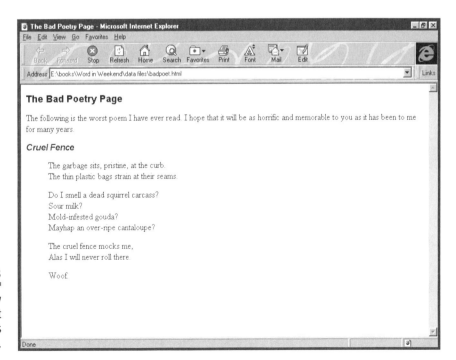

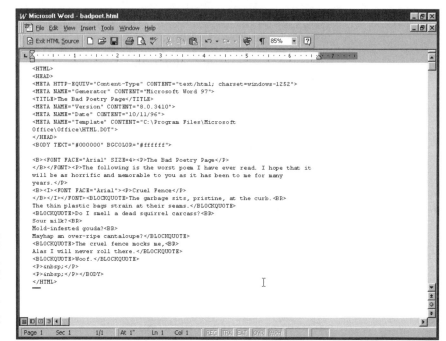

Figure 6.4

This is HTML source code. Don't let it scare you; you'll never have to work with it directly.

 Actually, creating a text-only page is not just an empty exercise. Many Web designers create text-only versions of their sites for readers who do not have graphics-capable Web browser programs or who have slow Internet connections and therefore want to avoid graphics. In earlier days, it was considered good form to have a text-only welcome page that included a hyperlink to a text-only version of your site. That way no potential reader would be left out. Nowadays, with technology advancing, it is unlikely that a reader would not have a graphical browser, so a text-only version of your site is probably not necessary, depending on the audience you are trying to reach.

Creating a Simple Web Site

If you're going to have more than one page on your Web site, you need to have a plan before you start. All the pages on your site should be

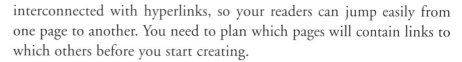

SUNDAY AFTERNOON Web Pages

interconnected with hyperlinks, so your readers can jump easily from one page to another. You need to plan which pages will contain links to which others before you start creating.

For this session's example, you'll design a personal Web site consisting of three pages: a welcome page, a hobby page (for your favorite hobby), and a links page (for listing your favorite Web sites). The structure will look something like Figure 6.5. Since there are only three pages, each one will be linked to both of the others.

For more complex Web sites with dozens of pages, you probably will not want every page to hyperlink to every other. Instead, you should designate a few main pages beneath the welcome page as "subject welcomes" and every page on the site should have a link to each of them. For example, a company's welcome page could have links to two pages: products and services. Each of these pages, in turn, could link to several pages related to their topic, as well as back to the welcome page and the other subject welcome page.

TIP You might want to create a new folder on your hard drive to store your Web pages and their associated files. This way, when you're ready to transfer them to the server, they'll all be in one handy location.

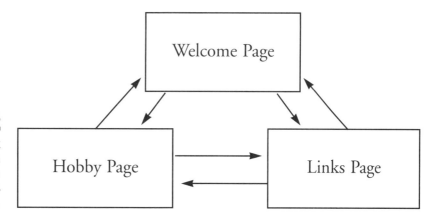

Figure 6.5

Each box represents a page, and each arrow represents a hyperlink.

Using the Web Page Wizard

The Web Page Wizard is a great way to make your Web pages look like you have a lot more experience with HTML than you actually do. (In fact, you don't need to have any experience with it at all!) You can create pages with graphics, fill-in forms, and all kinds of other fancy stuff. Try it out for your three-page example (the one in Figure 6.5).

1. Choose File, New, and click on the Web Pages tab in the New dialog box.
2. Double-click on the Web Page Wizard icon. A Web Page Wizard dialog box opens, along with a sample Web page in the background, as shown in Figure 6.6.
3. For this basic exercise, click on Simple Layout, if it is not already selected, and then click on Next.

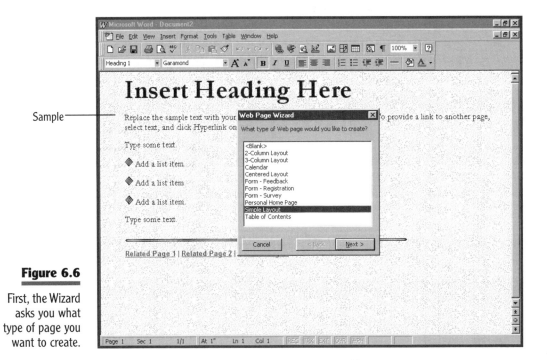

Figure 6.6

First, the Wizard asks you what type of page you want to create.

4. The dialog box now asks what visual style you want, and lists several styles. Click on a style name, and then wait a moment and the page behind the dialog box changes to show that style. Check out each of the styles, and when you find the one you like best, click on Finish. For the example, I used Festive.

Now you've got a template—a good start at a Web page—as shown in Figure 6.7. It contains the needed HTML styles on the Style list, a nice background, and some interesting fonts and bullets. All you have to do is fill in your own details.

Adding Your Text

By now, you are probably very familiar with text editing, so maybe you don't even need this section! But I thought I would tell you what I

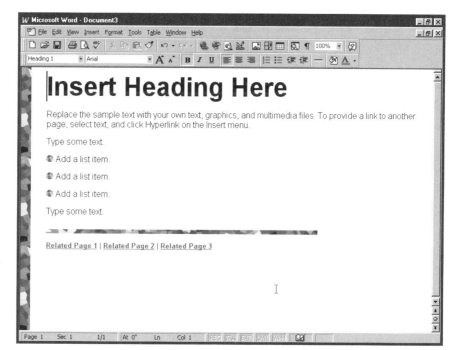

Figure 6.7

The Web Page Wizard leaves you with a nicely formatted generic page to customize.

did to customize the page, and you can either do the same or go your own way.

1. Select "Insert Heading Here" and type your own heading. I typed **Welcome to the Wempen Zone**.
2. Select the first paragraph and type your own introduction to your site.
3. Do the same for each of the other paragraphs and bullets; replace them with your own text. In Figure 6.8, you can see the text I used.
4. Choose File, Properties and type a page title in the Title box; then click on OK. I called mine **Welcome to the Wempen Zone**.

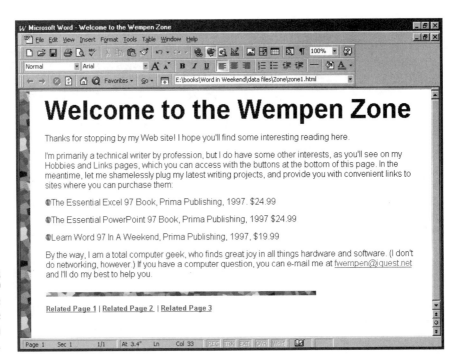

Figure 6.8

Here's how I chose to replace the generic text with my own material.

> **TIP** You can include your e-mail address on your page, and Word automatically makes it a hot link, which means that when people read your page, they can click on your e-mail address and send you mail using their e-mail program. Very handy! Just type your e-mail address in your text, as I did in Figure 6.8. Word will take care of the rest.

Adding Hyperlinks

Part of what makes Web pages so cool is that you can include clickable hyperlinks anywhere you want. For example, in Figure 6.8, I listed several books that I've written. In the following steps, I'll make them into hyperlinks.

Don't worry if you don't have any books that you've written in your bullets! Surely you can link to something on the Internet where more information is available. For example, suppose in one of your bullets, you mention that you own a Siamese cat. There are tons of great pages that contain information about Siamese cats, and you can link to any of them.

Finding the URLs for Your Links

Before you link to another page, of course, you need to know the exact address of that page. Even if you think you know it, it's a good idea to check it out, because addresses change frequently.

To find a URL, follow these steps. For example, here's how you would find a good Siamese cat site:

1. Start your Internet connection. Depending on who you use for your service provider, this could involve starting an online service (like Prodigy, CompuServe, America Online, or The Microsoft Network) or using Windows 95's Dial-Up Networking to dial a local Internet Service Provider.

Learn Word 97 In a Weekend

2. Open your Web browser. If you use Internet Explorer, you can just click on the Internet icon on your Windows 95 desktop.

3. For this exercise, you'll use AOL NetFind for the search because that's Internet Explorer's default. If you're using Internet Explorer or the America Online browser, click on the Search button on the browser toolbar. If you're using a different browser, type in **http://www.aol.com/search/** and press Enter.

4. At the search site (see Figure 6.9), type the keywords you want to search for. I looked for **Prima Computer Books**, but you can type **Siamese cats** or anything else. Then click on the Find! button.

The results of your search appear, as shown in Figure 6.10, with the sites listed by how closely they match your search (best results

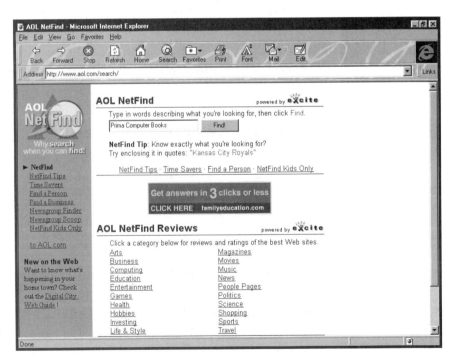

Figure 6.9

Type the terms you want to search for, and then click on Find!.

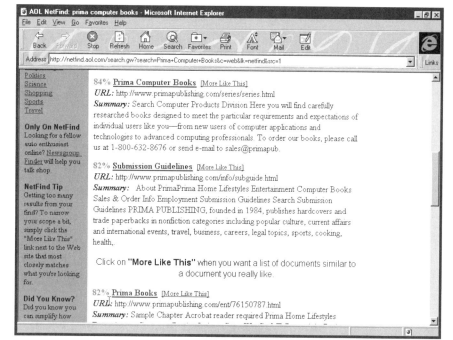

Figure 6.10

The results of the search appear here.

first). Your results may look a little different if you are using a different browser, but the steps are the same for working with them. Click on a hyperlink to jump to another page.

5. Click on the first site that looks relevant (they might not all be), and browse the site. Explore the whole site, looking for the exact page you want to link to. If it looks like a page you want to link to, skip to Step 7. If not, continue to Step 6.

6. Click on the Back button on your browser toolbar until you return to the list, and then repeat Step 5 for a different site.

7. When you are viewing a page that you want to link to, right-click on the URL that appears directly below the browser toolbar, and choose Copy from the shortcut menu.

Creating Hyperlinks in Word

Now you have a URL copied to the Windows Clipboard; now what? Now you paste it into Word, like this:

1. Go back to Word (by clicking on it in the Windows 95 Taskbar), where your half-completed Web page should still be open.
2. If you haven't done it yet, save your work. I saved mine under the name **Zone1**.
3. Select the text you want to make into a hyperlink. For example, I chose the title of my book, *The Essential Excel 97 Book,* but if you were linking to a cats page, you might select the words "Siamese cats" on your page.
4. Click on the Insert Hyperlink button on the Standard toolbar. (It looks like a globe with a piece of chain in front of it.) The Insert Hyperlink dialog box opens.
5. Press Ctrl+V to paste the URL into the Link to file or URL text box (see Figure 6.11).
6. Click on OK. The dialog box closes, and the text you selected is underlined, indicating it is now a hyperlink.

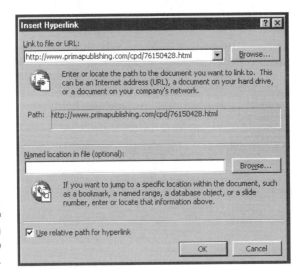

Figure 6.11

Insert the URL from the Clipboard into the text box.

SUNDAY AFTERNOON **Web Pages**

7. Repeat the process to create hyperlinks for any other words on the page for which you want to point the reader to more information. Figure 6.12 shows my page after I created hyperlinks for all three of my books.

Don't worry about the text at the bottom of the page that says Related Page 1, Related Page 2, and so on. You'll use these placeholders to tie all three of the pages together later.

Adding the Hobbies Page

Remember, you started out this project to have three pages: a welcome page, a hobbies page, and a links page. So far you have worked on the

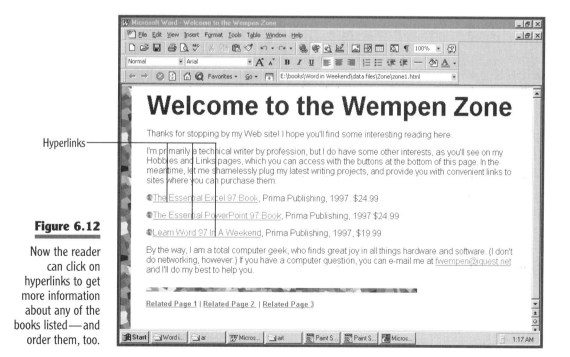

Figure 6.12

Now the reader can click on hyperlinks to get more information about any of the books listed—and order them, too.

welcome page. Now it's time to plan and create the other two. You'll start with the hobbies page.

1. Create another Web page using the Web Page Wizard and the Simple layout, and the same design as the one you chose earlier. (All your pages should have the same design, for consistency.)
2. Change the title of the page to **My Hobbies**, or a different title if you want.
3. Choose <u>F</u>ile, Proper<u>t</u>ies and enter **My Hobbies** in the <u>T</u>itle box; then click on OK.
4. Add an introductory paragraph (replacing the dummy text in the first paragraph). Delete the second dummy text paragraph.
5. Select one of the bullet lines, and press Ctrl+C to copy it. Then press Ctrl+V to paste it. Press Ctrl+V repeatedly until you have enough bullet lines to represent all your hobbies.
6. Replace the text for each of the bullets with a hobby you are interested in.
7. Save your work.
8. Create hyperlinks to your favorite Web pages that deal with each hobby.
9. If you want, add some concluding text under the bullets, or delete that paragraph.

Figure 6.13 shows my completed hobbies page.

Creating the Links Page

The links page is just like your hobbies page in structure; the only difference is the content. On the links page, you'll list your favorite Web pages that you've found and want to share with others, not necessarily ones associated with your hobbies. Follow the same steps as in the preceding section, but call the page **Favorite Links** and set up the bullets and hyperlinks to include links to other sites that you like. Figure 6.14 shows my favorite sites.

SUNDAY AFTERNOON Web Pages   363

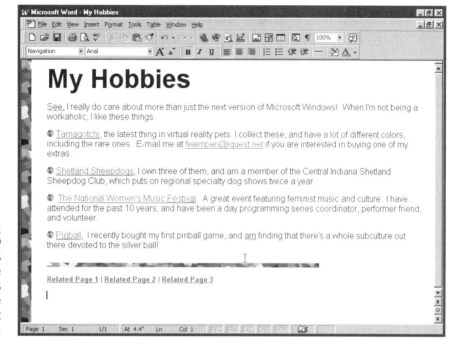

Figure 6.13

Here's my hobbies page, complete with hyperlinks that offer more information about each item.

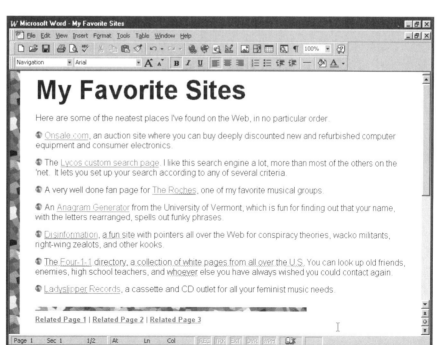

Figure 6.14

Here's my page of links.

Connecting the Individual Pages

Your final step is to replace all those placeholders at the bottom of each page with links to the other pages. Start with the welcome page, and work from there.

1. Open the document containing your welcome page.
2. Select the words "Related Page 1," and type **My Hobbies**. This replaces the old text with the new.
3. Select "My Hobbies," and click on the Insert Hyperlink button. The Insert Hyperlink dialog box opens.
4. Type the filename of your hobbies page in the Link to file or URL text box. I called mine zone2.html.
5. Make sure that the Use relative path for hyperlink check box is marked. This way, as long as all the pages are in the same folder (directory) on the same computer, they will always be able to find each other.
6. Click on OK. Now your hyperlink is *hot*—if you click on it, the named document will open.
7. Repeat Steps 2 through 6, replacing Related Page 2 with **My Favorite Sites**, and link it to your links page (mine is zone3.html).
8. Select Related Page 3 and press Delete; you won't need that one. When you're finished, your welcome page should look like Figure 6.15.
9. Save your file.
10. Open your hobbies page and replace the dummy text with links to your welcome page and links page. Save your work.
11. Open the links page and replace the dummy text with links to your welcome page and links page. Save your work.

When you finish, you should have links to both the other pages on each page. In other words, your reader should be able to hop from any page to any other page with a single click on a hyperlink.

SUNDAY AFTERNOON Web Pages

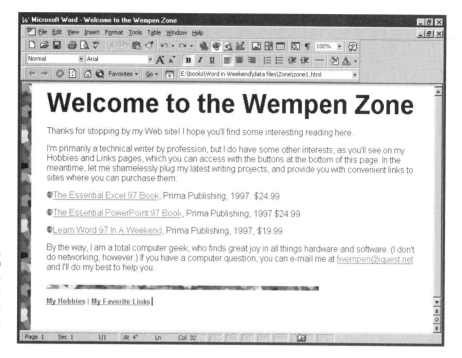

Figure 6.15

Replace the dummy links at the bottom of the page with actual links to your other pages.

Testing Your Links

You can test your links by opening your Web browser and opening your welcome page, and then clicking on the links to see if they work. Follow these steps if you're not sure what that entails.

1. Display your welcome page in Word.
2. Click on the My Hobbies link at the bottom of the welcome page. Your hobbies page should appear.
3. Notice that there is an additional toolbar at the top of the screen: the Web toolbar. It has a left-pointing arrow button (the Back button); click on it to return to your welcome page.
4. Now click on the My Favorite Sites link. The page should appear. Click on the Back button to return to your welcome page.

NOTE If a link doesn't work, check your link by right-clicking on the link and choosing Edit Hyperlink. If the correct filename does not appear, type it. If the correct name is there, make sure the Use relative path for hyperlink check box is marked.

5. Now click on the My Hobbies hyperlink again, and check the links in that document.

6. Check the links on the My Favorite Sites page the same way.

Once you've verified all your links, it's time to publish your page on the Internet. I'll teach you that later in this session. But first, look at some more complex Web pages you can create. Who knows—you may want to add one or more of the nifty elements I'm going to show you to your pages before you publish them.

Take a Break

You're halfway through this afternoon's session, so grab a snack, or at least something to drink. There's quite a bit more to learn about Web pages, but you can't do it on an empty stomach! When you're refreshed and revitalized, jump into the next section.

Creating Hyperlinks within a Page

Remember in the last example, I had you create three separate pages for the three types of information at your site. You did this so that your readers wouldn't have to wade through information that he or she didn't care about. Well, if you don't have very much information to put on each page, you might actually be better off putting it all on one page. You'll keep the readers from getting bored by including hyperlinks at the top of the page that jump to the various headings on the page.

You see, hyperlinks don't necessarily point to other documents; it's just been that way in all the examples you've seen so far. They can also point

SUNDAY AFTERNOON Web Pages 367

to bookmarks within the same document. This is the premise of Word's Personal Web Page design; all your info is on a single page, but you can jump from place to place in the document with hyperlinks. For example, in Figure 6.16, you can see that the first heading begins right after the list of hyperlinks.

TIP Hyperlinks can be used in regular documents too, not just on Web pages. If you are creating a long document (as in the Sunday Morning session) that your readers are going to read onscreen rather than in printed form, creating bookmarks for each heading and creating a hyperlinked table of contents is a good way to help people navigate the document (see the Time-Savers section at the end of this session).

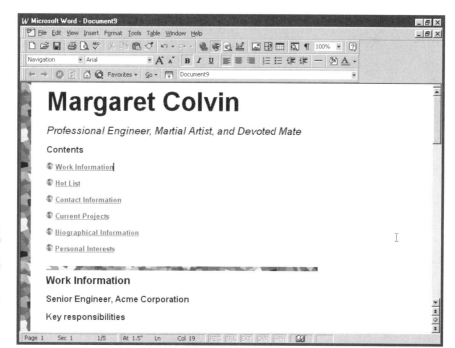

Figure 6.16

This page starts with a list of headings; you can jump to any heading by clicking on its hyperlink.

Use the Web Page Wizard to create such a page, and then I'll take you behind the scenes to show you how it works and how you can create the same effect manually in any document.

1. Choose File, New and double-click on the Web Page Wizard icon.
2. Choose Personal Home Page and click on Next.
3. Choose the visual style you want and click on Finish.
4. Replace the text that's there with your own text, customizing the page.

Pretty easy, eh? The hyperlinks that move to the headings are already hot. You can try them out by clicking on a hyperlink; the heading associated with that hyperlink immediately appears in the center of the Word screen. Now here's the cool part: how it works.

1. Choose Insert, Bookmark. The Bookmarks dialog box opens. (Remember, you worked with bookmarks this morning.)
2. Notice that there are several bookmarks already set up—A through F, as shown in Figure 6.17. There is also a bookmark for the top of the page, which returns the reader to the beginning of the document.

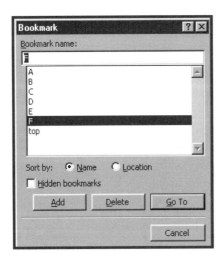

Figure 6.17

The template has already attached a bookmark to each heading.

3. Click on A on the list and then click on the Go To button. Notice the display jumps to the first heading, Work Information.
4. Click on each of the letters on the list in turn (B through F) and then click on the Go To button after each one, to see that these bookmarks do point to the headings on the page.
5. Click on Close to close the Bookmarks dialog box.
6. Point your mouse pointer to the first hyperlink at the top of the page: Work Information. Note that a ScreenTip appears that says "A," indicating that the A bookmark is associated with the hyperlink.
7. Right-click on that hyperlink and choose Hyperlink, Edit Hyperlink from the menu. The Edit Hyperlink dialog box appears.
8. Notice that there is no hyperlink in the top text box. Instead, the letter A appears in the Named Location in File box.
9. Click on Cancel to close that dialog box.

See how it works? Just for practice, try creating a new heading on the page and a new hyperlink for it at the top of the page. Here are the general steps:

1. Add the new heading.
2. Create a bookmark for it (see the Sunday Morning session).
3. Create the text for a hyperlink at the beginning of the document, with the other hyperlinks.
4. Select that text and click on the Insert Hyperlink button on the toolbar.
5. In the Named Location in File box, type the name of the bookmark.
6. Click on OK.

Creating a Page with Graphical Hyperlinks

Text-based hyperlinks are great because your reader knows right away what they represent. You can be very specific with your words: if you create a hyperlink out of the words "Elvis Museum," your readers can be pretty sure that they are going to be visiting the Elvis Museum page by clicking on that link.

But sometimes it's classier to have graphics for hyperlinks. Instead of clicking on some text to jump to a different page (or a different spot on the same page), the reader clicks on a graphical button or picture. For example, in Figure 6.18, the reader can click on one of the three buttons on the left. Text appears beside each button to clarify its meaning.

Preparing a Two-Column Page with Graphical Buttons

Word's two-column layout provides an excellent head start, so use it to create a page that uses graphical buttons as hyperlinks.

1. Choose File, New and double-click on the Web Page Wizard icon.
2. Choose 2-Column Layout and click on Next.

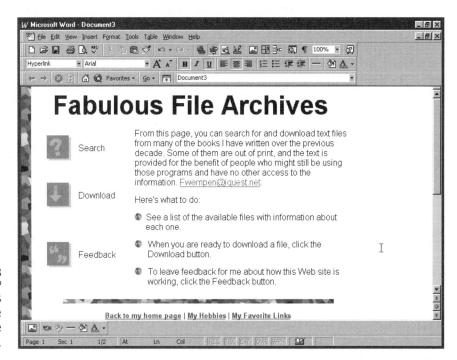

Figure 6.18

Graphical buttons make the Web page look more interesting.

3. Choose your favorite design scheme (I like Festive) and click on Finish.

4. Replace the text with your own text, and replace the hyperlink placeholders at the bottom with links to your other pages as appropriate.

5. Change the text beside each button as needed to change what you want the button to do. For example, if you want to provide more information about some files when the reader clicks on the question mark button, replace "Search" with "File Information" as I did in Figure 6.19.

6. Save your work.

Converting a Graphic to a Hyperlink

The buttons on the page are, so far, just graphics. You can click on one to select it like any graphic, and you can drag it around on the page if you

Figure 6.19

Customize the text on the page to make it your own, including the text explanations of the buttons.

want. But for now leave it in place, and follow these steps to make it into a hyperlink.

1. Click on the button to select it. Black selection handles appear around it.
2. Right-click on the button and choose Hyperlink from the shortcut menu. The Insert Hyperlink dialog box opens.
3. Type the URL or filename that you want the button to hyperlink to, and then click on OK.
4. Test the button by clicking on it. The specified file should appear in Word.

You aren't bound to these buttons; you can delete them and import your own graphics to use instead. (Remember, you learned how to import graphics into Word in the Saturday Afternoon session.)

Including Hyperlinks to Download Files

You are also not limited to using HTML files for your hyperlinks. Remember that you can also hyperlink to bookmarks in the same document. You can also hyperlink to a binary file to be transferred to the reader's computer via FTP. For example, suppose you want the Download button to automatically download the most recent version of some software to the reader's computer. You could enter a hyperlink for it like this:

ftp://ftp.iquest.net/~fwempen/mysoft.zip

A couple of things are different about this line from what you have seen so far. For one thing, it starts out ftp:// instead of http://. This warns the Web browser that an FTP address is forthcoming. If you don't specify http://, ftp://, gopher://, or whatever, most browsers (and Word) assume http://. This is why you haven't had to type it until this point.

Notice also that the line ends with a binary file (in this case a .zip file) rather than an HTML document. When your readers click on the hyperlink, the specified file will be sent to their computers and their browsers will do one of two things:

- If the browser is set up to handle that type of file automatically, it will handle it. For example, the browser may be set up to open .zip files with an unzipping program.

- If the browser is not set up to handle that file type, it will ask what to do with it, and offer the option of saving it to the hard disk (which is usually what the reader wants to do).

TIP A .zip file is a compressed binary file, which means it has been packed for shipping over the Internet with all its pieces consolidated into one convenient lump. If you had your readers download a compressed file like a .zip file, you would want to make sure that they had access to an unzipping tool like PKZIP. These days, it's fairly safe to assume that most people who use the Internet already have PKZIP, but you might also provide it (the shareware version) for download on your page.

Including Hyperlinks to Send E-mail

Remember early in this session, I had you type your e-mail address into Word, and Word automatically turned it into a hyperlink? That's the quickest way to create a hyperlink that the reader can use to open a window and send you an e-mail message. But suppose you want the "mail-to" hyperlink to be associated with a button—then what? It's easy. Just enter a hyperlink like this for the button:

mailto:fwempen@iquest.net

The "mailto:" part will inform the reader's browser that the link is meant as a convenience for sending e-mail, and the browser will open the appropriate mail-sending window. (Not all browsers support this, but most do.)

Inserting Images on a Page

You have already learned how to insert pictures into Word, and the procedure is not much different for placing pictures on a Web page.

CAUTION Pictures take a long time to load in readers' browsers, especially if a reader has a slow Internet connection. If your page takes too long to load, nobody will want to visit it again, so don't use too many images on a page, and keep the images small.

1. Position the insertion point where you want the picture.
2. Choose Insert, Picture, From File.
3. Choose the picture file you want to insert (see Figure 6.20).
4. Click on the Float over text check box, or not, depending on what you want:

    If you select the check box, the picture is in its own free-floating frame. You can drag the frame to position it precisely anywhere on the page. You cannot, however, drag it into a table within the page. (This works best for single-column layouts like the Personal Home

Figure 6.20

Choose the picture you want to include.

Page. The entire 2-Column Layout is a table, so if you use this feature with that type of page, the figure must be placed before or after all the rest of the page.)

If you do not select the check box, the picture is inserted at the insertion point, just like any character you would type. If the text moves, the picture moves along with it.

5. Click on Insert to insert the picture.
6. Resize the picture in the document as needed by dragging its handles.

NOTE Even though the procedure for placing an image in a Web page is much the same as placing an image in a regular Word document, what goes on behind the scenes is quite different. When you place an image in a regular Word document, that image is stored in the actual Word file. When you place an image in an HTML-format document, Word creates a separate image file (with a .gif extension) and saves it in the same folder as the HTML file itself. Then it creates a link from the HTML file to the .gif file so that whenever the HTML file loads, the .gif file loads and appears in the right spot. (It always needs to be in the same folder as the HTML file; otherwise the HTML file won't be able to find it.)

Changing Image Properties on a Web Page

Once you get the picture onto the Web page, the procedure for manipulating it is fairly different from what you may be used to in regular Word documents. There are fewer options because Web pages are more limited than native-format Word documents in how they can use graphics.

1. Right-click on the picture and choose Format Picture from the shortcut menu. A special Format Picture dialog box appears, as shown in Figure 6.21.
2. Click on the Settings tab if it is not already visible.
3. In the Text box, type any text that you want to appear while the file is loading.

Figure 6.21

Formatting pictures on a Web page is a little different from formatting them within a regular document.

 TIP I recommend that you enter some descriptive text in Step 3, even though it may not seem necessary. Sometimes Web pages take a long time to load, especially the graphics, and a reader who has an idea of what the graphic is going to be can make a more informed decision about whether to wait for it to load or move on.

4. Click on the Position tab (see Figure 6.22).
5. In the Text wrapping section, click on the button representing the alignment you want (left, right, or centered).
6. If you want the picture to be a specific distance from surrounding text, enter distances in the Vertical or Horizontal boxes, or both.
7. Click on OK.
8. Save your work.

Reviewing the Saved Images

Here's a little side trip (unnecessary, if you're pressed for time) that helps you understand what you just did:

1. Jump out to the Windows desktop, and open My Computer.

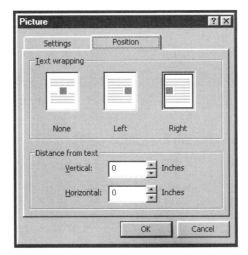

Figure 6.22

Here's the other tab full of picture-formatting options that you have to work with.

2. Open a window for the drive and folder containing your Word files (probably My Documents unless you changed the default saving location earlier in the weekend).

3. Notice all the image.gif files—image1.gif, image2.gif, and so on. These are the images used in your Web page, stored separately from the page itself.

4. Double-click on the one with the highest number (which is the picture you added to the page most recently). The image opens in your Web browser, all by itself. See, it really is saved as a separate file!

5. Close the Web browser and jump back to Word. Demonstration over.

 Want more images to use on your Web pages? Visit the Microsoft on the Web site, as you learned in the Saturday Afternoon Time-Savers. Here's another way to get there: Start your Internet connection, and then in Word choose Insert, Picture, Browse Web Art Page. This opens your Web browser and points it to the Microsoft Web Art Resource Page, where you can collect some more art.

Creating Horizontal Lines on a Web Page

One last exercise, and then I'll let you rest. I promise.

In this one, you'll start with a blank page and add some horizontal lines to it, just so you can see how that's done. Lines help separate text on a page—for example, on the Personal Home Page design, there is a horizontal line that separates the hyperlinks at the top of the document from the rest of the page.

The separator lines that you see in the predesigned Web Page Wizard pages are actually thin strips of artwork. Look back at the early figures in this chapter, for example, and you can see that there's a horizontal line in the Festive design that looks like a stained-glass window. Pretty, eh? When you incorporate lines like that, you treat them as what they are: images. It's just coincidental that they look like lines. You can place any of these artwork strips manually with the Horizontal Line command, as you'll see shortly. First, follow along with these steps to start a blank page:

1. Start a new Web page by choosing File, New and double-clicking on the Web Page Wizard icon.
2. Choose <Blank Page> and click on Next.
3. Choose any of the designs (I went with Festive once again) and click on Finish. Now you have a blank page that fits in with the design you've been using. See mine in Figure 6.23.

NOTE A blank page is not totally blank, because it contains the background image specified by the design. This is good, though, because it keeps the blank page looking like it fits in with the others. If you want a truly blank page, use the Blank Web Page template instead of the Web Page Wizard in the New dialog box.

Now insert some separator lines.

1. Type some text, and format it with Heading 2 style.
2. Press Enter to start a new line.

SUNDAY AFTERNOON Web Pages

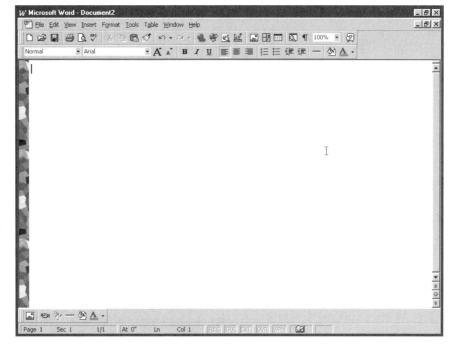

Figure 6.23

Sometimes you may want to start out with a blank page (no predesigned text, tables, or hyperlinks).

3. Choose Insert, Horizontal Line. The Horizontal Line dialog box opens (see Figure 6.24).

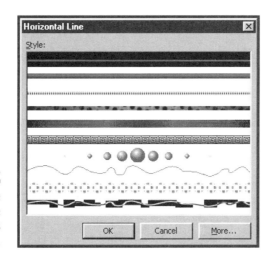

Figure 6.24

Choose the horizontal line that most appeals to you.

4. Click on the line that you want to insert, or click on the More button for access to the horizontal lines used by the Web Page Wizard designs.
5. Click on OK to place it.
6. Type some more text under the line, and then add another line. Figure 6.25 shows some text set off between two horizontal lines.

NOTE If you have graphics in other folders or on other drives that you want to use as horizontal lines, you can click on the More button to browse for them. You can download additional horizontal line graphics from the Microsoft Web site (Insert, Picture, Browse Web Art Site).

You can modify how these graphical lines look in your document for some very cool effects. I would love to tell you about them right now, but you're running out of daylight and you still have places to go in this

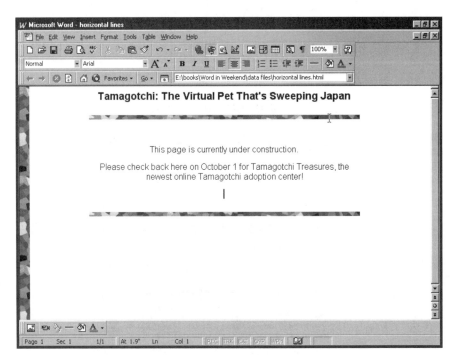

Figure 6.25

A pair of horizontal lines frames and accentuates this text.

Sunday Afternoon session. I'll save this treat for the Time-Savers section at the end of the session.

Publishing the Pages

Now you have some beautiful Web pages, but they aren't doing any good because nobody can see them but you. But that will change shortly.

Determining Your Save Location

Before you can publish your pages to the Internet, you need to contact your service provider and find out where on its server you need to put your pages. (If you are using a service like America Online, there is information available in the online help about this.) For example, your service provider might give you a path like this:

>ftp.servername.com/pub/web/homepage/members/yourname

This is the physical location on the server where you will send your files via FTP. This is *not* the address you will give to other people who want to access your page, however. The Web address to your page will likely be much simpler, like this:

>http://www.servername.com/~yourname

These addresses I'm showing you are just made-up examples; your service provider must tell you what real addresses to use.

Sending Your Work to the Server

When you publish your Web pages to the server, you must transfer all the following files:

- The welcome page
- All your pages that are linked to the welcome page
- All the image files associated with each page (image1.gif, image2.gif, and so on)

Here's the dilemma. You can transfer HTML files (the first two bulleted points) directly from Word to the server, and it's very easy. But Word provides no way to transfer the graphics to the server, so you need another way to transfer the graphics.

An FTP program can transfer both the HTML files and the graphic files easily, but you may not have an FTP program installed. Many good ones are available all over the Web, and most are shareware or freeware. However, finding and installing one could take at least a half-hour, and you probably don't want to take the time to do that now.

Microsoft offers a free Wizard called the Web Publishing Wizard that can easily transfer your pages and their accompanying graphics files to the server. There is a version on the Microsoft Office 97 CD, in the ValuePack/Webpost folder, so you don't need to download anything. Just install it right from there. However, when I tried to use the Web Publishing Wizard, it wouldn't work with my Internet Service Provider. I had to download the new version (1.5) from Microsoft's Web site to get it to work; so you may have to download it. (Exception: you're all set if you have already downloaded and installed Internet Explorer 4.0—it comes with the newest Web Publishing Wizard.)

Sigh. Don't you wish it were easier? Me too. In the following sections I'll explain a bit about each of your options, and I'll let you decide how to proceed based on what you've got and how much energy you have left this evening.

Publishing Your Work with the Web Publishing Wizard

Your Microsoft Office 97 CD comes with a program called Web Publishing Wizard that can transfer both HTML files and graphics files to a server. It's the ValuePack/WebPost folder on the Office 97 CD. You can install it from there, or you can download a more recent version from Microsoft's Web site.

If you want to install the version on the CD, here's how:

1. Use Windows Explorer to open the contents of the Microsoft Office 97 CD, and navigate to the ValuePack folder.
2. Double-click on the WebPost folder.
3. Double-click on the WebPost.exe file to run the installation program.
4. Follow the on-screen prompts to install.
5. Restart your computer before you attempt to use the Web Publishing Wizard.

To download and install the new version, do this:

1. Start your Internet connection if it is not already running, and open Internet Explorer.
2. Go to the following site:

    http://www.microsoft.com/windows/software/webpost/

3. Follow the downloading instructions and download the file to a temporary folder on your computer. (C:\Windows\Temp will do.)
4. Navigate to the new file on your hard disk using Windows Explorer and double-click on it to install the program.
5. Follow the on-screen installation prompts.
6. Restart your computer before you attempt to use the Web Publishing Wizard.

To start the Web Publishing Wizard, choose Start/Programs/Accessories/Internet Tools/Web Publishing Wizard. I won't give you specific steps for this because the steps are different depending on which version of the Wizard you are using. But the dialog boxes that appear are very clear in their instructions; you shouldn't have any problems.

You will be uploading either a single file or a single folder at a time, which means that you will have to run the Wizard many times if you have many files to upload. The shortcut, of course, is to create a separate folder on your hard disk and put into it all the files that you want to upload. Then just run the Wizard once and upload that one folder.

Transferring Files with an FTP Program

There are many good FTP programs out there, and most of them are shareware or free. You can use Internet Explorer to download such a program to your PC and install it, and then use that program to upload the files.

Two very good FTP programs are CuteFTP and WS_FTP. You can find them by visiting **http://www.shareware.com** and searching for either of those keywords. Then download and install the program. You may need to read the documentation that comes with the program to figure out how to use it, but both programs are fairly easy, with well-labeled buttons.

For example, if you're using WS_FTP, you first connect to the server using a dialog box like the one shown in Figure 6.26. This box appears automatically when you start the program.

Once WS_FTP has connected, you make sure the correct folder is showing on the server, and then select the file to transfer on your local hard disk and click on the right-arrow button, as shown in Figure 6.27. That's

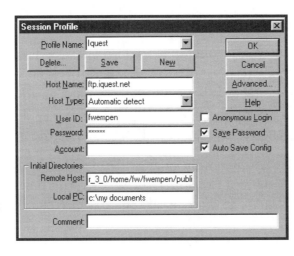

Figure 6.26

With an FTP program like WS_FTP, you first tell it what FTP site to connect with.

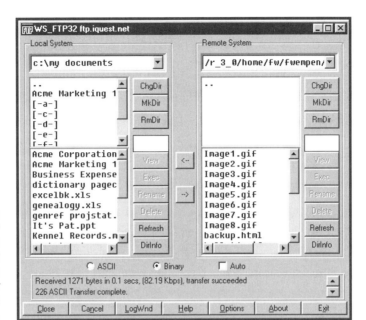

Figure 6.27

Once connected to the server, simply click on the file you want to transfer and click on the arrow button.

all there is to it! You can transfer multiple files at once by selecting more than one on your local hard disk.

An FTP program like WS_FTP can also be used to download files. In fact, most people used FTP programs to download files back in the days when Web browsers didn't have the capability.

Publishing Web Pages (Text Only) with Word

If you have text-only Web pages, this is definitely the method to use. It's also good if you have already saved the HTML files to the server once, and you are simply saving an updated version that doesn't include changes in graphics. You can also use this method to transfer your Web pages, and then one of the other methods to transfer your graphics. Follow these steps to save an HTML file to a server:

1. Start your Internet connection if it's not already running.
2. In Word, open the Web page that you want to save.
3. Choose File, Save As. The Save As dialog box appears.
4. Open the Save in drop-down list and choose Add/Modify FTP Locations (at the very bottom of the list). The Add/Modify Locations dialog box opens (see Figure 6.28).

NOTE The first time you save pages to the server, you use Add/Modify FTP Locations to set up the location. Subsequent times, the location will be listed on the Save in drop-down list, and you can choose it from there and save normally.

5. In the Name of FTP site text box, type ftp, a period, and the main address of the server that you want to log into. For example, my service provider is iquest.net, so I used **ftp.iquest.net**, as shown in Figure 6.28. Then I entered the rest of the address my service provider told me to use, as shown in Figure 6.29.

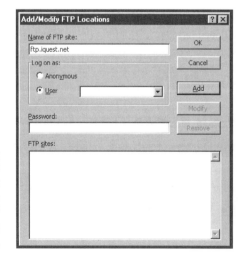

Figure 6.28

Choose Add/Modify FTP Locations to set up an FTP connection to the server.

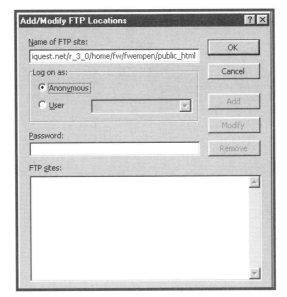

Figure 6.29

Your service provider should have provided the address at which to save pages.

6. Click on the User button, and type your user name in the text box next to it.
7. Type your password in the Password box.

 NOTE Word gives you the option of anonymous login instead of identifying yourself and giving a password, but almost every server requires you to log in with your name and password when you want to save files to its server. This is a security measure, so anonymous people don't upload destructive viruses.

8. Click on the Add button, and then click on OK. You return to the Save As dialog box, and your new FTP site is listed.
9. Click on your new site, and click on Open to connect to that site. A series of folders appears in the Save As dialog box, as shown in Figure 6.30.
10. Double-click on the first folder in the path that your service provider gave you to use. For example, if my service provider told

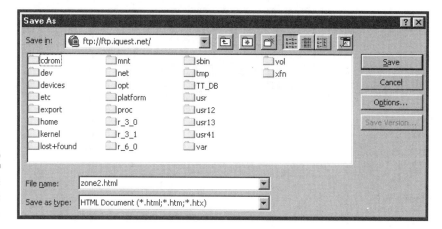

Figure 6.30

You are now in the top folder at the server site.

me that I should use /r_3_0/home/fwempen, I would first double-click on the r_3_0 folder.

11. Continue double-clicking on folders until you arrive at the one that you are supposed to use.

12. Click on Save. If you used any images in your page, you get a message like the one in Figure 6.31, telling you that you have some extra work to do. Click on OK.

13. Repeat this whole procedure for each Web page you want to save to the server.

If you received the graphics warning message shown in Figure 6.31, you will have to use one of the other methods to transfer the extra files. As the dialog box notes, the extra files have been copied to the C:\Windows\Temp folder; you can upload them from there, or you can

Figure 6.31

If you get this message, you will need to transfer some graphics files as an extra step.

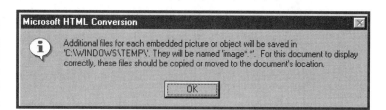

upload the originals from the location where you saved the HTML files on your hard disk. Both copies are the same.

Testing Your Web Pages

Now that your material is on the server, you should test it. This part's easy. Just open your Web browser (Netscape Communicator, Internet Explorer, or whatever browser you're using) and type in the address.

If your welcome page is named index.html, you don't have to type in the filename because index.html is the default name. However, if you've named the page anything else, you need to include the filename in the address you type. For example, my welcome page is zone1.html, so I typed:

> http://members.iquest.net/~fwempen/zone1.html

If your page doesn't appear onscreen, double-check that you have the right location and the right filename.

Once the page appears, test each of its links by clicking on it. The linked page should appear. Then click on the browser's Back button to return to the original page. This is just like the testing you did earlier in Word, but you're doing it on the live copy that's available all over the world through your Web site.

Getting More Visitors to Your Web Pages

Everything works? Congratulations! You are now "on the Web," and millions of people all over the world can read your pages!

Of course, in reality, you are not going to get millions of visitors to your pages, at least not right away. You can increase the number of visitors to your site in some of these ways:

- Provide content that people want to see. Even though it was fun to create a page with information about yourself, not many people are

going to find it fascinating reading, except maybe your family or potential suitors. To draw in the crowds, you'll want universally appealing content.

- Add a hyperlink to your site at the end of each e-mail message you send, and participate in Internet newsgroups that are related to your interests. People who read your posts in the newsgroup may want to check out your Web pages.
- Add your welcome page's address to your business card.
- Visit the various search engine sites and register to have your page included in their search. Click on the Search button in your browser to start with the default search site, and then follow links from that page to other search sites.
- Participate in link exchanges, where you list someone else's page as a link on your Favorite Links page and he or she, in turn, lists your site on their list of links.
- Add new content frequently! The same visitors will come back again and again if you give them new things to look at.

Editing Your Web Pages

Keeping fresh, updated content is one of the secrets of getting lots of traffic on your Web pages. You will want to update your content frequently.

You can open your pages directly from the server, in much the same way that you saved them there:

1. In Word, choose File, Open. The Open dialog box appears.
2. Open the Look in drop-down list and choose the FTP site where you saved your pages. If it's not on the list anymore, set it up again as you did when you saved.
3. Double-click on the page you want to edit.
4. Edit the page normally, and then save your work back to the server.

Time-Savers

I know this has been another power-packed session, so I'll keep the time-savers brief. Here are a couple of cool extras that you can use!

Modifying Horizontal Lines for Interesting Effects

Remember earlier in this session I showed you how to place horizontal lines on your Web pages? The lines are sometimes awfully thin in their original state, but you can thicken them up to make them more interesting and attractive.

1. Open a Web page that you've been working on, or start a new one.
2. Place a horizontal line on it. (Use Insert, Horizontal Line. For this example, I clicked on More and then chose Colorful Stone Stripe.)
3. Double-click on the horizontal line on your Web page to edit it. Gray lines appear at the corners, and a floating Edit Picture toolbar opens (see Figure 6.32).
4. Position the mouse pointer over the horizontal line, so the pointer becomes a four-headed arrow, and then click. This selects the graphic so that selection handles appear around it.
5. Position the mouse pointer over the bottom handle and drag down, making the line thicker, as shown in Figure 6.33. A dotted line shows where the bottom will be when you release the item.
6. Click on the Reset Picture Boundary button (the only other button on the Edit Picture toolbar besides Close), to tell Word that you want to keep the new size when you exit from picture-editing mode.
7. Click on Close. Your new-sized line appears.

Here's another cool thing you can do while you're editing the picture: right-click on the picture and choose Show Picture Toolbar. Then use the Contrast and Brightness buttons on that toolbar to change the appearance of the line.

392 Learn Word 97 In a Weekend

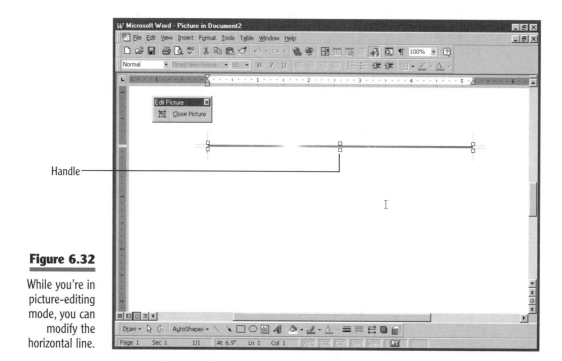

Figure 6.32

While you're in picture-editing mode, you can modify the horizontal line.

Handle

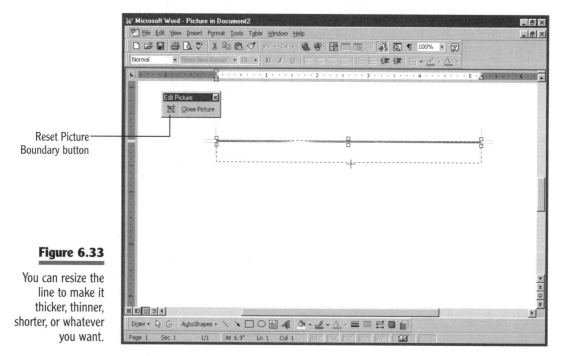

Figure 6.33

You can resize the line to make it thicker, thinner, shorter, or whatever you want.

Reset Picture Boundary button

Adding Scrolling Text to a Page

You have probably seen scrolling text (a.k.a. marquee text) on somebody else's Web page and thought it must be hard to set up. Not with Word! Scrolling text moves across the page as the reader views it, adding interest and calling attention to the words.

1. In Word, open a Web page to which you want to add scrolling text.
2. Choose Insert, Scrolling Text. The Scrolling Text dialog box appears.
3. Enter the text that you want to use in the Type the Scrolling Text Here box, as shown in Figure 6.34.
4. Use the other controls in the dialog box (which are fairly self-explanatory) to make the text scroll the way you want it to.
5. Click on OK.
6. Save your work.

Check out the result by choosing File, Web Page Preview.

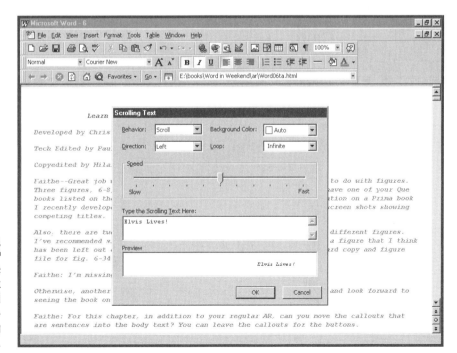

Figure 6.34

This easy-to-use dialog box helps you add professional-looking scrolling text.

More Web Page Ideas

There is a lot more you can do with Web pages. Here are some places to look for more information.

- Start a new document based on the More Cool Stuff template. It's on the Web Pages tab in the New dialog box, right next to the Web Page Wizard. The new document that appears contains information about add-in tools on the Office 97 CD.

- Choose Help, Microsoft on the Web, Free Stuff and check to see what add-ins are available for free download that can enhance your Web pages.

- If you're feeling adventurous, try out the Web Page Wizard's more advanced designs for forms and surveys. These require some integration with the server to work, so you'll need to talk to your service provider staff to discuss how to set up real surveys and forms. (It may be over your head if you don't have any programming experience.)

- Experiment with the commands on the Insert menu. You can insert background sounds that readers will hear when they open your page, and videos that will play themselves for your readers.

Using Hyperlinks in Non-Web Documents

Hyperlinks, as I've told you, don't necessarily have to point to Internet addresses. They can point to other documents on your local hard drive, or to bookmarks in a document.

You can use this to your advantage in long documents. Here are some ideas:

- Create bookmarks for each of the headings in the document. Then hyperlink each of the headings to its entry in the table of contents. Now your reader can browse the TOC and skip immediately to any specific section.

- If you need to refer to other sections of the document, set up hyperlinks in the document for cross-references. For example, if

you say "See the Integration section" in your document, select the words "Integration section" and insert a hyperlink there to the Integration heading elsewhere in the document.

- If there is information available on the Internet (or on your company's network) about something you talk about in a document, create a hyperlink to a Web address or to the document on your local server. For example, you might distribute a memo to all employees reminding them of a personnel policy, and include a hyperlink to the corporate Employee Procedures manual that's available on your local area network.

Conclusion

Congratulations! You made it through the weekend, and now you know more about Word than 90 percent of the folks out there who say they are Word users. Do you realize what a phenomenal feat you've accomplished by completing the book? You've traveled from basic file handling through tabs, bullets, fonts, text boxes, and even powerful features like indexes and Web pages, all in a little more than 48 hours. Very few computer courses, even those that cost thousands of dollars, cover this much material in such short a time. Pat yourself on the back—you've earned it in a big way.

As you complete your journey, take a moment and glance back through the sessions. There are probably topics that you will want to review later to make sure that you understand the features thoroughly. Do you remember how to change the bullet character? How to import graphics? How to create a bookmark hyperlink? Don't worry if the details don't spring to mind immediately. I certainly don't expect that you'll have perfect recall for everything that you've covered.

I hope that you'll continue working with Word, using it for all your home and work projects, and continue learning new features and skills with it. Appendix A, which follows this session, lists some resources that can help you take the next steps. Good Luck!

APPENDIX
Online Resources

If you're an Internet user, you have lots of information at your disposal that can help you become a more informed Word user. The following listing gives you some places to start.

Technical Support

On these Web pages, you can find the most recent telephone numbers and other contact information for Microsoft. If you don't want to wait on the telephone for technical support, you can request support via e-mail. You can also explore the Microsoft Knowledge Base, which contains thousands of articles about known problems with Microsoft products and suggested work-arounds for them.

Telephone numbers for technical support:

>   http://www.microsoft.com/supportnet/phonenumbers.htm

For general support information:

>   http://www.microsoft.com/support/

Troubleshooting assistance:

>   http://www.microsoft.com/support/tshooters.asp

The Microsoft Knowledge Base:

>   http://www.microsoft.com/kb/default.asp

Upgrades and Add-Ins

These free downloads can update your copy of Word 97, and can add new functionality to Word (like support for NetMeeting, additional Office Assistants, additional AutoShapes, and so on).

Just for Word:

> http://www.microsoft.com/OfficeFreeStuff/Word/

For all of Microsoft Office, including Word:

> http://www.microsoft.com/OfficeFreeStuff/Office/

For information about and a download link to the most recent version of Internet Explorer:

> http://www.microsoft.com/ie/ie40/

For information about other Microsoft products that you may find useful:

> http://www.microsoft.com/products/default.asp

Newsgroup Discussions

On newsgroups, you can read about problems and solutions from other users, and you can post your own questions for help from other users.

> http://www.microsoft.com/support/news/default.asp

INDEX

3-D tool, 175

A

Access, Microsoft, 244–245
Add/Modify FTP Locations, 386
Address Book, 133
addresses, sorting, 267
addressing envelopes, 126–128
advertising flyer, 180–183
alignment buttons, 15
America Online (AOL), 357
    NetFind, 358–359
    publishing Web pages on, 381
anonymous login, 387
Answer Wizard, 33
AOL NetFind, 358
Arial font, 95
arrow keys, moving insertion point with, 44
Arrow Style tool, 175, 178
articles, multicolumn, 191
Attention style, 290
authoring tools, Web page, 347
AutoCorrect feature, 107, 110, 139–140
Auto Hide feature, Windows Taskbar, 9
AutoMap Streets Plus, 169
AutoShapes, 171–172, 175, 179–180

AutoText, 135–137, 307–310
Avery labels, 252

B

Barbe Display SSi font, 189
binary files, 373
Bitmap Image Format, 181, 203–204
Blank Document template, 84–85, 289
Blank Web Page template, 378
.bmp files, 181, 203
Body Text style, 295–296
boilerplate text, 135–137
Bold button, 104–105, 119
bookmarks, 322, 323–324, 368–369, 395
books. *See* long documents
Border button, 119
borders
    adding to letterhead, 117–119
    dotted line, 152
    headers and footers, 311
    letterhead, 117–119
    Page Border feature, 156–157
breaks
    column, 215
    page, 215
    section, 213–215, 239, 240, 316

browser, Web, 344, 358
bulleted lists
    changing bullet character, 165–166
    for flyers, 162–168
    for letters, 102–105
business letters, 114–115. *See also* letters

C

callouts, 179–180
Cancel buttons, dialog box, 23
capitalization, automatic, 140
Caps Lock, correcting accidental use of, 140
carbon copy (cc:) field, 133
cascading menus, 13
case-sensitive searching, 76
catalog listing, 257–259
categories, changing clip, 208–209
cells, table, 224
    resizing, 262–263
    splitting and merging, 263–265
centering text with Vertical Alignment, 93
character styles, 298
check boxes, dialog box, 22, 23
Check for Errors feature, 235–237
clip art
    Clip Gallery, 201–202, 204–207, 208–209
    color, 156
    downloading from Internet, 204–207
    importing, 202–204
    for newsletters and flyers, 201–202
Clipboard, 41, 53–54, 360
Clip Gallery, 201–202, 204–207, 208–209
Close button, 8, 9
closing
    documents, 65–66
    Print Preview, 80
    Word window, 6
Collapse Subdocuments, 332
collapsing outline levels, 285–288
collating documents, 72
color borders and clip art, 156
column breaks, 215
columns
    adjusting width, 260–263
    breaks, 215
    creating documents with multiple, 191, 192–193, 211–212
    displaying vertical guides for, 192–193
    inserting and deleting in tables, 226–227
    selecting, 226–227, 228
command buttons, dialog box, 22, 23
commands
    menu, 11, 12–14
    unavailable, 14

communicating with Word, 11–12
Communicator, Netscape, 344
Company Name style, 290
compressed binary files, 373
CompuServe, 357
concordance file, 319, 325–327
connecting Web pages, 364–365
Contemporary template
    letters, 85–88, 290
    reports, 329
Contents command, Help system, 37
controls
    dialog boxes, 21–23
    Word program, 5–7
Convert Text to Table, 247–248
Copy command, 53–55
copying
    with Copy command, 53–55
    Help topics to Clipboard, 41
    lines and shapes, 172–173
    text, 52–56
cross-references, 322–323, 395
customizing
    bulleted lists, 165–166
    letter templates, 86
    Office Assistant, 35
Cut command, 53–54
CuteFTP, 384

D

database programs, 242, 244–245
data entry form, 248–250
data sources, mail merge
    Access, 244–245
    Excel, 242–244
    text file, 245–248
    Word form, 248–250
date codes, inserting
    in headers and footers, 307, 308
    in letterhead, 122–123
Decrease Indent, 97
Default Paragraph Font, 289

deleting
    columns in tables, 227
    lines and shapes, 172–173
    styles, 296, 300–301
    text, 48–51
desktop publishing, 149–150, 165
dialog boxes, 13
    common controls, 21–23
    purpose of, 20–21
Dial-Up Networking, 357
dictionary, adding words to Word, 110
displaying
    nonprinting characters, 30–32, 121
    Windows Taskbar, 9
documents. *See also* flyers; letters; long documents; newsletters; Web pages
    closing, 65–66
    combining into master document, 330–333
    creating and editing, 43
        deleting text, 48–51
        finding and replacing text, 56–59
        moving and copying text, 52–56
        selecting text, 47–48, 49, 50
    finding, 68–70
    inserting section breaks, 213–215
    merged (*See* mail merge)
    moving around in, 43–45
    multicolumn, 191, 192–193, 211–212
    opening, 66–70, 105
        multiple, 10–11
    printing, 70–73
    saving, 60–62
        choosing location for, 62–64
        to a different name, 67
        in other formats, 64–65
    switching between open, 11
    viewing, 24, 26–30
    window controls, 6, 10–11
    zooming in on, 24–26
dot matrix printers, 126, 253
dotted lines, 151–154
double spacing documents, 102

downloading
    files with hyperlinks, 372–373
    patches from Microsoft, 4, 75–76
drag-and-drop, 55–56, 284
dragging windows with mouse, 11
Drawing toolbar, 143, 144, 157, 169–171, 174–175
drawing tools, 169
    3-D tool, 175
    AutoShapes, 171–172
    lines and shapes, 170–171
drive, selecting, 62–64

E

Edit Data Source, 237–238
editing
    documents, 43
        Cut, Copy, and Paste, 53–55
        drag-and-drop method, 55–56
    headers and footers, 303–307
    Web pages, 390
    WordArt, 210–211
Elegant template
    letters, 85
    reports, 329
ellipses, 13, 170
e-mail, Web page hot link, 357, 373
employee procedures manual, 395
enclosures, letter, 134–135
end-of-file marker, 6–7
end-of-paragraph markers, 30
envelopes
    creating, 126–128
    merged, 254–256
    sorting by ZIP code, 267
    testing and printing, 128–131
errors. *See* mistakes
Excel, Microsoft, 242–244, 268
exiting program, 4
Expanding Subdocuments, 332
exporting files, 64–65
extensions, file, 67

F

fields, 219, 222–223, 231, 232, 249
files. *See also* documents
    binary, 373
    common file extensions, 67
        .bmp format, 181
        .gif format, 181, 375
        .htm format, 345
        .jpg format, 181
        .pcx format, 181
        .pic format, 181
        .rtf format, 64–65
        .tif format, 181
        .txt format, 245
        .zip format, 372–373
    compressed, 373
    downloading, 204–207, 372–373
    exporting, 64–65
    index.htm, 345
    multimedia, 201, 204–207
    naming, 67
    organizing with master document, 330–333
    plain text, 245–248
    saving to Internet, 64
    scanned image file formats, 181
    splitting long documents into multiple, 288–289
Fill Color tool, 174, 177, 180
filters, 240, 269–271
"Find all word forms" option, 77
Find and Replace feature, 56–59, 76–78
Find command, Help system, 39–40
finding documents, 68–70
flipping lines and shapes, 173–174
Float Over Text option, 182, 374
flyers
    creating
        clip art, 201–202
        formatting text, 151
        importing scanned images, 181–183
        page borders, 156–157
        tear-off lines, 151–154
        text and bulleted lists, 162–168
        WordArt titles, 157–162

flyers (*continued*)
　examples
　　advertising flyer, 180–183
　　map, 169, 175–180
　　party invitation, 155–168
　　permission slip, 150–154
folders
　finding, 68–70
　specific
　　documents, 62–64
　　Letters & Faxes, 124
　　Templates, 124
　　Web page, 353
fonts
　Arial, 95
　Barbe Display SSi, 189
　choosing for letters, 94–95
　entering sizes manually, 189
　Times New Roman, 94
footers. *See* headers and footers
Format Picture, 375–376
formatting
　documents (*See* styles)
　headers and footers, 311
　indexes, 328
　searching for, 77
　with styles, 289
　table of contents, 317–319
　tables, 265–266
Formatting toolbar
　buttons, 18–20, 119
　changing font and size from, 94
　description of, 7
　setting indents, 97
form letters. *See* mail merge
forms, advanced designs for, 394
for-sale flyer, 180–183
Free Stuff page, Microsoft, 75, 394
Frequently Asked Questions, Microsoft Word, 75, 76
FTP
　anonymous login, 387
　downloading files with, 344, 372
　programs, 384–385
　setting up location on server, 386
Full Block letter style, 95, 132
Full Justify alignment, 119–121

G

.gif files, 181, 375
Gopher, 344
grammar-checking
　entire letter, 111–112
　individual words and phrases, 107–108
　setting options, 137–139
　turning off, 108, 112
graphical hyperlinks, 369–372
graphics
　inserting on Web pages, 374–375
　reviewing saved, 376–377
green underlining, words with, 107–108

H

"Happy Chef" letterhead, 113, 141–145
hard disk, saving documents to, 60
Header and Footer toolbar, 303–307
header record delimiters, 231
headers and footers
　for different document types
　　documents with multiple sections, 314–315
　　long documents, 302–313
　　newsletters, 199
　different first page, 311–313
　formatting, 311, 313–314
　inserting page, date, and time codes, 307, 308, 313–314
　toolbar, 303–307
　varying for odd and even pages, 311–313
headings, document
　collapsing and expanding, 285–288
　creating table of contents from, 315–317
　examples, 277–278
　meaning of plus and minus signs, 280
　styles for, 289–290
Help system, 32
　choosing Help topics, 36–40
　Microsoft Web site, 75–76

letterhead

Office Assistant, 5, 33–36
What's This?, 42
working with Help topics, 40–41
hiding
    nonprinting characters, 30–32
    Windows Taskbar, 9
Hobbies page, 361–362, 363
horizontal lines on Web pages, 378–381, 391–393
hot links, 345
.htm files, 345
HTML, 344–345, 351, 352
    templates, 346–347
http://, 372
hyperlinks, 345
    adding to Web pages, 357–361
    connecting Web pages with, 353, 364
    creating in Word, 360–361
    creating within a Web page, 366–369
    downloading files with, 372–373
    graphical, 369–372
    testing, 365–366
    using in non-Web documents, 394–395
Hypertext Markup Language, 344–345, 351, 352
    templates, 346–347

I

icons, 13
images
    importing scanned, 181–183
    reviewing saved, 376–377
Increase Indent, 97
increment buttons, text box, 21, 22
indents, 95, 97–98
Index command, Help system, 37–39
index.htm files, 345
indexing long documents, 319–325, 328–329
Information Superhighway, 344. *See also* Internet
inkjet printers, 126, 128–130, 253
Insert Columns button, 227
Insert Hyperlink, 360
insertion point, 6, 44–46, 225
Insert Merge Field button, 231–232

Insert mode, 44
Insert Rows button, 228
Insert Table button, 224
installing
    graphics import filters, 181
    templates, 85
    Web tools, 347
Internet
    downloading
        clip art, 204–207
        multimedia files, 204–207
    Microsoft Web site, 4, 75–76, 204–207, 377, 380
    saving files to, 64
    search tools, 358–359
    service providers, 343
    terminology, 343–346
    Web browsers, 344, 358
Internet Explorer, Microsoft, 344, 358

J

.jpg files, 181

L

labels. *See* mailing labels
landscape *vs.* **portrait printing**, 72–73
laser printers, 126, 128–130, 253
layout, page. *See* Page Setup options
leading, 99
letterhead
    adding border, 117–119
    adding extra spaces, 119–122
    aligning, 119–122
    creating
        "Happy Chef," 140–145
        simple, 114–115
    designing, 112–114
    inserting date code, 122–123
    inserting symbols, 115–117
    making name bold, 119
    sample personal and business, 113–114, 140–145
    setting defaults, 115
    using preprinted, 125–126

letters
  checking for errors, 106–112
  creating
    adjusting line spacing, 98–102
    boilerplate text, 135–137
    bulleted lists, 102–105
    cc: field, 133
    choosing font, 94–95
    enclosures and reference lines, 134–135
    margins and page alignment, 89–93
    tabs and indents, 95–98
    typing text for, 89
  designing letterhead, 112–123
  envelopes for, 126–128
  methods of creating
    from scratch, 88–95
    from templates, 85–88
  personalized. *See* mail merge
  styles, Semi-Block *vs.* Full Block, 95
  types of, 83–84
  using preprinted stationery, 125–126
Letters & Faxes folder, 124
Letter Wizard, 85, 131–135
light bulb, Office Assistant, 35
Line Color tool, 174
lines
  adjusting spacing of, 98–102
  copying and deleting, 172–173
  drawing, 170
  moving, 172
  rotating and flipping, 173–174
  styles, 119
Line Style tool, 175
Line Thickness tool, 174
Line tool, 178
links. *See* hyperlinks
Links page, 362–363
Link to File option, 182
lists, bulleted, 102–105, 162–168
long documents
  concordance file, 319, 325–327
  headers and footers, 302–313
  indexing, 319–325, 328–329
  organizing files with master document, 330–333
  outlining, 276–288
  problems with, 275–276
  splitting into multiple files, 288–289
  table of contents, 315–319
  using hyperlinks in, 394–395
  using styles for, 289, 290–302
  writing, 288–289

M

mailing labels, 251–254
  sorting by ZIP code, 267
mailings, mass, 219, 251. *See also* mail merge
mail merge
  applications
    catalog listing, 257–259
    envelopes, 254–256
    letters, 229–232
    mailing labels, 251–254
  basic steps, 219–221
  changing record data, 237–238
  data sources
    Access, 244–245
    Excel, 242–244
    text files, 245–248
    Word form, 248–250
  errors
    checking for, 235–237
    preventing, 233–235
  executing merge, 232–235
  merging to new document, 239–241
  previewing letters, 237
  printing letters, 240–241
  saving, 241–242
  sorting and filtering data, 267–271
  table
    assembling data, 222–223
    creating, 223–224
    typing table data, 225–229
Mail Merge Helper, 229–230, 238–239, 248, 253
Mail Merge toolbar, 231, 233, 234–235
mailto: hyperlink, 373
map, creating with Word, 169, 175–180
mapping programs, 169

margins, 7, 89, 91–92, 153
marking terms for indexing, 320–322
mass mailings, 126, 219. *See also* mail merge
master document, organizing files with, 330–333
Master Document view, 29–30, 330–333
masthead, creating, 186–191
"Match case" option, 76
maximizing Word window, 6, 8
memory, computer, 60
menus
    cascading, 13
    menu bar, 7
    menu commands, 11, 12–14
    shortcut, 12, 20
Merge Cells, 263–264
merge codes, 220, 229
merge fields, 231, 232, 253
merge letter, creating, 229–232
Merge to New Document, 239
Merge to Printer, 241
Microsoft
    applications
        Access, 244–245
        Excel, 242–244, 268
        Exchange, 133
        Internet Explorer, 344, 358
        Mail, 133
        Network, 357
        Office, 74, 242, 382
            patch for Office 97, 4, 75–76
        Outlook, 133
        Schedule+, 133
    ValuePack/WebPost folder, 382–383
    Web site, 4
        Clip Gallery, 201–202, 204–207
        Free Stuff page, 75, 394
        Web Art Resource Page, 377
Minimize button, 8
minimizing Word window, 6, 8
misspelled words, 106–107, 108–112
mistakes
    AutoCorrect feature, 139–140
    fixing with Undo and Redo, 51–52
    grammar, 108–112

mail merge, 233–237
spelling, 106–107, 108–112
Modified Block letter style, 132
More Cool Stuff template, 394
mouse
    drag-and-drop editing, 55–56
    moving insertion point with, 44–45
    pointer, 7
    selecting text with, 47–48, 49
    using right and left buttons, 20
Move Down button, 282, 284
Move Up button, 282, 284
moving
    lines and shapes, 172
    text, 52–56
    windows, 11
multicolumn documents, 191, 192–193, 211–212
multimedia files
    Clip Gallery, 201
    downloading from Internet, 204–207
    importing, 204
My Computer, 74, 75

N

names, sorting, 267
naming documents, 67
NetFind, AOL, 358–359
Netscape Communicator, 344
newsletters
    clip art, 201–202
    creating
        with Newsletter Wizard, 184–185
        from scratch, 186–196
    finishing touches, 195–196
    headers and footers, 199
    inserting articles, 194–195
        multicolumn, 191, 192–193, 211–212
    mailing, 242, 251
    mastheads, 186–191
    multiple pages, 193–194
    numbering pages, 199
    saving template, 200
    text box tricks, 197–198

Newsletter Wizard, 184–185
new-user quiz, 3
nonprinting characters, 30–32, 121
Normal style, 289, 295
Normal view, 26, 27, 30, 303, 333
numbering pages, 199, 307, 313–315, 333

O

Office Assistant
    character, 5, 34
    customizing, 35
    dialog box button, 22, 23
    searching for help, 34–36
    turning off and on, 33
OK buttons, dialog box, 23
Online Layout view, 26–27
opening documents, 10–11, 66–70, 105
option buttons, dialog box, 21, 22
orientation, page, 72–73
outlines
    collapsing levels, 285–288
    moving lines, 284–285
    Outlining toolbar, 277, 281, 282–283
    promoting and demoting lines, 281–283
    purpose of, 276–278
    starting, 278–280
Outline view, 27–29, 279
Outlining toolbar, 277, 281, 282–283, 284
Overtype mode, 44

P

Page Border feature, 156–157
page breaks, 215
Page Layout view, 27, 28, 303
PageMaker, 149
page numbering, 199, 307, 313–315, 333
page orientation, 72–73
Page Range, 71–72
Page Setup options, 72–73, 91–93
paper-clip character. *See* Office Assistant

paragraphs
    adjusting space between, 43, 98–102
    alignment options, 132
        Full Justify, 119–121
    assigning style to, 290
    bulleted, 102–105
    markers, 30
    rearranging, 53
    styles, 298
    underlining, 118
party invitation flyer, 155–168
Paste command, 53–55
patches, downloading from Microsoft, 4, 75–76
.pcx files, 181
permission slip flyer, 150–154
personalized letters. *See* mail merge
personal letters, 113. *See also* letters
.pic files, 181
pictures
    downloading from Internet, 204–207
    importing, 181–183, 204
    inserting on Web pages, 374–375
PKZIP, 373
plain text, saving documents in, 64–65
portrait *vs.* landscape printing, 72–73
preprinted stationery, 125–126
printing
    documents, 70–73
    envelopes, 128–131
    Help topics, 41
    mailing labels, 252, 253
    merged letters, 240–241
    on preprinted stationery, 125–126
    previewing documents before, 78–80
    reverse side of flyer, 169
    selecting printer, 71
Print Preview, 78–80, 91
Prodigy, 357
Professional template
    letters, 85
    reports, 329
Properties, document, 348
publishing Web pages, 366, 381–389

Q

QuarkXpress, 149
query
    Access, 244, 245
    filtering records with, 269–270
quiz, new-user, 3

R

records, 219, 220, 250
    changing data in, 237–238
    filtering, 269–271
rectangles, drawing, 170
Rectangle tool, 177
Redo command, 51–52
red underlining, words with, 106, 107
renaming documents, 67
Replace feature, 56, 58–59
resizing
    table columns, 260–263
    windows, 11
Restore button, 8
restoring Word window, 6, 8–9
Return Address style, 290
reverse video, 47
right mouse button, 20
rotating lines and shapes, 173–174
rows, table
    inserting and deleting, 228–229
    selecting, 228
.rtf files, 64–65
Ruler line, 6, 7, 152–153
running headers and footers, 302–313

S

salutation, 132
Save As feature, 61–62, 64
Save With Document option, 182
saving
    changing default location for, 78
    documents, 60–62, 78
    mail merge letter and table, 241–242
    templates, 124, 200

scanned images, importing, 181–183
ScreenTips, 7
Scrolling Text, 393–394
Search button, Office Assistant, 35
search tools, Internet, 358–359
section breaks, 213–215, 239, 240, 316
selecting text, 47–48, 49, 50
Semi-Block letter style, 95, 132
separator characters, 245, 246
shading, 118
Shadow tool, 175
shapes
    copying and deleting, 172–173
    drawing and manipulating, 170–172
    moving, 172
    rotating and flipping, 173–174
shortcut keys, 11, 14
    assigning to styles, 334–335
    moving insertion point with, 45–46, 225
    selecting text, 50
shortcut menus, 12, 20
Show/Hide button, 31, 121
Show Picture toolbar, 391–393
single spacing documents, 102
Slogan style, 290
sorting data, 267–269
sound files, 204–207
sounds, Web page, 394
"Sounds like" option, 77
source code, HTML, 351, 352
spaces, 30
special characters, searching for, 77
spell-checking
    entire letter, 108–110
    individual words, 106–107
    turning off, 108
Split Cells, 264–265
spreadsheet programs, 242–244
Standard toolbar
    buttons, 16–18
    description of, 7
starburst AutoShape, 179–180
starting program, 4, 74–75

Start menu, Windows Taskbar, 4
stationery, using preprinted, 125–126
styles, 289
    assigning shortcut keys to, 334–335
    assigning to paragraphs, 290
    borrowing from other templates, 299–300
    creating new, 295–299
    creating toolbar for, 336–340
    deleting, 296, 300–301
    modifying existing, 291–295
    paragraph contrasted with character, 298
    table of contents, 319
subdocuments, 29, 332
subheads, 280
surveys, advanced designs for, 394
symbols
    for bullet character, 165, 166
    selecting and inserting in letterhead, 115–117

T

Table AutoFormat, 266
table illustrations
    Buttons for Changing Drives and Folders in Windows 95 Dialog Boxes, 63
    Formatting Toolbar Buttons, 18–20
    Header and Footer Toolbar Buttons, 304–305
    Merge Function Buttons on the Mail Merge Toolbar, 234–235
    Moving Insertion Point in a Table, 225
    Outlining Toolbar, 282–283
    Selecting Text with Mouse, 49
    Shortcut Keys for Moving Insertion Point, 46
    Shortcut Keys for Selecting Text, 50
    Standard Toolbar Buttons, 16–18
    WordArt Toolbar Buttons, 210
table of contents, 276, 278, 315–319, 333
tables
    adjusting column widths, 260–263
    creating, 223–224
    formatting, 265–266
    inserting and deleting rows and columns, 226–229
    sample, 220
    sorting and filtering merge data, 267–271
    splitting and merging cells, 263–265
    suggested uses for, 260
    typing data into, 225–226
tabs, dialog box, 21, 22
Tab stops
    displaying or hiding, 30
    searching for and replacing, 246
    as separator characters in text files, 245, 246
    setting, 7, 95–96, 154, 186–188
Tagged Image Format, 181
tear-off line, 151–154
templates, 43. *See also* Wizards
    borrowing styles from, 299–300
    deleting styles from, 300–301
    HTML, 346–347
    installing, 85
    letterhead, 114–115, 140–145
    newsletter, 200
    report, 329–330
    saving, 124, 200
    specific
        Blank Document, 84–85, 289
        Blank Web Page, 378
        Contemporary, 85–88, 290, 329
        Elegant, 85, 329
        More Cool Stuff, 394
        Professional, 85, 329
    using saved, 124–125
testing
    envelopes, 128–131
    hyperlinks, 365–366
    Web pages, 389
text
    deleting, 48–51
    finding and replacing, 56–59
    moving and copying, 52–56
    selecting, 47–48, 49, 50
text boxes
    creating multicolumn documents with, 191, 192–193
    dialog box, 21, 22
    resizing and moving, 168
    tricks for improving layout, 197–198
    when to use, 165
    widening, 197

text files, converting to tables, 245–248
theme shift, long document, 277
three-dimension (3D) tool, 175
.tif files, 181
time of day, inserting, 307, 308
Time-Savers
   clips
      downloading from Internet, 204–207
      importing, 202–204
      modifying WordArt, 210–211
      recategorizing, 208–209
   general Word
      changing default save location, 78
      Find and Replace options, 76–78
      getting help from Microsoft Web site, 75–76
      previewing print jobs, 78–80
      setting custom grammar-checking rules, 137–139
      starting Word, 74–75
      upgrading Word 97 to latest version, 4
      using AutoCorrect to fix common typing errors, 139–140
   letter-writing
      creating fancy letterheads, 140–145
      Letter Wizard, 131–135
      using boilerplate text, 135–137
   multicolumn documents
      creating without text boxes, 211–213
      using section breaks in, 213–215
   reports and long documents
      assigning shortcut keys to style, 334–335
      creating toolbar of style buttons, 336–340
      organizing files with master document, 330–333
      using report templates, 329–330
   tables
      adjusting column widths, 260–263
      formatting, 265–266
      sorting and filtering merge data, 267–271
      splitting and merging table cells, 263–265
   Web pages
      adding scrolling text, 393–394
      modifying horizontal lines for interesting effects, 391–393
Times New Roman font, 94

tips
   correspondence
      choosing fonts for business letters, 95
      installing letter templates, 85
      using Letter Wizard, 132
      using names and addresses from other Microsoft applications, 133
      using Vertical Alignment to center text for letters, 93
   flyers and newsletters
      adding text box to maps, 179
      choosing colored borders and clip art, 156
      clip art, bypassing message about additional artwork on CD, 202
      creating extra pages, 194
      cutting and pasting from mapping programs, 169
      dealing with multi-page articles, 195
      drawing more of the same shape, 171
      increasing your options for fonts and font sizes, 189
      printing double-sided flyers, 169
      using Format AutoShape to control shapes and lines, 175
      using Newsletter Wizard, 185
      using Ruler line to control paragraph margins, 153
      working with WordArt, 160
   general Word
      changing from Insert mode to Overtype mode, 44
      displaying nonprinting characters with Show/Hide button, 121
      identifying default printer, 70
      installing Word's graphics import filters, 181
      navigating dialog boxes, 230
      Office Assistant, choosing character, 34
      Office Assistant, responding to light bulb, 35
      opening a recently used file from File menu, 105
      positioning Tab stops, 154
      saving documents, setting preferred format for, 65
      saving documents in other formats, 64
      saving documents to Internet locations, 64
      selecting text on a page, 72
      shrinking Find dialog box during text searches, 78
      sorting paragraphs by first letter, 267
      turning off bullets feature, 167
      unassigned shortcut key combinations, 335
      using alignment buttons on toolbar, 15

tips (*continued*)
    using mouse to drag a window, 11
    using shortcut keys, 14
    using Undo and Redo commands, 52
    using What's This? feature for identifying on-screen elements, 42
    using wildcards to locate documents, 68
mail merge and tables
    changing return address for envelopes, 256
    choosing which records to print, 241
    converting text to tables, 246
    mailing labels, 252
    moving from field to field, 224
    resizing column widths, 261
    starting new row, 225
reports and long documents
    adding table of contents, 316, 317
    advantage of working in Normal view, 333
    creating an index or concordance file, 320, 321, 327, 328
    formatting headers and footers, 311
    inserting page numbers in headers and footers, 303
    moving lines in outlines, 284
    using headings to organize, 278
    using Tab in Outline view, 279
Web pages
    creating text-only version, 352
    getting images from Microsoft Web Art Resource Page, 377
    including descriptive text for images, 376
    including e-mail hot link, 357
    providing visitors with PKZIP, 373
    saving documents as HTML files, 347
    separating public and restricted-access Web pages, 345
    storing in separate folder, 353
    using hyperlinks in, 367
title bar, 7
TOC (table of contents), 276, 278, 315–319, 333
toolbar buttons
    communicating with Word via, 12
    determining function of, 16
    Formatting toolbar, 18–20
    Standard toolbar, 16–18
    using, 14–15

toolbars
    Drawing, 143, 144, 157, 169–171, 174–175
    Formatting and Standard, 7
    Header and Footer, 303–307
    Mail Merge, 231, 233, 234–235
    Outline, 277, 281, 282–283, 284
    Show Picture, 391–393
    WordArt, 160, 210
.txt files, 245
typing letters, 89

U

underlining, 14, 118
Undo command, 51–52
Uniform Resource Locator (URL), 345, 357–359, 360
upgrading Word 97, 4
URL. *See* Uniform Resource Locator (URL)

V

ValuePack/WebPost folder, Microsoft, 382–383
Vertical Alignment, 92, 93
video files, 204–207
videos, Web page, 394
View buttons, 7
viewing documents, 24, 26–30
View menu, 7
View Merged Data, 237
views
    Master Document, 29–30, 330–333
    Normal, 26, 27, 30, 303, 333
    Online Layout, 26–27
    Outline, 27–29, 279
    Page Layout, 27, 28, 303
visitors, Web page, 389–390

W

wallpaper, 204
Web Art Resource Page, Microsoft, 377
Web browser, 344, 358
Web Page Authoring, 347

Web pages
    changing image properties, 375–376
    connecting, 364–365
    contrasted with other documents, 346–347
    creating
        inserting images, 374–375
        simple, 347–352
        text-only version, 352
        with Web Page Wizard, 354–357
        with Word, 343
    editing, 390
    examples
        Hobbies page, 361–362, 363
        Links page, 362–363
        Welcome page, 345–346, 353
    hyperlinks, 357–361
        creating within a page, 366–369
        graphical, 369–372
    increasing traffic, 389–390
    installing Word tools for creating, 347
    planning for multi-page site, 352–354
    previewing, 351
    publishing, 366, 381–389
    reviewing saved images, 376–377
    separating public and restricted-access, 345
    special effects
        horizontal lines, 391–393
        scrolling text, 393–394
        sounds and video, 394
    testing, 365–366, 389
    text-only, 385–389
    titles, 350
Web Page Wizard, 354–357, 368, 378–381, 394
Web Publishing Wizard, 382–384
Web site, Microsoft, 4, 75–76, 204–207
What's This? feature, 22, 23, 42
widening text boxes, 197
wildcards, 68, 77
window controls
    documents, 6, 10–11
    Word program, 6, 8–9

windows, moving and resizing, 11
Windows Clipboard. *See* Clipboard
Windows Explorer, 74, 75
Windows Taskbar
    Auto Hide feature, 9
    Start menu, 4
Wizards. *See also* templates
    Answer Wizard, 33
    Letter Wizard, 85, 131–135
    Newsletter Wizard, 184–185
    Web Page, 354–357, 368, 378–381, 394
    Web Publishing, 382–384
WordArt, 143–145
    editing, 158, 210–211
    for newsletter masthead, 188–189
    positioning and sizing, 159–162
    titles for flyers, 157–162
    toolbar buttons, 210
WordPerfect
    exporting to, 64–65
    opening documents from, 67
work area, 11
Works, exporting to, 64–65
World Wide Web, 344. *See also* Web pages
Write, exporting to, 64–65
writing style. *See* grammar-checking
WS_FTP, 384–385

X

X (Close button), 8, 9

Z

ZIP code, sorting by, 267
.zip files, 372–373
Zoom feature, 24–26, 195

OTHER BOOKS FROM PRIMA PUBLISHING
Computer Products Division

ISBN	Title	Price
0-7615-1175-X	ACT! 3 Visual Learning Guide	$16.99
0-7615-0680-2	America Online Complete Handbook and Membership Kit	$24.99
0-7615-0417-6	CompuServe Complete Handbook and Membership Kit	$24.95
0-7615-0692-6	Create Your First Web Page In a Weekend	$29.99
0-7615-0743-4	Create FrontPage Web Pages In a Weekend	$29.99
0-7615-0428-1	The Essential Excel 97 Book	$27.99
0-7615-0733-7	The Essential Netscape Communicator Book	$24.99
0-7615-0969-0	The Essential Office 97 Book	$27.99
0-7615-0695-0	The Essential Photoshop Book	$35.00
0-7615-1182-2	The Essential PowerPoint 97 Book	$24.99
0-7615-1136-9	The Essential Publisher 97 Book	$24.99
0-7615-0752-3	The Essential Windows NT 4 Book	$27.99
0-7615-0427-3	The Essential Word 97 Book	$27.99
0-7615-0425-7	The Essential WordPerfect 8 Book	$24.99
0-7615-1008-7	Excel 97 Visual Learning Guide	$16.99
0-7615-1194-6	Increase Your Web Traffic In a Weekend	$19.99
0-7615-1137-7	Jazz Up Your Web Site In a Weekend	$24.99
0-7615-1217-9	Learn Publisher 97 In a Weekend	$19.99
0-7615-1193-8	Lotus 1-2-3 Visual Learning Guide	$16.99
0-7615-0852-X	Netscape Navigator 3 Complete Handbook	$24.99
0-7615-1162-8	Office 97 Visual Learning Guide	$16.99
0-7615-0759-0	Professional Web Design	$40.00
0-7615-0063-4	Researching on the Internet	$29.95
0-7615-0686-1	Researching on the World Wide Web	$24.99
0-7615-1192-X	SmartSuite 97 Visual Learning Guide	$16.99
0-7615-1007-9	Word 97 Visual Learning Guide	$16.99
0-7615-1083-4	WordPerfect 8 Visual Learning Guide	$16.99
0-7615-1188-1	WordPerfect Suite 8 Visual Learning Guide	$16.99

TO ORDER BOOKS

Please send me the following items:

Quantity	Title	Unit Price	Total
_____	_____	$_____	$_____
_____	_____	$_____	$_____
_____	_____	$_____	$_____
_____	_____	$_____	$_____
_____	_____	$_____	$_____

Subtotal $_____
Deduct 10% when ordering 3–5 books $_____
7.25% Sales Tax (CA only) $_____
8.25% Sales Tax (TN only) $_____
5.0% Sales Tax (MD and IN only) $_____
Shipping and Handling* $_____
TOTAL ORDER $_____

Shipping and Handling depend on Subtotal.

Subtotal	Shipping/Handling
$0.00–$14.99	$3.00
$15.00–29.99	$4.00
$30.00–49.99	$6.00
$50.00–99.99	$10.00
$100.00–199.99	$13.00
$200.00+	call for quote

Foreign and all Priority Request orders:
Call Order Entry department for price quote at 1-916-632-4400

This chart represents the total retail price of books only (before applicable discounts are taken).

By telephone: With Visa or MC, call 1-800-632-8676. Mon.–Fri. 8:30–4:00 PST.

By Internet e-mail: sales@primapub.com

By mail: Just fill out the information below and send with your remittance to:

PRIMA PUBLISHING
P.O. Box 1260BK
Rocklin, CA 95677-1260

http://www.primapublishing.com

Name_____ Daytime Telephone_____

Address _____

City _____ State _____ Zip _____

Visa /MC# _____Exp. _____

Check/Money Order enclosed for $_____ Payable to Prima Publishing

Signature _____

Prima's In a Weekend™ Series

Create Your First Web Page In a Weekend
Steven E. Callihan
416 pp. • 0-7615-0692-6 • CD-ROM
$24.99 (Can. $34.95)

Jazz Up Your Web Site In A Weekend
Paul E. Robichaux
456 pp. • 0-7615-1137-7 • CD-ROM
$24.99 (Can. $34.95)

Learn Publisher 97 In a Weekend
Nancy Stevenson
336 pp. • 0-7615-1217-9
$19.99 (Can. $27.95)

GOOD NEWS! You can master the skills you need to achieve your goals in just a weekend! Prima Publishing's unique *In a Weekend* series offers practical fast-track guides dedicated to showing you how to complete your projects in a weekend or less!

Also Available

Create FrontPage Web Pages In a Weekend
David Karlins
364 pp. • 0-7615-0743-4 • CD-ROM
$29.99 (Can. $41.95)

Increase Your Web Traffic In a Weekend
William R. Stanek
480 pp. • 0-7615-1194-6
$19.99 (Can. $27.95)

Coming Soon

- Create PowerPoint Presentations In a Weekend
- Learn HTML In a Weekend
- Learn the Internet In a Weekend
- Learn Windows 98 In a Weekend
- Organize Your Finances In a Weekend with Quicken Deluxe 98
- Upgrade Your PC In a Weekend

To Order, Call 1-800-632-8676 • www.primapublishing.com

Prima Publishing and In a Weekend are trademarks of Prima Communications, Inc. All other product and company names are trademarks of their respective companies.